THE BATTLE OF
VERNEUIL
1424

THE BATTLE OF
VERNEUIL
1424

A SECOND
AGINCOURT

RICHARD WADGE

The
History
Press

First published 2015 by Spellmount, an imprint of The History Press
This paperback edition published 2019

The History Press
97 St George's Place, Cheltenham
Gloucestershire, GL50 3QB
www.thehistorypress.co.uk

British Library Cataloguing in Publication Data.
A catalogue record for this book is available from the British Library.

ISBN 978 0 7509 9268 8

Typesetting and origination by The History Press
Printed and bound in Great Britain by TJ International Ltd

Contents

Acknowledgements

People in all three of the countries involved in the Battle of Verneuil have freely given me generous help while I have been writing this book.

Roselyne Millet, the Directrice of the Jérôme Carcopino Municipal Library in Verneuil supplied material which gave the French point of view. Jean Baptiste Pierrat and Frédéric Jurczyk in the Tourist Information Office in Verneuil were very patient and helpful with the random Englishman who appeared in the office one damp Saturday.

Staff of Historic Scotland, particularly Malcolm Irving, sorted out pictures of monuments in response to my enquiries. Jason Sutcliffe, who works for East Ayrshire Council in the Future Museum, also made sure I found the best images from their collection to meet my needs.

Just as happened in the battle, the Italians made an important contribution, thanks to the staff of the photographic office of the Uffizi Gallery in Florence.

Yet again the cheerful professionalism of the staff of the Bodleian Library in Oxford has been a great help.

My son Edmund read the early chapters and provided penetrating advice which made me clarify things.

Finally, but by no means the smallest contribution, Eleanor gave cheerful, tolerant support to a husband living in the fifteenth century.

Thanks to you all.

I

The Hundred Years War

E ngland and France waged the Hundred Years War between 1337 and 1453. While relations between the two kingdoms were more likely to be hostile than amiable between the Norman Conquest and the end of the Napoleonic Wars, hostility was more persistent during these years. There were times, such as *c.*1340–56 and 1415–35, when the fighting was almost continuous with some large-scale battles and sieges, and there were other times, such as *c.*1390–1410, when life was almost peaceful. The original cause of the war was that according to English law, Edward III had a good claim to the French throne through his mother, Isabella, who was daughter of Philip IV of France. Unsurprisingly, the French claimed that the ancient Salic law of the Franks excluded inheritance of royal power through the female line. Edward was not prepared to accept this slight. However, relations between the kings of England and France were made more complicated by the English king claiming to be Duke of Normandy and Duke of Aquitaine, which meant that he owed feudal fealty to the King of France for these lands. These were matters that were never going to be resolved solely by diplomacy or legal argument. But it is also fair to say that war became something of a habit among the English at this time.

This habit was fuelled by the longer running warfare between England and Scotland. Once the Hundred Years War[1] started England was in a pincer between Scotland to the north and France over the Channel to the south. There were two major areas of dispute between

England and Scotland in the Middle Ages, which were as insoluble as was the dispute over the French throne: where was the border between the two kingdoms, and was the King of Scotland subject to the English king? Edward I had managed to establish a shaky English suzerainty, but it crumbled under his weak successor, Edward II. He could not counter Robert Bruce, Robert I of Scotland, a heroic figure who led his kingdom to independence. While a series of victories in Edward III's reign taught the Scots to avoid provoking the English king, these two issues ensured that there was never more than a truce on the border. The Scots and the French agreed treaties in the fourteenth century to support each other against England – the Auld Alliance, which is described in a later chapter.

England's two long wars came together in the fateful meeting of the armies of the three kingdoms at Verneuil in 1424.

The years of the Hundred Years War would have been eventful enough in western Europe without warfare between the two kingdoms. In 1347–50 the Black Death killed around 40 per cent of the population of Europe, but this only quietened the war for a couple of years. This dreadful cull of the population gave opportunities to the survivors; ordinary men and women had a scarcity value which gave them some economic power and choice. Towns and cities continued their rapid growth in much of western Europe, despite the ravages of war in France in particular. Local and international trade grew with the towns, and the great commercial cities of the Italian peninsula began to send their trading fleets full of exotic goods (and more ordinary items like high quality bowstaves for the English war-bow) to the ports of northern and western Europe.

What is perhaps most surprising in the period between 1380 and 1420 is the remarkable coincidences in the political upheavals in the three kingdoms of England, Scotland and France. There were deeply divisive struggles between the king and the magnates and among the magnates themselves in all three countries. All three countries had an incompetent king for a period. Robert III of Scotland may have had some long-term physical disability after his accident in 1388 but he seems to have become vacillating and desperate to please many of his nobles. He was succeeded by a minor, James, who also happened to be a prisoner in England. Richard II of England became a capricious, self-indulgent ruler who found it very difficult to trust anyone outside his immediate circle. His successor Henry IV always had a problem because some people felt he was not a legitimate king because he had deposed Richard II. This may have led to him being plagued by self-doubt. But as his reign progressed, he increasingly suffered from sustained serious ill health which affected his ability to rule. At the same time, France was rent by feuding between the royal dukes and their supporters, because King Charles VI of France had increasingly frequent bouts of insanity, which necessitated a regency for much of the last thirty years of his reign. Yet despite these problems the three kingdoms managed to continue their desultory, often bloody struggles for supremacy.

At this time of tragedy and change, when the people needed spiritual support the most, the papacy was in a state of decay. It had been based in southern France at Avignon since 1309 where it gained an unenviable reputation for corruption and partiality. Then, from 1378 western Christendom ended up with two popes for forty years. Despite these problems with the leadership of Christendom, this was a period of deep personal faith, but that could be something very different from a deep faith in the spirituality of the Catholic Church. Some theologians and preachers put forward ideas that, with hindsight, we would regard as being the foundations of Protestantism.

The Hundred Years War inevitably led to a number of developments in military practice. The best known of these are the use of the English war-bow and the development of gunpowder artillery[1]. The development of professional non-noble armies was just as important. The success of the English armies, wherein everyone fought on foot regardless of rank and most of the soldiers were archers, was a great surprise in Continental Europe. It went against the tradition that noble, mailed and armoured horsemen were the most important and effective fighting men on the battlefield. The English armies weren't the only ones that demonstrated the power of good infantry against armoured cavalry. The Scots showed that pike-armed infantry could defeat cavalry at Bannockburn against the English and the Flemings proved much the same point at Courtrai against the French. But the English were the only ones who used infantry archers to defeat armoured cavalry. The other surprise was that it was the English who were so successful. They had never been a major European military power in their own right before, although England had been an important part of Henry II's Angevin Empire in the twelfth century.

It has been suggested that Edward III had a very small number of primitive cannons at the Battle of Crécy, but they had no effect on the outcome of the battle. However, by the fifteenth century gunpowder artillery had developed sufficiently to give a great advantage to besiegers, and by the end of the Hundred Years War it was becoming an effective force on the battlefield. Other nations took to hand-held gunpowder weapons rather than the war-bow, leaving England and Wales with their 'eccentric' choice of missile weapon until the sixteenth century. It was pike-armed infantry assisted by infantry armed with gunpowder weapons that ended the reign of heavy armoured cavalry as kings of the battlefield in western Europe. By the fifteenth century, many of the companies that made up the English armies in France, and even more of the individuals who served as archers and men-at-arms, were professional.[2] Many of these professionals came from the ordinary people, not from the nobility or what would later be called the gentry. In his efforts to both counter the English and control his fractious kingdom, Charles VII of France also came round to encouraging the development of professional soldiers by establishing the gendarmes d'ordonnance. Interestingly, it was the kingdom of France that maintained and developed these professional soldiers in the later fifteenth and sixteenth centuries, while in England, suspicion of standing armies and royal tight-fistedness prevented the continued development of a professional army.

The Hundred Years War made a notable and lasting contribution to popular self-image of what it was to be English. In the fourteenth century, Edward III's campaigns brought considerable wealth to England in the form of loot and ransoms. His victories brought pride to many English people. Both the wealth and the pride were spread to local levels by the involvement of ordinary men as archers in the wars. When Henry V reinvigorated the English war against the French, he won what became a near mythic victory at Agincourt. Again the stalwart English (and Welsh) archers were key contributors to English success. Although the Hundred Years War ended in defeat for the English, they maintained a healthy contempt for the French, which Henry VIII exploited. An expression of this well-established contempt for the fighting qualities of the French can be found in the description of the Battle of Verneuil in Edward Hall's *Chronicle*, which was written in Henry VIII's reign. Hall commented 'for surely the nature of the Frenchman is not to labor long in fighting and muche more braggeth than fighteth'.[3] In the nineteenth century, the no-nonsense English longbowman was built up into an archetype of what Englishmen could achieve. Three key events in this process of building the archers' reputation were the battles of Crécy, Poitiers and Agincourt. But the question this book raises is 'Why is the Battle of Verneuil not the fourth battle in this list?' A history which describes only the events of battles can be very sterile. A battle happens as part of a chain of events in history, and these events are what give the battle its significance. As this account of the Battle of Verneuil will show, the behaviour of the soldiers in a battle can turn the battle one way or another, and so they can also influence the path of history after the battle one way or another. These are the battles that historians call decisive. It is almost certain that the leaders and captains of the forces engaged in the Battle of Verneuil were aware that they and their men were engaged in just such a battle. Like the battles of Crécy, Poitiers and Agincourt, the Battle of Verneuil was the culmination of one side following a battle-seeking strategy. But, as the outcomes of these four major battles demonstrate, having a battle-seeking strategy and winning the sought-for battle were two very different things. This was why large battles were rare in the 116 years of the Hundred Years War. Leaders on both sides understood the strategic risks inherent in any battle, let alone a large-scale, decisive one. Therefore, as will become clear in the account of the years preceding the Battle of Verneuil, strategy was advanced by raids, sieges, ambushes and surprise assaults, rather than through a series of great set-piece battles such as happened in the Crimean War or the First World War.

Military activity is only half a war; diplomacy makes up the rest. Diplomatic activity during the Hundred Years War had various strands. There was the struggle for what we would now call the 'moral high ground'. Whose cause was 'more right'? While both sides sought rulings from the law departments of the great universities of western Europe, papal support was the key to establishing this. The papacy's other role was to try to lead peace negotiations in an attempt to stop the shedding of Christian blood. At the same time as there was conflict and uncertainty at the top of secular society, there was conflict and division in the Church. In 1377 Pope Gregory XI ended the Avignon papacy by returning to Rome. He hoped that, by returning to his see, he would be able to re-establish the independence of the papacy. The standing of the papacy had been weakened by more than sixty-five years' residency in Avignon where its decisions and actions were effectively controlled by the French kings. Something most clearly demonstrated by all seven Popes who reigned from Avignon being French. Unfortunately Gregory died a year later, before he had been able to do much to improve the papacy's reputation. When the cardinals met to choose his successor, the Roman mob rioted, demanding that the conclave elect an Italian pope. Fear and national pride had more effect on the papal election than spiritual considerations, with the cardinals electing the Archbishop of Bari, who became Pope Urban VI. However, Urban was autocratic and intemperate and soon antagonised the cardinals, particularly the many French ones appointed during the time of the Avignon papacy. They met at Anagni, about 70km south-east of Rome, where they declared Urban's election invalid. Fearing Urban's reaction, the cardinals moved to Fondi further away from Rome, where they elected Robert, a son of the Count of Geneva, who became Pope Clement VII. This so outraged Urban that he had five of the cardinals tortured and killed![4] Clement needed to find a sympathetic haven to be secure from Urban's outrage, and so re-established a papal court at Avignon. France and its supporters (many ruled by relatives of the French king), including Burgundy, Aragon, Castile and Naples, supported Clement. Scotland, honouring the Auld Alliance, also accepted Clement. England, Flanders, the Holy Roman Empire and a number of north Italian city states supported Urban. Naturally both popes declared the other to be an antipope. All this was worse than anything that happened in England, Scotland or France in their divisions at this time.

The Papal Schism continued until the election of Martin V in 1417. The Schism affected the Hundred Years War since both the English and the French could gain papal support for their claims. They could do this knowing that the papacy did not have the standing to lead a peace process because of its divisions. This changed with Pope Martin's election, but he was unable to negotiate even a temporary truce between the warring nations. However, his successor managed to promote negotiations in the early 1430s which brought lasting harm to the English cause. It is difficult to know what effect the Schism had on the ordinary men and women of England, Scotland and France. But it must be no coincidence that the philosopher and theologian John Wyclif, who questioned the Church's right to its authority and vast properties, thrived at this time.

Diplomacy was also part of the practical aspect of war making; the kings of England and France made serious efforts to build up alliances. Firstly, there were attempts to gain active military support, more commonly by the French kings. The make-up of the army that fought for Charles VII of France at Verneuil is the clearest proof of the success of these efforts. Both the French and English kings made treaties with the great dukes of France and with the dukes of Brittany to try to gain some military advantage. Secondly, the kings of both realms made serious diplomatic efforts to build alliances which contained their enemy, rather than actively participating in the wars. Henry V's negotiations with the Holy Roman Emperor are an example of this. The most robust result of the diplomatic efforts throughout the Hundred Years War was The Auld Alliance between Scotland and France. Although they played their part earlier in the Hundred Years War on occasion, the Scots were particularly active in the wars in France in the period between the battles of Agincourt and Verneuil.

The Battle of Verneuil marked a high point for the kings of England in their efforts to win the Crown of France. The outcome of the battle ensured that Henry V's legacy, both military and diplomatic, survived and was built upon. The story of how the armies of the kingdoms of England, Scotland and France came to meet on a hot summer's day in the open fields just north of Verneuil in 1424 is a neglected tale. While it is overshadowed in popular history by other great battles of the Hundred Years War and later wars, it is one of the great achievements of English soldiers, as this book will recount. But it is more important than just another notable English military success; it was a decisive battle that affected the course of history in England and France for some years. It was part of a complex sequence of events following the shock of Henry V's victory at Agincourt that ultimately led to consolidation of the kingdom of France as a European power after a century and half of disorder, and left England with the reputation of being a pugnacious neighbour in Europe; part of it, but also at the edge of it.

2

England and France at the beginning of the fifteenth century

I n the decades immediately before and after 1400, England, France
and Scotland all endured their own particular version of the
same political problem; conflict between the king and the great
magnates of the nation. Sometimes this involved physical violence
but more usually it was political plotting for supremacy. In all three
countries this conflict concerned the rights of the king, the nature of
kingship and the rights of the magnates. Kingship at this time was very
personal. Robert I of Scotland, Edward III of England and Charles V of
France were examples of successful kings who commanded the loyalty
of the magnates and their people. In the heyday of their reigns, they all
chose highly competent loyal servants. Robert and Edward were also
heroic military figures. But if the king was a child or an incompetent,
problems could arise. In all three kingdoms, there were senior relatives
who could act as regent; men whose right to be regent would be
questioned only by their own relatives but not by the nobility or the
Church in general. If a kingdom was ruled by a weak king or a regent
revolt and civil war were not inevitable, as the situation in Scotland at
this time proved, but they did happen in England and France. Meanwhile
the magnates, whether relatives of the king or not, were concerned with
the maintenance of their own rights: primarily the security and integrity
of their estates and access to the king for influence and patronage. In
general they did not consider themselves as aspirants to the throne,
except when the king had left no clear heir. Equally they were reluctant

to accept a magnate succeeding or replacing the king. In both England and Scotland the Parliament had some restraining effect on both kings and magnates mainly through its powers to authorise the collection of specific taxes, but it was only able to influence the outcome of conflicts between the king and the magnates when acting in concert with one party or the other. The Church could only influence these struggles when the archbishops and bishops used their political skills and wealth in a secular manner by behaving very like lay magnates.

England

Two dramatic events showed the condition of England in the late fourteenth century. Firstly, in 1381 the Peasants' Revolt showed that the ordinary people, including many wealthy peasants and merchants, would not just quietly pay taxes and 'know their place'. The revolt is often said to have been a protest against the Poll Tax, which bore little relation to a person's ability to pay in contrast to the more traditionally levied taxes on moveable property. While this is true, it was as much a revolt against landlords oppressively, and on occasion illegally, enforcing their 'rights' for fees and labour services. In addition, a series of laws had been enacted with the aim of keeping the mass of the population in their place after the Black Death and subsequent outbreaks of plague. These included the Statute of Labourers which tried to limit wages and workers' rights to choose their employer, sumptuary laws restricting clothing types, fabrics and colours to particular social groups and even the laws requiring archery practice which restricted leisure activities for the good of England. These various restrictions were attempts to contain the freedoms that the ordinary people had gained because of the Black Death. Between 1348 and 1351 it killed as much as 40 per cent of the population of the British Isles, which meant that workers became a scarce commodity. These attempts at repressing the freedoms that ordinary people had gained built up a powerful sense of discontent which the demands of the Poll Tax ignited into actual revolt. The rebels invaded London and confronted the young King Richard II. He showed courage (and possibly faith in his divinely ordained role as king) and led the rebels from the city after their leader Wat Tyler was killed.

But all the promises he made to them came to nothing in the aftermath of the revolt. However, the revolt was not a failure, since Poll Tax was dropped, and there was no sustained attempt at systematic repression of the 'peasants'.

The second of these events happened in 1400 when Henry Bolinbroke, a grandson of Edward III, deposed his cousin Richard II to become Henry IV. This action was the culmination of nearly two decades of tension and dispute between the established magnates and the Parliamentary Commons on the one hand and the king and his 'court party' on the other. Richard's success with the rebels in 1381 seems to have reinforced his feeling that the king was appointed by God and that his will was paramount in ruling England. In his mind this meant that there was no need to consult either the magnates or the Parliamentary Commons. How much this view was reinforced by the theories of John Wyclif is uncertain. Since Wyclif was under the protection of Richard's uncle, John of Gaunt, it is possible that he may have preached before the young king. But since the Peasants' Revolt seems to have left Richard with a distrust of the mass of his subjects, he may have had little sympathy for much of Wyclif's thinking, which was potentially revolutionary in the way it attacked the structures of spiritual power and authority. In 1382 the old magnates such as his uncles John of Gaunt, Duke of Lancaster and Thomas of Woodstock, Earl of Buckingham, and the Earl of Arundel pushed to restart the war with France. At the same time a number of younger men such as Robert de Vere, Thomas Mowbray, Peter Courtenay and John Montagu came into the king's household and began to form a counterbalance to the power and influence of the older magnates. While Richard didn't have access to great wealth or patronage, what he did have he lavished on this group of younger courtiers. As a result he was able to surround himself with a group of nobles and knights whom he had chosen and who held strong personal and political loyalty to him. In this they differed from the nobles of the older generation like the king's uncles, who had bonds formed through their military service, experience that the court circle lacked. In 1385 Parliament demanded that Richard reform the royal finances, particularly by spending less and granting less of the royal income as annuities to his courtiers. Since taxation had to be approved by Parliament, financial pressure was its most powerful weapon. While

Gaunt objected to some of the proposals made by Parliament to achieve this, a majority of the politically powerful lords supported Parliament by issuing 'Articles of Advice' proposing that Richard attend council more frequently and accept its decisions. Richard accepted the advice and nine lords were appointed to provide guidance to the king on reforming his financial affairs. But Richard managed to avoid having to provide any detailed account of his household's expenditure to Parliament, in part because the magnates were unwilling to undertake concerted action with the Commons at this time.

1386 was a turning point. Firstly, John of Gaunt left the kingdom with an army to pursue his ambitions in Spain. Richard encouraged this, quite probably calculating that if his powerful uncle was out of the country, the criticism of his court would be less effective. Knowing that Gaunt was absent from England, Charles VI of France collected a very large army at Sluys in preparation for mounting an invasion of England. Meanwhile, French and Castilian ships added to the threat by raiding the south coast. Parliament tried to fund a fleet to guard the Channel with limited success, and in September ordered the array of a large number of men to guard London against invasion. However there was insufficient money to pay these men so they started to live off the land in Kent and the south-east of England. Fortunately for England the French king abandoned the idea of an invasion in November. However, this did nothing to reduce the level of dissatisfaction that Parliament, the magnates and the taxpaying population at large felt with the king and courtiers. The sustained threat of invasion and the coastal raids by the French had demonstrated that Richard's policy of trying to 'buy' peace with the French by offering to return some of his grandfather's territorial gains was a mistake. This policy was promoted by his courtiers against the advice of many other peers who wanted to restart the war with France. Not only had he followed an ineffective policy towards France, Richard had done nothing to reform the royal finances. The Parliamentary Commons and the magnates now united in an attempt to get Richard to change his ways and govern within what they considered the traditions established in Edward III's reign. Richard could not resist this combined pressure. In 1387 Henry Bolinbroke, Earl of Derby, became a junior member of the Lords Appellant. This group of peers forced King Richard to banish some of his favourites and to accept themselves as his councillors. However, Richard was soon able to reclaim power. In 1387 he put a series of questions about the legal status and extent of his royal prerogative to a group of judges led by the Chief Justice of Common Pleas. They pronounced in his favour, which allowed the offence of treason to be extended to include peaceful political opposition to the policies and actions of the king's government. Then in 1389 Richard declared his majority, and with it his intention to become the ruler of England, taking power away from the various councils that had held it to greater or lesser extent up to this point. These actions caused much unease among the magnates and political classes. This unease was reinforced by Richard's recruitment of a large personal retinue of Cheshire archers. These men came from his own estates – Richard was Earl of Chester – and acted as a personal bodyguard, the core of an army when necessary, and as enforcers of the king's rule. The final provocation came in 1398 when Bolinbroke accused the Duke of Norfolk of treasonable activities. Richard banished both men, Norfolk for life and Bolinbroke for ten years. But shortly afterwards John of Gaunt, Duke of Lancaster, Bolinbroke's father and the king's uncle, died. His enormous estates and wealth passed to the banished Bolinbroke, but Richard was not prepared to allow this. He recalled the committee that had judged the case and persuaded it to do as he wished and banish Bolinbroke for life and disallow his inheritance, which meant that all of Gaunt's enormous wealth reverted to the Crown. Not surprisingly, Bolinbroke refused to accept this and returned to England from Flanders with a small company. Richard was in Ireland trying to stabilise his rule there at the time of Henry's invasion and so was unable to make a rapid response. More seriously for him, there was no one in England with sufficient power and influence to keep the kingdom safe in these circumstances. Richard had been in conflict with many of the long-standing magnates throughout his reign, and this attack on Henry's rights of inheritance made many nobles great and small fear that the king meant to threaten the family rights of the nobility at large. This fear went to the core of the relationship between the English king and his nobles so that many either actively joined Bolinbroke or, more importantly for Richard, did nothing to support the king. Nor could Richard look to the English Church for support since he had driven Archbishop Arundel into exile in 1397. Indeed, Henry and Arundel had joined forces as fellow exiles and Arundel's acute advice and guidance was of great value to

Henry in the deposition of Richard and his succession to the throne. Richard, who had a clear belief in his prerogative rights as divinely approved king, ignored the political realities and hurriedly returned from Ireland. He had little support and had no choice but to accept Henry's demands and allow Parliament to impeach some of his closest councillors. While on his way to meet Henry he was seized and imprisoned in the Tower before being moved to Pontefract Castle later in the year. Meanwhile, Parliament withdrew its fealty to Richard and Henry claimed the throne by right of blood and conquest. Henry was crowned in October 1399. Henry and Arundel found themselves having to manage the accumulated ill feeling towards Richard and his supporters that had built up particularly in the last three years of his reign. Initially Henry managed to avoid bloodshed, but the younger magnates who had gained lands and status as supporters of Richard found themselves losing both their titles and properties. These included the earls of Huntingdon, Kent, Rutland, Salisbury (father of Thomas who was so successful in the wars in France under Henry V & Henry VI) and Gloucester. Faced with the loss of both wealth and influence, they plotted to seize Henry and his sons during the Twelfth Night celebrations and restore Richard to the throne. It is probable that one of the plotters panicked and told Henry, who was able to escape. When the plotters tried to flee they were killed by angry townspeople in Cirencester and Bristol. Henry was now acutely aware of the danger the living Richard posed and it may be that orders were given that the former king should be kept in severely straitened conditions. Richard died in February 1400 at Pontefract Castle and his body was briefly displayed in St Paul's Cathedral to publicise his end before being quietly buried. There is no clear evidence of the cause of Richard's death but the general view has always been that it was the result of serious neglect rather than violence.

Henry IV immediately applied himself to building up enough support and approval to give him a realistic sense of security on the throne. Unfortunately for him there was another magnate, Edward Mortimer, Earl of March, who had as good a claim to the throne by blood although he was no threat at this date because he was a minor. But there were two major threats facing Henry before he could feel secure on his throne.

In 1403 the Percys led a serious military revolt against Henry. He had antagonised Henry Percy, known to all as Hotspur, in a dispute over ransoms for some of the Scottish prisoners Hotspur had taken at the Battle of Homildon Hill in the previous year. King Henry also owed the Percys payments for their duties as Wardens of the Marches. So Hotspur and his father the Earl of Northumberland agreed to ally with Owain Glyndŵr in the hope of trapping Henry IV between their two armies. The Percys raised an army in the north, particularly from Cheshire, including many erstwhile members of Richard's infamous bodyguard of Cheshire archers, and marched south. Glyndŵr was either unable to move fast enough or too cautious, so Hotspur had to face the king's army alone. The two armies met at Shrewsbury where a bloody battle took place. It was one of the rare battles with a substantial number of English war-bow archers on both sides. So the battle began with a devastating archery duel in which the rebellious Cheshire archers, who had been unable to fight for their king in 1399, were able to fight in Richard's memory. They seem to have got the best of the shoot-out and some of the royal army melted away. But once the battle came to close quarters it is likely that the royal army had an advantage because Hotspur was killed in his personal assault on the king's standard (and he hoped the king's person). The dangers archery presented to men in full armour were demonstrated in this battle. Hotspur was said to have been killed by an arrow to the face because he had raised his visor to breathe in the heat of battle and Henry of Monmouth, the future Henry V, was certainly wounded in the face by an arrow. After his son's defeat, the Earl of Northumberland managed to make his peace with the king in the aftermath of the battle, an arrangement which was more like the way that Scottish magnates worked through their disputes with the Scottish throne in this period. Two years later there was more trouble in the north of England which led to the Earl of Northumberland fleeing to Scotland and Richard le Scrope, Archbishop of York, being beheaded. The archbishop and his supporters had been objecting to the level of taxation and the apparent anticlericalism of Henry's administration. They were also antagonised by the greed of Henry's supporters and household, including the Neville family who had gained status and wealth at the expense of the Percys and their supporters in the north. Quite why Henry decided to make such an example of Archbishop Scrope is not clear. Archbishop Arundel pleaded for Henry to respect clerical immunity from the death penalty, but to no avail. Henry may just have lost patience with the north and felt the need to make an example of someone; it may have been the climate of anticlericalism which made it difficult to allow any special treatment for Scrope. Whatever the reasons for this action, Henry faced no major threats to his rule for the rest of his reign, except for some tensions with his oldest son, Henry of Monmouth. Henry's reign was one of the quiet patches in the Hundred Years War, since he followed Richard II's example and didn't actively prosecute the war with France. This was despite the perception in France, voiced by the Duke of Berry, King Charles's brother, that 'it [Henry IV's coronation] is a great tragedy and a signal misfortune for our country. For as you well know, Lancaster governs by the will of the English people and the English people like nothing better than war.'[5] Later in his reign he came near to proving the duke right by allowing English forces to fight in France in support of one or another of the factions struggling for control of France. However, England's neighbours were able to take advantage of the uncertainty that affected England in the years immediately after Henry's seizure of the throne. In 1401 Henry attempted to negotiate peace with Scotland, believing that he was in a powerful position after he had led a large English army into Scotland in the previous year, reaching Edinburgh in what amounted to a demonstration rather than an invasion. He raised the old English claim that the Scottish king should do homage to him for his kingdom, and thought he had a clever way of achieving this by proposing that this matter should be referred to arbitration. However, the Bishop of Glasgow countered with the proposal that Henry's right to the throne of England could also be referred to arbitration. The conference ended abruptly.[6] But after Hotspur's victory at Homildon Hill in 1402, which resulted in the death or capture of some of the more bellicose Scottish leaders including Archibald Douglas, Earl of Douglas, and Murdoch Stewart, Earl of Fife, the Scots were less inclined to put serious pressure on northern England. The Earl of Douglas was a significant enemy of the English kings until his death at the Battle of Verneuil. He even fought for Hotspur at the Battle of Shrewsbury. Then in 1406 Henry IV had one of his rare pieces of good luck when James, the young heir to the Scottish throne, was captured by English pirates. James was kept as an honoured prisoner by the English kings until 1424. For the rest of

Henry IV's reign the Scots had their own difficulties to deal with and largely left the English alone. From Henry's point of view, relations with Scotland were dominated by discussions of the ransoms to be paid for James, who became King of Scotland early in his captivity, and for the earls of Douglas and Fife.

The Welsh, led by Owain Glyndŵr, revolted in 1400. In part this was because of Welsh dissatisfaction with English rule; Glyndŵr himself had a real grievance with the English Lord Grey of Ruthin, but there was also a strong feeling that Henry IV was not a legitimate king. If Henry was not the rightful King of England, then neither he nor any of his sons could be the rightful Prince of Wales. So Owain claimed to be the legitimate Prince of Wales. The French sent Owain help on several occasions, but after 1404, the tide began to turn against the Welsh despite their (possibly) gaining a victory over an army led by Henry IV himself, in the bloody Battle of Stalling Down in Glamorgan in the following year.[7] By 1409, the Welsh effort was exhausted by persistent military pressure from the English, compounded by the particularly harsh winter of 1408–09. The revolt fizzled out, although Owain Glyndŵr was never captured.

The problems in Wales, his own health, money problems and probably personal inclination led Henry to concentrate on domestic matters for much of his reign. In 1406 Henry was temporarily incapacitated by ill health. A peaceful agreement was quickly made that a council made up of magnates both lay and clerical would rule the kingdom until Henry recovered. This council would concentrate on restoring the financial and political stability of the realm which had not recovered from Richard II's time. Importantly the loyalty of the Parliamentary Commons was not in doubt even when they criticised the royal administration. This council remained active for the rest of Henry's reign. However, Henry recovered sufficiently to be an influential player in the politics of England for much of the rest of his reign. Henry was able to manipulate the membership of the council to ensure that it tended to support him as ruler of England.[8] His health collapsed again in 1409, when it was feared he would not recover, but he did. On this occasion, his heir Henry of Monmouth moved to become leader of the council, an act which marked the beginning of the struggle between the two Henrys. While this struggle never became violent it certainly became dangerous to the peace of England in 1412. Henry IV accused Prince Henry of having profited illegally from his captaincy of Calais. Prince Henry was able to clear himself but this episode ensured that he never trusted his father or those around him again. Henry IV seems to have favoured his second son Thomas of Lancaster, Duke of Clarence over Henry, which only added to the tension.

In the last two years of his reign Henry IV started to dabble in the murky politics of France, allowing small-scale English support for one side or the other. In 1412 Henry sent an expedition to support the Armagnacs led by his favourite son, Thomas of Lancaster, Duke of Clarence. This achieved nothing except some financial rewards because the Armagnacs and Burgundians reached one of their many short-term agreements to end the fighting between them. But it exacerbated the ill feeling between the two Henrys.

When Henry V succeeded in 1413, there were still mutterings about his right to rule. The Scots stirred the pot by providing refuge and some support for Thomas Ward, who claimed to be the deposed Richard II. A small group of plotters were arrested and their leader, a yeoman named John Whitlock, was tried for plotting rebellion and the assassination of Henry so that Thomas Ward could take the throne as Richard II restored. A more serious plot against him happened as Henry was preparing for his invasion of France in 1415. This time the plan was to put the Earl of March, Edmund Mortimer, on the throne. Henry was a very different character to his father in that he seems to have had a deep personal feeling that he was the true King of England in God's eyes, whereas his father never seemed so confident. Moreover he seems to have been both a good judge of men and charismatic, and so was able to build a group of loyal, competent men about him.

People believed that the victory against the odds at Agincourt demonstrated that Henry was in receipt of God's favour, and so must be the rightful King of England. For the rest of his reign he was a largely unchallenged hero king. However his early death in 1422 when his son was only 9 months old brought another of the problems of medieval monarchy to the fore – the need for a regent. The problems this led to are recounted in later chapters.

France

In 1380, three years after the 10-year-old Richard II came to the throne in England, Charles VI became King of France, aged 11. In another parallel with the situation in England, the royal uncles ruled, with one, Philip the Bold, Duke of Burgundy, taking the lead. Charles was declared of age in 1388 and began his personal rule. However, this was short-lived since he had his first episode of madness four years later. He recovered fairly quickly on this occasion, but the attacks continued throughout his reign and became longer in duration. Philip of Burgundy, who was with Charles when he went mad in 1392, declared himself regent. He was the senior royal relative at the time, and had already had successful experience in the role, so it seemed reasonable to both Burgundy and many others that he should be regent. But this decisive act antagonised the king's brother, Louis, Duke of Orléans. In 1402 Charles recovered his sanity for an interval and declared a regent was no longer necessary so Burgundy's pre-eminence was temporarily ended. However, Charles soon lapsed into insanity again and Orléans managed to become regent on this occasion. He was an extravagant spendthrift without Burgundy's abilities or experience and so was soon replaced by Burgundy. In 1404, the elder statesman Philip of Burgundy died. His son John succeeded as duke and soon rivalled Orléans as the leading figure in the court of King Charles. One of the keys to the success of the dukes of Burgundy at this time, namely Philip the Bold and his son John and grandson Philip, was that not only were they basically competent and shrewd, but they cultivated popularity with the population at large, and with the citizens of Paris in particular. It was difficult for Queen Isabeau of France to gain any power and influence in these times of uncertainty, in part because Charles often seemed unable to recognise her in his bouts of madness, and in part because she was a foreigner (she was a Bavarian princess). She was unable to build up power and influence outside the royal court in the way the Burgundian dukes did and concentrated on the more limited aims of protecting her own rights and those of her son, the Dauphin. It was suggested that she became closer than was decent to Louis of Orléans in her efforts to achieve this, and that Charles, her fifth son, who later became Charles VII, was the result of this closeness.

John of Burgundy seems to have been more ruthless than his father since in 1407 his agents assassinated Louis of Orléans. John gained several years' dominance of France by this action, although he was not unopposed. Louis' successor as Duke of Orléans, Charles, was married to the daughter of Bernard VII, Count of Armagnac, an alliance that proved vital to the opposition of the dukes of Burgundy. Bernard was the major figure in League of Gien which came into being in 1410 to co-ordinate the opposition to the dukes of Burgundy. The opposition to the Burgundians never seems to have been called the Orléanist party, but after the formation of the league, contemporaries thought of the power struggle as being between the Armagnacs and the Burgundians.[9] Although both parties asked the English for troops late in Henry IV's reign, the English neither took advantage of the situation in France nor had any real effect on the standing of either party. Both kingdoms seem to have broadly adhered to the terms of the Truce of Leulinghem agreed in 1389 until Henry V's invasion of France in 1415. This is not to suggest that all was peaceful; trading or fishing in the Channel could still be dangerous with freebooters active on both sides. But the fact is that the near civil war in France seemed more intractable than the Hundred Years War, since there were seven reconciliations or peace treaties made between the Armagnacs and the Burgundians between 1405 and 1415, none of which brought any real period of peace![10]

After the formation of the League of Gien, the Armagnac party gained ground against the Burgundians, particularly in Paris, where Duke Bernard seems to have been an effective leader. This may have led Louis, Duke of Anjou to join them, an alliance cemented by the betrothal of Charles, the fifth son of Charles and Isabeau (eventually becoming the fifth Dauphin in 1417 after the early deaths through ill health of his four older brothers) to Louis' daughter, Marie. The long-term advantage for the Armagnac party from this was that Charles (the fifth Dauphin) came under the advice and influence of his formidable mother-in-law Yolande of Anjou and other Angevin counsellors. Indeed, Yolande seems to have become a maternal figure for Charles, replacing the unfortunate Isabeau, who was distracted by the need to protect the interests of whichever of her sons was Dauphin and her own feckless nature.

Once Henry V came to the English throne, and made his ambitions in France clear, these divisions among the French nobles became even more significant for the wellbeing of the kingdom of France. Historians agree that without the active support of some French nobles, or at least their neutrality or apathy, it was probably impossible for the English to achieve their war aims, even when they were led by someone as able as Henry. But at the Battle of Agincourt, both sides fought the English. While the Armagnac party lost more major figures in the battle, the Burgundians also took part. Duke John himself appeared to have delayed in a very calculating fashion, but two of his brothers were killed in the battle. The defeat at Agincourt shook all parties in France but they were unable to unify, perhaps understandably, since poor mad King Charles hardly made a credible figurehead. Duke John of Burgundy carefully consolidated his position of power in the years following the battle. Then in 1418 the Burgundians re-established their control of Paris on the back of a bloody popular rising against the Armagnacs in which Duke Bernard was killed. The journal written by an anonymous Parisian cleric at the time (misnamed the *The Journal of a Bourgeois of Paris*) described the events, writing, 'there was not one of the principal streets of Paris that did not have a killing in it … they [the corpses] were heaped up in piles in the mud like sides of bacon'.[11] But it is unlikely that this was part of a plan by the Duke of Burgundy to replace King Charles and follow the example of earlier events in England. He seems to have been content to expand his duchy and maintain control of royal authority.[12] But the storm of popular feeling that was released in Paris in 1418, in part fomented by the Duke of Burgundy, proved very difficult to contain. The same journal contains accounts of several more 'purges' against Armagnacs in which attacks were made on Armagnac properties and purely personal scores were settled. Charles the Dauphin was quite sensibly fearful of the situation in Paris and fled the capital as soon as the Burgundians approached at the start of these troubles. He went south of the Loire and set up an independent administration with a Parliament and Chancery at Poitiers.[13] He had his own court which included his mother-in-law and other Angevin advisors, which when it wasn't travelling about southern France was based at Bourges and Poitiers.

The political situation in 1419 was very volatile with first one party then the other gaining some advantage, but by the end of the year matters had settled into the pattern that held for about ten years. The Armagnacs were militarily active all round Paris, leading the writer of the Paris journal to comment that '... the Armagnacs were everywhere all the time as has been described. They killed, stole and burned everywhere, men, women and grain. They were worse than Saracens ...'[14] Henry maintained the English drive for control of northern France by taking Pontoise, and following this up by sending his brother Clarence on by a chevauchée (raids by an army on horseback, which covered considerable distances looking for booty and reputation) which went right up to the gates of Paris. These advances seem to have made Duke John of Burgundy consider rethinking his allegiances. Perhaps the English were becoming too powerful and threatening his interests; maybe he began to think that Frenchmen should combine against the traditional foe. Whatever his thinking, he and the Dauphin managed to agree to a meeting where they might negotiate some sort of agreement. But, in what was an exceptionally short-sighted act, Duke John of Burgundy was assassinated on the bridge at Montereau as soon as he came into the presence of Charles the Dauphin of France, allegedly in revenge for the assassination of Louis of Orléans twelve years earlier. This was a remarkable case of the needs of the present being brushed aside by demands from the past. While no one accused Charles of actually striking a blow, many people found it unbelievable that he had no inkling of what was going to happen to the duke.

After the murder of his father, the new Duke of Burgundy, Philip, was an implacable opponent of the anti-English Armagnacs, including the Dauphin, although he continued to pay lip service to Charles as King of France. The situation had reached the point where 'the seriousness of the divisions in France is further demonstrated by the numerous French chroniclers who depict Henry as the only man capable of bringing peace to a divided nation.'[15] Although his father disinherited him under English and Burgundian pressure as a result of the events at Montereau, the Dauphin was not left helpless or friendless. In Bourges south of the Loire, he sheltered behind the formidable moat that the river provided against the English. In general Philip, Duke of Burgundy concentrated his efforts on securing his influence over the king and consolidating his hold on the areas linking the Duchy of Burgundy to his holdings in Flanders. The Armagnacs may not have been able to regain control of Paris but they harried the area around the capital and tried to disrupt communications between the various lands held by the Duke of Burgundy. All this stopped the Burgundians putting any significant pressure on the Dauphin south of the Loire. The Dauphin also provided a figurehead for all the French who wanted to resist the English conquest of northern France. This resistance effort included the activities of formal armies raised by the Dauphin to harass the English by carrying out chevauchées or recapturing towns and castles. These forces also supported the Armagnac held castles and fortified towns whose garrisons could influence the surrounding areas. There was also partisan type activity much of which was local and unco-ordinated in scope, but no less irritating to the English and their supporters for all that. But the Dauphin knew better than to risk a battle-seeking strategy against Henry V.

Charles VI's mental incapacity made it much easier for Charles the Dauphin and the Armagnac party to ignore the statement of disinheritance. As a result, when both Henry V and Charles VI died in 1422 he was able to claim that he, not his nephew the infant Henry VI of England, was the rightful King of France. However, bad blood still existed between him and Philip of Burgundy and it was to be another thirteen years before they made their peace and France began to make a unified effort against the English and their supporters.

3

Scotland and
the Auld Alliance

The political situation within Scotland was just as changeable
as that in England and France. The reigns of David III
(1329–71) and Robert II (1371–90) had allowed Scotland
to grow in confidence as an independent kingdom.
This was despite David being a captive of Edward III for eleven
years, after his defeat in the Battle of Neville's Cross. After about 1350
Edward III was more concerned with trying to establish a peaceful
northern border than making efforts to pursue the claim of English
overlordship. In November 1355 the Scots attacked Berwick, encouraged
by the French to do something to distract Edward. He responded by
making a devastating invasion in 1356, which became known as Burnt
Candlemas, to remind the Scots that it was unwise to provoke him. They
learnt this lesson and truces were negotiated for most of the rest of the
fourteenth century. But truces did not mean that a state of peace spread
through the borders. The Scots were aggrieved that the English king still
held large areas of land in the Scottish marches, and the comparatively
rich towns and farming areas of the English marches were always
attractive targets for border raids.

When Robert II died in 1390 he left Scotland in a strong position
with regard to England. Indeed when Walter Bower was writing
his *Scotichronicon* in the 1440s he looked back to 'the tranquillity and
prosperity of peace' in Robert II's reign.[16] In his reign, the Scots had
recovered much of their land from English suzerainty and won a

famous victory two years before his death over the renowned Henry Hotspur, son of Henry Percy, Earl of Northumberland. Unfortunately his son and successor Robert III (actually he was christened John, but this was considered an ill-omened name for a Scottish king since it brought up memories of John Balliol) was not of the same calibre as his predecessors. John, Earl of Carrick had had experience of substantial power since 1384 when his father, who was aged about 68, relinquished his executive power as king to him. But when Carrick was badly injured in a riding accident in 1388 he had in turn relinquished these powers to his brother the Earl of Fife, who was actually christened Robert. When Carrick became king as Robert III, he seems to have been weak and easily biddable. He was 53 at the time, two years younger than his father was when he came to the throne, so age does not seem to have been the explanation for this. Royal resources and revenues were granted away as pensions to a wide range of applicants, for no obvious reasons. Nicholson describes the motivation behind this generosity: 'Usually no reason is given in the exchequer accounts for the grant of pensions. They may be attributed to Robert III's desire to please all men, especially those of the name of Stewart.'[17]

However, there may have been some political planning behind this generosity as well. King Robert III, or his immediate advisors and supporters, were exploiting the Scottish king's position as the wealthiest of the Scottish magnates, to build up an affinity in the way that John of Gaunt, Richard II and subsequently Henry IV did in England. This all seems to have weakened Fife's position as Governor and his influence over the policies and politics of Scotland declined. In 1398 Robert III attempted to satisfy the ambitions of both his brother Robert, Earl of Fife and David, his son and heir, by making the former the Duke of Albany and the latter the Duke of Rothesay. These honours, which effectively made them Scotland's premier nobles, did nothing to dampen the rivalry between the two men. Rothesay encouraged the auditors to query Albany's actions, and in January 1399, a General Council Meeting in Perth attacked Albany for misgovernment. But his brother the king stepped forward and took the responsibility for this, with the result that Albany suffered no more than being formally replaced by Rothesay as the King's Lieutenant. It is difficult to get any clear insight into what the king's role was in all this. The power struggle between Albany and his supporters on the one hand and the king's party on the other is clear, but why King Robert decided to rescue his brother is not so clear. It may just have been that Albany persuaded him to do it; it could be that Robert III knew his son Rothesay's character and wanted to limit his triumph. It may just have been another example of what was noted above; Robert III looked after members of his extended family. This sort of power struggle was very like what was happening in France throughout the reign of Charles VI (and what would happen in England in Henry VI's reign) in that the person of the king was above the struggle. There was no threat to Robert III's position in all of this. This was all a marked contrast to what was happening in England at the same time, where Richard II was deposed and his death encompassed. Rothesay seems to have been a very different character to both his father and his uncle, Albany. He seems to have been arrogant and careless of his major subjects' concerns. He tended to ignore the council appointed to advise him, just listening to the members of it who were his supporters. One important example of his arrogance and lack of understanding of the need to maintain a balance between his own interests and those of the other nobles was the way he alienated George Dunbar, Earl of March. In 1400 he married March's daughter, and then almost immediately repudiated her to make what he considered a better alliance by marrying the daughter of Archibald the Grim, Earl of Douglas. The insult of the repudiation was bad enough, but Rothesay also refused to return the bride price. The net result was that March went to England, declaring enmity towards Rothesay and the Douglas family. He allegedly went on to play a major role in the tactics used in the devastating English victory at Homildon Hill in 1402. Rothesay didn't even gain a powerful ally by his actions, since Archibald Douglas died soon after the wedding and his son and successor, also called Archibald, only supported his brother-in-law as long as it served his own interests. As will become clear later in this book, while there is no doubt about Archibald the younger's courage in battle or his loyalty in broad terms to Scotland, his true loyalty was to his own self-interest.

Rothesay's power ended in 1402 since he had been appointed as the king's lieutenant for only three years. As soon as his term expired Albany and the Earl of Douglas arrested him. He died in one of Albany's castles, like Richard II either deliberately murdered or sufficiently neglected.

A parliamentary enquiry attached no blame to either Albany or Douglas over Rothesay's death, which cleared the way for Albany to re-establish his political leadership of Scotland. The Scottish defeat at Homildon Hill made his recovery of power even easier because so many of the major nobles were killed or captured there, including both his own son Murdoch and the Earl of Douglas. This left no one in Scotland with sufficient standing to challenge him. But this didn't mean that he ruled unchecked. Firstly, he was not king. Robert III tended to remain on Bute, concentrating on trying to ensure the personal and political wellbeing of his surviving son and heir, James, who had been born in 1394. It is not known if he believed that the young prince's uncle had murderous designs on him, but Robert was determined that James should grow to adulthood outside his uncle's influence. He continued to maintain his affinity, and used his large personal landholdings to give the young prince an estate for his maintenance. Finally, in 1406 Robert decided to take advantage of the 'Auld Alliance' and send David to France where he would be free of any threats from his uncle. Unfortunately his ship was captured by English pirates and David became an honoured prisoner first of Henry IV and then Henry V. The news seems to have killed his father, so that once again Scotland's king was a captive in England. Robert III seems to have been deeply aware of his failings as a king. Bower records him as saying, in reply to a question from his wife as to when he was going to plan his epitaph and burial, 'I would prefer to be buried deep in a midden, providing that my soul be safe in the day of the Lord. Wherefore bury me I pray in a midden and write for my epitaph "Here lies the worst of kings and the most wretched of men in the whole realm".'[18] Whatever the truth in this sad tale, it may well reflect Robert's cast of mind, and why he was unable to influence events, in much the same way that Charles VI of France's mental state reduced him to a figurehead. Albany, who ruled Scotland as governor until his death in 1420, may or may not have ensured the English knew of Robert III's plans for his son, but he made sincere efforts to ransom the young king without success. Keeping hold of the King of Scotland was too much in English interests for him to be given up without a great deal of thought.

However, while these political and dynastic struggles were going on, there was another long-running area of tension within Scotland, namely the relations between the two linguistic and cultural groups.

For much of the fourteenth century, it would be a mistake to suggest that the two cultural groups were at peace, either with each other or indeed within themselves. But there wasn't the clear sense of division and even alienation between them that became apparent in the last decades of the century. This change was marked by the rise of Alexander Stewart, the 'Wolf of Badenoch'.[19] He was the son of Robert II and brother to Robert III, and was made Lord of Badenoch, one of the lordships that made up the extensive Stewart estates, in 1371. He rapidly established himself in the area by force and in 1382 was made Earl of Buchan. It is clear that Alexander, while not unique in being disruptive (Alastair Carrach, Lord of Lochaber was another disorderly noble), was exceptional in the amount of disorder he caused in the north of Scotland, something recognised at the time by the Council General Meeting in 1385.[20] But Grant makes it clears that the way he established himself was not uncommon in the Scottish Highlands at the time, it is just that he was particularly aggressive in his behaviour. He describes the technique used by the Highland lords to extend their power as follows:'[It] was to exert armed pressure in areas where legal lordship was weak or missing, achieve de facto superiority over the inhabitants and appropriate the rents …'[21] Alexander crowned his reputation in 1390 when he led a force of 'wyld wykkyd helandmen' to burn Elgin Cathedral as part of a dispute with the bishop.[22] His sons were no better behaved, for in 1392 they led a large-scale raid into Angus which was only stopped at the Battle of Glascune. This battle, like the bigger one fought at Harlaw, seems to have been a bloody stalemate, wherein the 'Highland' raiders, who were mainly lightly armed caterans,[23] were mauled by the more heavily armoured troops attempting to maintain the king's peace, but these troops in turn suffered such losses that they couldn't take any further effective action against the retreating 'Highlanders'.[24] By the beginning of the fifteenth century contemporary Scottish historians and chroniclers were beginning to make a clear separation between the 'domesticated', 'civilised' or 'tame' lowlanders, broadly those who spoke Scots English, and the 'wild' Scots, namely the Gaelic speakers. One of the clearest demonstrations of how Scotland at this time was perceived as being divided into two cultural and social traditions is the encounter known as 'the Battle of the Clans' at Perth in 1396. Clan Chattan and Clan Kay were in a dispute which threatened to become a war between these two large confederations of clans. The Earl of Crawford and the Earl of Dunbar attempted to resolve the matter through negotiation without success, so the Chiefs of the two clans agreed to what amounted to a judicial duel between thirty men from each side. Lists were set up on the North Inch at Perth to contain the fighting and, no doubt, provide seating for the important spectators. These included the king himself, Robert III, who had to be present to recognise the solution to the dispute that victory would bring. Many Scottish nobles were present, as were some English and French knights. It is probable that the king gave the signal for the fighting to start, just as he might at a more traditional tournament, but after that this fight would have borne no resemblance to a chivalric tournament. It was a ferocious fight to the death between men who at best would have worn mail shirts and open helmets, if they were equipped in line with the slightly later descriptions of gallowglasses.[25] According to the traditional accounts, when the king dropped his baton to declare the fight over, eleven men of Clan Chattan were still alive (but all were wounded), and one man from Clan Kay.[26] Whatever else this amazing spectacle demonstrated, it showed that Robert III could not control the north and west of his kingdom in the way he did in the south and east, but only legitimise matters as they were resolved in ways very different from the methods used in the more European-focussed half of his kingdom.

In the last decades of the fourteenth century and the first decades of the fifteenth century, the greatest of the Gaelic magnates, the Lords of the Isles, were expanding their influence. In the first decade of the fifteenth century Donald, the second Lord of the Isles, determined to take possession of the Earldom of Ross, which he claimed through marriage. Albany was unprepared to allow a noble as powerful as the Lord of the Isles to have the earldom and raised a large army, mainly from the English speaking areas of Scotland. Fortunately for him the Earl of March, the most consistently successful Scottish military leader of the period, was available to lead this army. In 1411 Donald seemed to be willing to confront Albany; the captive king James may have encouraged him in this. He led a large army eastwards on a great plundering raid towards Aberdeen and was intercepted by the royal army under March at Harlaw. It is difficult to reconstruct the events of the battle but it is clear that it was both on a large scale and very bloody. The Macdonald

accounts say that Donald's men broke two of the battles of the royal
army and the third took refuge in a large walled enclosure and beat off
the attacking gaelic forces. If this was the case, Donald's men may well
have taken such casualties that they had to rethink their raid, but just
as likely was that in the aftermath of a hard battle they felt that they
had gained enough booty that further fighting wasn't worth the trouble.
However, when Albany led a large army north in the following year,
Donald had to make submission to him and abandon his claims to the
Earldom of Ross. This may suggest that the Macdonald account of the
battle was biased, and made the best of what was probably a stalemate.
The importance of Harlaw is not so much which noble won or lost
but that it may well have been decisive culturally, in that it marked the
end of the expansion of 'Gaelic' Scotland and ensured that the kingdom
of Scotland continued to develop its European cultural heritage.[27]
This account of the state of Scotland makes it sound as though it was a
disorderly place racked by disputes and actual conflicts between the king
and his magnates and amongst the magnates themselves, but this was
not really the case. Compared with England in the fourteenth century
and the first two decades of the fifteenth century, where two kings were
deposed and killed and several magnates executed by the various kings
for treason, it was an orderly state. This was despite two kings of Scotland
being imprisoned in England for a number of years, royal minorities and
sustained rule by a governor (effectively a regent). Grant has suggested
that the underlying principle in the governance of Scotland was that
when the king or one of the magnates achieved some purpose by
circumventing the law and customary practice, maybe even by the use
of violence, the other leading figures in Scotland found a way to accept
this and adapt to the new circumstances. This was made easier because
most of the leading figures in Scotland in this period seem to have
been reluctant to use fatal violence on their main opponents (Robert
Bruce, later Robert I, was a notable exception to this, as was the Duke
of Albany in the first decade of the fifteenth century). A simple example
of this is the way that Donald, Lord of the Isles, was allowed to make
his submission in 1412, the year after Harlaw. This was the second time
that he had had to make submission to royal authority, but this wasn't
held against him. English kings tended not to be so understanding.
Grant suggests that in England, neither the king nor the magnates were

prepared to accept this sort of political shake-up and the natural reaction to pressure was the threat of violence or actual violence.[28] While his account is perhaps biased in favour of Scotland and the Scots, his point is well made. Scotland survived the absence of a competent ruling king better than either England or France.

The Auld Alliance and the Auld Inemie

The Auld Alliance dominated the relations between Scotland, England and France from the end of the thirteenth century. It was an agreement between the kings of Scotland and France to support each other against their mutual enemy, the King of England. It began with the agreement between John Balliol of Scotland and Philip IV of France in 1295. It was reinforced in 1326 when Robert I of Scotland and Charles IV of France agreed the Treaty of Corbeil binding themselves and their heirs to aid each other against England in both war and peace. When Edward III started to assert himself in his relations with his neighbours in the 1330s, the French kings recognised the importance of an independent Scotland as part of their policies towards the English king. Unlike so many medieval treaties which were very short-lived in their effects, this agreement was maintained through the following two centuries. But it would be wrong to think that there was wide-ranging and deep-seated animosity between the English and the Scots throughout this period. For example, in the second half of the fourteenth century there was regular trade between the two kingdoms. The Scots particularly desired English grain, and there was a steady export of English wool to Scotland, in part to try to smother the smuggling activities from England which affected the English king's tax revenue. Also, a considerable number of safe conducts were issued to Scottish students in these years to allow them to attend English universities since there was no Scottish university until 1413.

Until the fifteenth century, the Scots took very little direct part in the fighting in France in the Hundred Years War, despite this long-standing alliance with France.[29] It is worth outlining their activities in the previous 100 years because their actions between 1419 and 1424 marked a major change in their involvement in the war.

Relations between Scotland and England in the fourteenth and fifteenth centuries were bedevilled by the English king's insistence that he was Scotland's overlord. Peace treaties could only be agreed when the English put no emphasis on this, or made attempts to insert a member of the English Royal Family into the succession to the Scottish throne. But this doesn't mean that the northern marches were in a state of perpetual warfare; truces could be agreed when peace could not. This problem is most clearly demonstrated in the reign of Edward III, who, after his spectacular victory at Crécy in 1346, had a fearsome military reputation. In the same year, David III of Scotland felt honour-bound to try to help his French allies, and distract Edward from his siege of Calais. However, he was defeated and captured at the Battle of Neville's Cross. Although the English took control of large areas of Scotland south of the Forth and the Clyde in 1347, they could not establish secure control over these areas. The ravages of the Black Death in 1348–50, and Edward's focus on the war in France, allowed the Scots to regain ground slowly until, in 1355, some of the Scottish magnates attacked Berwick-upon-Tweed. Edward immediately raised an army, went north and wasted Lothian in February 1356, in what became known as Burnt Candlemas. This showed the Scots that they needed to come to terms with Edward, particularly once it became clear that they could expect no help from France after the King of France was captured later in the same year at the Battle of Poitiers. For the next twenty years or so relations between England and France settled down. In 1365 Edward III had agreed a five-year truce with Scotland, and in 1370 this was extended for another fourteen years and the ransom payments still outstanding as a result of David III's capture at the Battle of Neville's Cross in 1346 were reduced. The Scots continued to pay instalments of David III's ransom until the death of Edward III in 1376, although David had died in 1371. Robert II, David III's successor, showed notable confidence in dealing with his two larger and more powerful neighbours. He kept the French at arm's length, observing through his ambassadors in 1375; could he trust Charles V in large matters, such as French military aid for Scottish attacks on northern England, when he had let him down on small matters? The French put up with this assertiveness because they knew the long-term value of Scotland to their policy towards England. At the same time, despite the truce, the Scots increased their border raids and pressure on English-held Scottish territory in the Borders. Robert balanced this apparently freelance military activity with careful diplomacy so as not to provoke the English into taking a more aggressive interest in Scotland. So much so that when, in 1378, some Scottish Borderers took Berwick-upon-Tweed in a surprise attack, Robert did nothing in support so that English Warden of the March could quickly recover the town.[30]

However, when the truce expired in 1384, military activity increased from border raiding to become outright warfare. At this time, Robert continued in his attempts to downplay the purpose of the Scottish border activities by apparently claiming that he wanted peace but could not keep his nobles in check.[31] In 1385, Jean de Vienne, the Admiral of France, sailed to Scotland with at least 1,300 men-at-arms, 250 crossbowmen, a supply of armour and, most importantly in Robert's eyes, a substantial amount of gold.[32] In July de Vienne and the Earl of Douglas invaded England's East March. Richard II led a large army in response but the Scots (and probably the French) evaded him and attacked the West March before retiring. In November the French went home feeling that they had achieved nothing in a strategic sense with this adventure, which was the only invasion of England by a substantial French force in the whole Hundred Years War. The problem for the French was that neither David III nor his successor Robert II was really interested in the expensive gamble of war with England, but they did appreciate the French gold. The Scottish Marcher lords were the most determined party of Scots in favour of war. Robert II and Richard II both came to the conclusion that war between their countries was not to their advantage, even if some of their subjects were determined to continue military activity. In 1388 a Scottish army under the Earl of Douglas crossed the border as part of a large-scale assault on northern England. He managed to provoke Henry Percy to live up to his nickname Hotspur, and attack the Scots as night was falling. This, and the close-quarters nature of the fighting, neutralised the English advantage in archery. The Earl of Dunbar brought the main body of the Scots army up to assist Douglas. The Scots won the drawn-out, confused Battle of Otterburn, despite Douglas being killed, and returned home rich in booty and prisoners, including Hotspur himself. England's foreign policy in the 1380s oscillated between the more outward looking policy established by Edward III with adventures in France and Spain, and a quieter, more inward looking policy favoured by

Richard II, which concentrated on keeping the realm of England, Wales and Ireland peaceful and prosperous. Richard seems to have felt that the grandiose campaigns in France were a waste of money which could be better spent on material and cultural benefits. However, Richard was no pacifist as his two effective expeditions to Ireland demonstrated, and he did mount one large expedition into Scotland, but he had to concentrate more on establishing his power and control over his own kingdom than on trying to interfere in other kingdoms. By 1388, after unsuccessful expeditions to France led by his political opponents among the nobility and the defeat at Otterburn, the financial resources of England were nearing exhaustion. The French were in a similar position and so were quite prepared to negotiate a truce with the English. This was agreed in 1389 and, despite English opposition, the French insisted that Scotland be allowed to become a party to this truce as well. The Scots thought about this and agreed to it, particularly since they were not required to return to England the lands in the Border areas that they had recovered from English hands. Robert II may well have appreciated that this kind of help, French persuasion of the English to allow Scotland to be part of their diplomatic agreements, was more beneficial to his kingdom than offers of military support. Also he would have realised the potential risk of Scotland being left isolated in opposition to England. From the Scots point of view, this diplomatic support was one of the greatest gains from the Auld Alliance.

His successor, Robert III, inherited a kingdom that was in a strong position in relation to its powerful southern neighbour. The truce between England and Scotland was maintained throughout the 1390s. This period of relative peace gave the magnates on both sides of the border the opportunity to consolidate their local position, and to follow their ambitions in regard to both rivalries with their opposite numbers across the border, and their power and influence within their respective kingdoms. These manoeuvrings are outlined above, and the most significant event in Scottish military activity at this time was the Battle of Homildon Hill in 1402.

By this date the Scottish nobles felt extremely confident in their abilities to carry out successful military operations against the English. Over the preceding generation the Scots had reclaimed most of the land they had to give up to Edward III, and had won a resounding victory at Otterburn, the only large-scale battle in the Borders in the second half of the fourteenth century. Henry IV made a powerful expedition into Scotland in 1400, which, like a number of English invasions, threatened much but achieved little because the Scots did not get drawn into losable battles when they could rely on supply problems to force the English to retreat. The Scots lords quite rightly felt that Henry was insecure on his throne, and so might well not be able to respond to any military activities of theirs. They also felt that the English Marcher lords, especially the Percys, had been provocative, raiding into Scotland. So in 1402 the earls of Douglas and of Fife led a large Scottish army, perhaps 10,000 strong, into England. They raided and pillaged as far as Newcastle on Tyne and then, laden with plunder, turned back towards Scotland. An English army led by Hotspur and George Dunbar, the Earl of March, who defected from Scotland in part because the king's son jilted his daughter, caught up with the Scots near Wooler. Douglas and Fife decided to take up positions on Homildon Hill (also known as Humbleton Hill) and challenge the English to attack. This must have seemed a good plan because Douglas's grandfather James had beaten Hotspur at Otterburn with a similar tactic. Also the Scots may have felt that they now had an answer to the English archers because they had developed their own bodies of archers and had acquired a number of sets of plate armour, mainly from the French. However, Douglas was wrong. The Earl of March managed to contain Hotspur's impetuousness; indeed, Hotspur may have learnt from his previous defeat, and the English stood back and let their archers destroy the Scottish army as it stood in its serried ranks of pikemen. The English Chronicler of St Albans says of the English in this battle: 'No lord, knight or esquire took a step until the archers had defeated the enemy.'[33] Neither the Scottish archers, who were unlikely to have been present in anything like the numbers of the English archers, nor the plate armour, could save the Scots from a bloody defeat. The Earl of Douglas and a number of other Scots made brave but doomed charges to try to turn the battle but to no avail. Douglas himself was reputed to have been wounded five times including losing an eye, despite wearing armour that was said to have been three years in the making. In all, eighty-two Scots nobles were killed or captured in the battle including Douglas, Murdoch, the Earl of Fife, the king's nephew, three other earls and twelve other magnates.[34] Homildon Hill shattered the Scots' confidence that they had the measure of England militarily and diplomatically, which had been carefully built up over the preceding four decades. But Henry IV was unable to take advantage of the victory since he was distracted both by rebellion in Wales and in England. Owain Glyndŵr and the Welsh had revolted against English rule in 1400, and they were still maintaining their independence. Henry then provoked Hotspur by taking control of his noble prisoners captured at Homildon Hill without offering any real compensation. Henry recognised the diplomatic value of some of the prisoners and wanted to use them to influence relations with Scotland. This led to the Battle of Shrewsbury in 1403, where the rebellious Hotspur was killed. But things did not become quiet on the Borders yet. In 1405 James Douglas, Warden of the March (and the Earl of Douglas's younger brother), burnt Berwick. After the capture of James, heir to the Scottish throne, by the English and the death of his father Robert III in 1406, the Scots became more subdued for a while. The year of 1409 was an important one for Scotland since Archibald, Earl of Douglas, Tyneman, broke his parole to Henry IV and chose to remain in Scotland and abandon the hostages left as surety for his parole in England. Why did he do this? Probably because the Earl of March and his family were becoming re-established in Scotland, and Douglas felt the need to concentrate on maintaining his political position and his family's economic and social positions. Also, he was struggling to raise the necessary ransom, so probably decided that his freedom was more important than any debt of honour to the English king. It is a mark of the attitudes of the Scottish nobility, particularly their estimation of Henry IV and the Douglas family's power in Scotland, that breaking his parole seems to have had no effect on Douglas's standing in Scotland. Whatever was happening in the internal politics in Scotland, small-scale border raiding seems to have become the norm for the rest of Henry IV's reign.

Once Henry V came to the English throne things changed. The Scots nobles seem to have decided to act out their traditional role in the Auld Alliance. In 1415 they raided northern England while Henry was in France establishing his international reputation at Harfleur and Agincourt. The Scots were quiet while Henry was in England in 1416, but on his return to France the following year, Albany and Douglas decided that this was a chance to regain Berwick and Roxburgh for Scotland.

They advanced separately to achieve this but both turned tail on hearing that John, Duke of Bedford, Henry's brother, was heading north with a large army. Bedford made a point about Albany and Douglas's incompetence by wasting Teviotdale and Liddesdale and burning Selkirk, Jedburgh and Hawick. This adventure became known as the Foul Raid because of Albany and Douglas's behaviour and Bedford's fierce response.

After this the Scots took a different approach and in 1419 the first of several large Scottish forces landed in France. Thereafter, while the Scots sent significant forces to fight the English in France, the Border truce held.[35] This may have been because enough of the militarily active men of Scotland south of the Highlands were out of the country to mean relative peace just happened in their absence. But it is as likely that the Scottish government worked to keep the borders quiet because it benefited them. The English were sufficiently distracted by their wars in France to have no interest in attacking Scotland unless provoked. The Scots had nothing to gain by provoking the English, since recent events showed that the English could raise a large enough force to spread devastation through Scottish border areas in retaliation. So relations between Scotland and England came to be dominated by the negotiations for the return of James I.

While the borders were hardly peaceful for the rest of the fifteenth century, there wasn't another major battle until the Battle of Flodden in 1513, which was even more disastrous for the Scots than any of the earlier ones.

4

Tactics and strategy in the Hundred Years War

This book focuses on the decade between two great English victories in the wars in France, Agincourt and Verneuil. The men of France, Scotland and England who dominated the fighting in this short period had developed their own military practice in the thirteenth and early fourteenth centuries. They had done this mainly through fighting each other, and also through civil strife. During the Hundred Years War itself the English tactical system was dominant and the problem for the French and Scots was how to defeat it. The key difference of this tactical system from any other experienced by men fighting in medieval Europe was that it relied on infantry archers using powerful hand bows (that is, bows relying on the power of the archer to extract the optimum force from the bow) to control the battlefield.

Tactics

The first battle fought using the tactics that became common English practice in the Hundred Years War was fought in 1138 at Northallerton against the Scots. But after that notable victory the system wasn't used again until the first three decades of the fourteenth century and continued to be used broadly unchanged by English armies until the early sixteenth century. How did this very successful tactical system work? It revolved about the longbow, or as it has increasingly become known, the English war-bow, a description of which can be found below.[36] English armies from the fourteenth century to the first half of the sixteenth century usually fought their battles entirely on foot, as did the Scots and Welsh, but this was in marked contrast to military practice in Continental Europe, until the rise of the Swiss infantry and the Landsknechts. Edward III may have had a mounted force as a reserve in one or two of his early battles and the Black Prince's great victories at Poitiers and Nájera definitely included a timely contribution from cavalry to what were largely infantry victories. This meant that English nobles from earls and dukes to the lowliest rural knight were prepared to dismount and form up in line of battle with their paid men-at-arms and work in close cooperation with the archers, who came from the broad lower social groups. At Agincourt even the king, the charismatic Henry V, stood and fought in the battle line. When it came to a fight, there was none of the snobbery that bedevilled some French armies at this time. The men-at-arms enabled the archers to do their work in safety by providing a solid battle line that could absorb the impact of the enemy attacks whether on foot or on horse. Throughout this period the English armies drew up with the largely armoured infantry making a battle line in the centre while the archers formed up on the wings, often angled forwards slightly. At Agincourt and Verneuil there is clear evidence that the archers also formed a sort of skirmish screen in front of the men-at-arms, which probably fell back through the men-at-arms, when the enemy were close.[37] To protect themselves against the onset of the enemy, especially cavalry, the archers either took advantage of natural features like hedges and natural banks or planted hedges of stakes in front of themselves.

How many of the enemy did the archers kill or disable? Contemporary accounts rarely give us enough clear information to know. In the fourteenth century, against the Scots, they inflicted serious casualties; against the French the answer is less clear. But even if the archers at Crécy didn't kill a large number of knights, they certainly broke their charges by killing their horses. In the second half of the fourteenth century and into the fifteenth century, as plate armour became more widely worn and improved in quality, the archers probably killed fewer men. This was despite arrowsmiths developing more effective types of arrowhead and royal commands that arrowheads should be made of steel. But the archers were not rendered ineffective by good armour, which in any case could only be afforded by a limited number of fighting men. Even good armour had weak points that an arrow might find. Recent analysis of Agincourt has suggested that proud, well-armoured men shrank from the pounding of the arrows even when they were not taking wounds. The archers disrupted attacking forces on foot because of the natural instinct of men when threatened by missiles to bunch together, trying to get shelter from their comrades. This meant that, at Agincourt at least, by the time the attackers reached the English battle line many of them were disorganised and so crammed together that some proportion didn't have space to use their weapons effectively. Alternatively, men-at-arms could try to hurry through the arrowstorm to spend as little time under it as possible. This again would lead to their ranks being disordered, and more importantly, the men would be hot and out of breath. Despite the skill of the armourers a major drawback with plate armour remained; it is heavy enough that even fit, practised knights and men-at-arms got hot and tired wearing it, particularly when expending energy marching and fighting on foot. A recent article has given a valuable insight into the way wearing armour can constrict the sustained performance of the wearer.[38] When many of the armoured men began to feel too hot and breathless in battle they raised their visors to breathe more easily. There is plenty of evidence that some of the archers at least were skilled enough to notice this and shoot the armoured men in the face. Even Henry V had learnt this danger the hard way in the Battle of Shrewsbury where an arrow (probably a ricochet since he survived) struck him in the face. The archers very rarely destroyed the enemy without any real contribution from the men-at-arms, but they weakened the onset so that the men-at-arms – with the support of the archers who as they proved in battle after battle were ferocious light infantry – could defeat the enemy attacks.

Cavalry provided a different challenge to the English armies. Success in the battles of Edward III's reign came because the tactical system was unfamiliar and plate armour was just developing. At Crécy the French cavalry, in their determination to attack their equals standing in the battle line under their standards, were steered by the shape of the rising land across the front of the archers who were standing on that higher ground.[39] As a result they made little effort to threaten the archers.

At Poitiers all of the archers had some protection from the onset of the French cavalry: some used hedges (remember hedges in the Middle Ages often meant banks with the hedge plant growing on them, not just a plant barrier); others had dug small pitfalls to hinder the enemy's onset; while those on the left flank seem to have been standing in soft ground unsuitable for heavy cavalry. According to Froissart, these archers had discovered that their arrows wouldn't penetrate the armour and trappers of the knights and their horses and so had moved out to the side so that they could shoot at the much less well-protected flanks of the horsemen with devastating effect. But armoured cavalry remained the real threat to the archers. The French realised this from experience but their practice was also driven by class pride; nobles must be able to crush these lowly peasants and townsmen. There are two surviving French battle plans, compiled in October 1415 as Henry V was marching from Harfleur to Calais, which lay out how the French commanders were planning to defeat the English.[40] One survives in a document in the British Library and the other was prepared in Rouen, where substantial French forces had been gathering, initially to make some sort of demonstration in support of the besieged port of Harfleur. Both take a very similar approach to the problem of defeating the English. Both use powerful forces of cavalry to ride down the archers while the main battles attacked on foot with the support of archers and crossbowmen. However, the layout of the battlefield area at Agincourt and the ground conditions made it difficult to implement the plan; moreover, Henry was aware of the dangers cavalry posed to his archers and had them all cut a stake to make a protective hedge. This may not have been his idea, or even a European one, since Sultan Beyazid had used stakes at the Battle of Nicopolis in 1396 to protect his foot archers in this devastating victory over the European Crusader army. First-hand accounts of this battle circulated in western Europe as captured nobles were ransomed. But at the battles of Valmont in 1416, La Brossonière in 1423 and at Verneuil in 1424 well-armoured cavalry caused the English serious problems by being able to attack in sufficient numbers and too rapidly for the archers to break up the attack. Cavalry could be successful against archers despite the threat that the archers posed to their horses. This threat was minimised by the speed of a cavalry attack and was being nullified to some degree by the development of good horse armour at this time.

The English tactical system is often described as a defensive system which relied on the enemy attacking to be effective. At Crécy and Poitiers, the English army just stood defiantly before the French and the French attacked them, but matters were different in the two great battles of the fifteenth century, Agincourt and Verneuil. At Agincourt, Henry advanced on the French lines from his original position and had the archers replant their defensive stakes before launching flights of arrows. This was provocation! The French nobles were shocked that this tired, scruffy army, the majority of whom weren't even knights or men-at-arms, was advancing on them. But the real provocation came from the showers of arrows which must have caused confusion and some casualties. At Verneuil John, Duke of Bedford showed similar confidence and advanced towards the enemy until he had them in arrowshot. At both battles the advance of the English archers left the French with no choice but to attack. There is no doubt that by the start of the fifteenth century, the tools for defeating the English tactical system were in existence and were understood. These were up-to-date plate armour and speed of assault so that the attackers were under arrowshot for as short a time as possible. The twin problems for the French and their allies were firstly that they seemed to be unable to benefit from this understanding and secondly, the quality of the English armies in the first three decades of the fifteenth century.

The Scots' battle tactics had notable similarities to the English tactical system, such that it has been said that the English system was a response to the humiliation of Bannockburn. This is a reasonable argument but must not be overstated since the English military tradition always was to fight on foot. The Norman Conquest could not change this since there weren't enough incomers. But the Norman Conquest did bring English military practice more into line with what was happening in the rest of Continental Europe for maybe two centuries because the Norman and Angevin kings of England needed military forces that were effective in France to defend their lands there. But at the same time as more mailed knights were being raised in England, the Battle of Northallerton was fought in 1138 by the northern English and Normans against the Scots. The English army contained substantial numbers of archers and the knights and men-at-arms in it fought on foot, just like the armies that Edward III and Henry V used. Indeed, it is likely that more men fought as cavalry on the Scots' side than on the English. But the tactics used in this battle were a bit of an aberration for both sides as the events two centuries later showed.

In the Wars of Liberation against the English in the thirteenth and fourteenth centuries, the Scots had to find a way to defeat the English mailed horsemen. While these were available in small numbers when compared with the numbers that could be raised by the kings and princes of Continental Europe, they greatly outnumbered those that could be raised in Scotland. The Scots' solution was the schiltron; a large body of pike-armed infantry who stood on the defensive, often with their pikes facing out in all directions to make them impervious to cavalry attacks. The only problem with this tactic was that it largely relied on the enemy being so foolish as to try and attack the schiltron on horseback. At the battles of Falkirk and Bannockburn the English obliged them by doing so. Falkirk was a bloody defeat for the Scots because Edward I had control of his army, and pulled the cavalry back to allow the infantry and archers to break holes in the schiltron so that cavalry could charge home. Bannockburn was very different! Edward II had no real control over his army; the knights made fruitless attacks on the schiltrons, English archers were sent forward to shoot at the Scots but were given no protection from the Scottish cavalry, who scattered them, and finally the schiltrons ground slowly forward pressing the disorganised English back until they broke. Despite a number of disasters at the hands of the English and Welsh archers this remained the basic Scottish battle tactic until the sixteenth century.

The fundamental difference between the Scottish and English tactical systems was the archer. The Scots never produced enough competent archers to turn a battle, nor to protect their pikemen from enemy archers. Yet Scotland produced archers; they had some at the Battle of Falkirk in 1297 and they had useful bodies of archers in their armies in France in the early fifteenth century as will be described below. The tactics used within Scotland possibly differed in that there was no need to fear the charge of armoured cavalry. They probably concentrated on using blocks of infantry, 'battles' in medieval terms, which included knights and men-at-arms (including what became known as gallowglasses) reinforcing bodies of lighter armed men. In battles involving the Highland Scots swarms of light infantry, caterans, would skirmish and charge around the better-protected men. Because of the presence of these unarmoured men, local archers could be significant even in relatively small numbers.

French tactical practice was potentially the most sophisticated of the three kingdoms. Despite its divisions France was much richer than either England or Scotland and, as a result, could support many more armoured horsemen of varied social status. In addition, because of the level of wealth within the kingdom, the French knights and men-at-arms tended to have more and better plate armour at any particular time than their English or Scottish counterparts. Up to the fourteenth century, the French developed their military practice to deal with enemies in mainland Europe, not to deal with the ambitions of the English kings. Therefore they based their tactics around a hammer blow delivered by the armoured men either on horseback or on foot. The preference was the mounted charge; an obvious choice since a charge by armoured horsemen was the most powerful offensive action any European medieval army could take until the Swiss infantry tactics as practised in the fifteenth century. But the French always learnt from their defeats. Flemish infantry defeated mounted French knights at Coutrai in 1302 and in other battles, so the French knights dismounted and defeated the Flemings by fighting as heavy armoured infantry. But it would be wrong to think that the French kings were only interested in raising armies of armoured cavalry. Many of the cities and large towns in France had competent infantry militias that often included bodies of crossbowmen. At this time the crossbowman was the dominant type of missile-weapon using troops in Continental Europe and bodies of professional crossbowmen developed in addition to those who made up the often well-trained urban militias. The availability of bodies of skilled mercenaries gave another advantage to the French kings in comparison to their English royal opponents in that they had sufficient revenue from their kingdom to hire these specialist troops if necessary. However, as the events at the Battle of Crécy proved, hiring good mercenary troops, Genoese crossbowmen on this occasion, and knowing how to use them effectively, were two different things. It must also be said that, despite having realised that stalwart Flemish infantry could defeat mounted knights, the French commanders didn't seem to think other armies fighting on foot might achieve the same result. By 1346 the French had had six years of often painful experience of the English and

Welsh longbowman and of fighting dismounted English knights and men-at-arms, but they still believed armoured cavalry charges would win the battle at Crécy. They learnt quickly from this shocking defeat and, as the Hundred Years War progressed, the French proved to have experienced and thoughtful leaders who readily drew up and in many cases implemented realistic plans to defeat the English. The plans created in the lead-up to Agincourt demonstrated this ability. But the French armies often had a problem with command structures when it came to a battle. This was not just the standard medieval problem that once battle was joined the commanders(s) often led by example and so were unable to exercise any control over the army. Edward I at Falkirk and Edward III at Crécy stood back and had some control over their army in the battle, Henry V at Agincourt did not, but his example was more important. On a number of occasions some of the French princes and magnates disputed the command of the army on the day of battle even while the enemy were forming up. Such a dispute led to the Agincourt plans being poorly implemented on the day. Many nobles present at this battle seemed to be reluctant to be part of the cavalry forces whose tactically vital role was to charge down the archers, allegedly because there was no honour (or opportunity for ransoms) to be had fighting ordinary men. This was compounded by many of the leading nobles wanting to be the first into battle in their overconfident belief that they were going to 'steamroller' the English because they had so few knights and men-at-arms. As a result there was no one outside the hand-to-hand fighting with sufficient authority to make decisions when things began to go wrong for the French.

But other battles, such as at Baugé in 1421, the French and Scottish commanders kept firm control over their army and implemented their plans.

The French and the Scots both realised that the most effective way of neutralising the threat posed by the English and Welsh archers was to close with the English battle line as quickly as possible so that they were exposed to the arrowstorm for as short a time as possible. This was potentially easier for the French, with their relatively large numbers of mounted men and the more widespread ownership of good plate armour. However, until the use of horse armour became more common in the fifteenth century, the warhorse could be more of a liability than a help when facing English and Welsh archers. It presented a large target for the arrows and became difficult to control once wounded. On the rare occasions that English armies faced enemies with powerful forces of archers, mainly in civil strife such as the Battle of Shrewsbury in 1403 and the battles of the Wars of the Roses from 1455–87, they followed the same practice and closed with the enemy as fast as was possible on foot while maintaining an ordered battle line.

Strategy

As far as we can tell with our retrospective (and no doubt patchy) view of the fighting in France between 1415 and 1425, Henry V and his immediate successors and the Armagnacs both had strategic visions of what they hoped to achieve. Henry after about 1417 and John, Duke of Bedford as Regent of France, followed a strategy with three major components. If they could, they were always prepared to fight a battle, confident that the English soldiers would win. Secondly, they had a long-term strategy of reducing castles and towns and so slowly gaining control of Normandy and much of northern France. Thirdly, they tried to win over the Normans and the French by including as many as they could in their administration and attempting to run a fair and efficient administration. This approach can be cited as evidence of Henry's subtlety as a military thinker. He seems to have understood the need to try to avoid fighting the French population at large if he was to succeed in his ambitions in France. He recognised that he needed to win 'the hearts and minds' (a term first used in a military context by the British during the Malayan Emergency from 1948–60) of the population to avoid repeating the mistakes made by his predecessors in their invasions of both Scotland and France. In this he showed an understanding of warfare far in advance of most of his contemporaries, an understanding that his brother John, Duke of Bedford shared. The aim of this strategy was to secure an English King of France, something achieved on parchment at least in the terms of the Treaty of Troyes. A more realistic second best to this was to secure a division of France, with England holding the Duchies of Normandy and Aquitaine protected by extensive marcher areas, accepted by a quiescent King of France. This was more positive than Edward III's strategy of attempting to break the will of the French kings and their people by destructive raids and successful battles. But the problem with Henry V's strategy is that it required patience and didn't produce a wealth of booty in the way that a more destructive strategy did. However, it was the only way of even half-achieving Henry's ambitions. Not every English commander saw things his way. Even two of Henry's brothers, Thomas, Duke of Clarence and Humphrey, Duke of Gloucester, were keener to follow Edward III's strategy, although when Henry was in France they had to follow his plans. Ultimately this division in the strategic visions of the English governing group gave the French opportunities which, particularly from 1430 onwards, they slowly took advantage of to recover sovereignty of France.

In the first thirty years of the fifteenth century, the French developed their strategy largely in reaction to that of the English and the resources they committed to achieve it. After Agincourt they avoided battle with Henry but were quite prepared to fight smaller battles with his subordinate commanders and allies. The English commanders often presented opportunities for these actions by going on expeditions that ranged from foraging for supplies because of need, to mounting ambitious chevauchées. The French had mixed success against these but achieved significant victories at Baugé in 1421 and La Brossonière in 1423 by taking calculated advantage of the opportunities presented by careless English commanders. The French countered the English strategy of taking castles and towns by following the same strategy. In general they did not sit down for sustained sieges because they feared the approach of English relieving forces. But they had plenty of success through sudden assaults and subversion. Although Henry and the Duke of Bedford did their best to win over the French, there were always plenty of individuals who were prepared to help their countrymen by opening gates or surprising English guards.

The French had two significant strategic advantages: they had internal communications and they were of course working among fellow countrymen. Their advantage from internal communications arose because the Armagnacs led by the Dauphin Charles (eventually Charles VII) controlled most of the heartlands of France, while their enemies held the lands around the edges. The English held Aquitaine in the south and Normandy in the north, but they never managed to link the two despite holding considerable lands in Maine and Anjou. The dukes of Burgundy had a similar problem of linking their duchy in central south-east France to their lands in Flanders. When the English and Burgundians gained some level of control over Paris and the Île-de-France they at least had easy communications with each other and the Duke of Burgundy had better communications with the northern lands. The Armagnacs also had the advantage of the Loire, which formed a 'moat' between their heartlands and disputed lands in Maine and Anjou. If the English were going to defeat Charles they had to take and hold one of the well-defended Loire bridges first. Ultimately, this proved to be too great a task.

The French people fell into three groups: those who actively supported the English; those who supported whoever brought relative peace and didn't make too heavy demands on them; and those who supported the Armagnacs. The majority of this last group lived south of the Loire, just as the majority of the first group lived in Normandy and Aquitaine. But Armagnac supporters north of the Loire were a persistent problem for the English and source of hope and support for the Armagnacs. Burgundian supporters did not fall into groups quite so clearly. While a number had reservations about their dukes' relations with the English, very few changed allegiance and joined the Armagnacs.

The Scots did not have independent strategic aims in a military sense. Their traditional role in the 'Auld Alliance', of distracting the English by invading northern Britain, was in abeyance since the defeat at Homildon Hill in 1402 and the capture of the heir to the Scottish throne in 1406. After more than a decade of relative peace, Charles of France reinvigorated the Auld Alliance in his search for allies and mercenaries to maintain his resistance to the English. For five years until its destruction at Verneuil the 'Army of Scotland' was a vital part of Charles's strategy.

5

Recruiting armies in England, Scotland and France in the Middle Ages

Two methods for raising armies were used in the three kingdoms. Firstly, there was the feudal summons whereby able-bodied men were required to come to specified muster points with their arms to take part in the defence of the kingdom from an outside threat. They served at their own expense for a specified number of days and thereafter could go home unless the king paid them. The core of the feudal army was the mailed horseman. Wherever it was established in western Europe the purpose was to provide a select group of men with the resources (usually land but sometimes an annual payment) to allow them to practise arms and afford to own arms and armour. In addition to these often highly skilled fighting men the feudal host would also include infantry levies of greater or lesser military skill. The second method was the use of what was called an indenture in England and Scotland; a contract agreed between the king (or one of the great magnates) and a captain. This contract specified the number of men, their weaponry, their period of service, their pay and the muster date and place. This second method of raising armies encouraged the development of a wider range of professional fighting men, both mounted and infantry.

England

The system for raising armies changed from simple feudal summons and terms of service to the use of a majority of troops raised through indentures earlier in England than it did in Scotland or France. The feudal summons raised forces to defend the kingdom through men serving for forty days at their own expense. In the twelfth and thirteenth centuries the English kings issued a series of Assizes of Arms, culminating in the Statute of Winchester issued by Edward I in 1285. These laid down the arms and armour that should be owned and used by each category of Englishman as defined by the value of their lands and property. These requirements were over and above the feudal duty of knights of whatever standing to be able and willing to serve the king as mailed cavalry when he summoned them. Since armoured horsemen were potentially available through this feudal duty, the Statute of Winchester required most Englishmen to be prepared to serve as infantry; only a relatively small group of wealthier landholders were expected to have a horse. To ensure that men met their duty of holding and practising with arms, a View of Arms was held twice a year. In comparison with the military skills and equipment expected of the men of France noted below, English kings concentrated on summoning large bodies of infantry rather than cavalry. In part this happened for economic reasons; England just could not support numbers of mounted knights and men-at-arms to rival France, but it also reflected the military tradition of the English who had always fought on foot.[41] What was particularly noteworthy in the Statute of Winchester was that two of the categories of men were required to serve as archers. One group was drawn from the peasants and townsmen who had sufficient wealth to keep their family without fear of dearth in normal circumstances, those who had '… from 40/- land and more unto 100/- of land, sword, bow and arrow and a knife'. Beneath these was another much larger group of those with little land and few goods whose duty is defined as 'all others that may shall have bows and arrows …'.[42] Medieval Englishmen thought of this statute as defining the nature and limits of their military dues to the nation and the king for the following two centuries. Once the value of military archery had been established by the great victories at Sluys, Crécy and Poitiers, the English kings were concerned that the Englishmen should practise archery to ensure a ready supply of men capable of using the war-bow. In 1363 Edward III issued a proclamation that required '… every able bodied man on feast days when he has leisure shall in his sports use bows and arrows, pellets and bolts, and shall learn and practice the art of shooting …'.[43] No doubt obedience to this proclamation was patchy, and later kings certainly felt the need to make similar legal demands on their male subjects, but there doesn't seem to have been a shortage of competent archers until the sixteenth century, by which time the war-bow was being superseded by gunpowder even in English practice.

Both cavalry and infantry raised through feudal summons had received pay for their service in the reign of Edward I because of the length and frequency of his wars. This practice of paying feudal levies was continued in Edward III's reign and was the mechanism that supported much of the infantry used at Crécy and the siege of Calais. But using feudal levies for the fighting in France was no cheaper than raising forces through indentures – the men had to be paid for all their service in France since it was outside the realm of England. Both Edward I and Edward III wanted their armies to serve longer than that and outside the kingdom in Scotland and France. As the Battle of Crécy proved, the infantry raised by a feudal summons could be very effective. The archers raised this way may have been of varying skill and quality but their effectiveness at Crécy showed that many ordinary English and Welsh men had practised archery enough to be very useful in battle. To complement this introduction of regular paid service for feudal forces, the kings of England had been issuing indentures since the 1330s at least.[44] By the second half of the fourteenth century the English armies engaged in the Hundred Years War were all raised through indentures for paid service. This meant that the English kings knew how many soldiers they would have (at the muster points at least) for their campaigns. By the fifteenth century, English armies raised this way tended to consist of up to three archers for every man-at-arms. One interesting small change in the men recruited into the English forces in France is that the number of criminals drafted into them to earn a pardon declined markedly in the fifteenth century, in particular when compared with the number in Edward III's armies.[45] This may have made the maintenance of discipline easier, an important factor once the English forces were holding lands in France and were required to do as little as possible to alienate the

French population. Raising forces through indentures made a major contribution to the success of the English military effort in northern France in the fifteenth century because it made the numbers of soldiers available much more predictable and encouraged the development of professional forces as men signed on under one indenture after another. Curry has commented on the 'high degree of cohesiveness' of the individual companies under Henry V and the early regency of the Duke of Bedford, while being less certain about how the companies depended on each other.[46]

This is another example of the much noted characteristic of soldiers throughout recorded history; namely that they fight to support their comrades in their unit rather than necessarily fighting for any larger ideal, such as a country. Inspiring leaders like Henry V, Thomas Montague, the Earl of Salisbury, Joan of Arc and John Talbot, the Earl of Shrewsbury were all able to connect with this basic unit loyalty and forge formidable field armies out of these potentially disparate units. I believe, judging from the performance of the English army at Verneuil, John, Duke of Bedford was another such leader. The main problem for Bedford in his Regency of France was not finding competent men willing to serve in France, but finding the money to pay them. This was not an English problem alone; it affected the French to a greater degree until some time in the 1430s. After Henry V's death, money became a major determining factor in the size of the English armies serving in France rather than strategic demands. One sign of this is the term of many of the indentures. Those covering key garrisons and the retinues of a few key officers were long-term, being in force for as long as the officer held his post. Others were issued for a six-month period of service to cover what was conventionally thought of as the campaigning season. This was an unrealistic economic measure that did not seriously damage the English war effort because the Armagnacs were having even more trouble raising money to pay their soldiers through much of the 1420s. But it did have two bad consequences for the English war effort. Firstly, it left the English government in France with the issue of disorder caused by unemployed soldiers in the reign of Henry V and in Bedford's regency. While both these rulers made broadly successful efforts to contain this problem, it was a distraction. Secondly, by reducing the number of English troops available to maintain the English hold over northern France between late autumn and late spring, it made it easier for the French to take towns and fortresses by surprise and disrupt communications and supplies. Small bodies of French professional soldiers in personal retinues and local irregular forces took advantage of this. The English military effort in France from Henry V's campaign of conquest starting in 1417 to the end of the Hundred Years War depended on the coordination of three components: 'expeditionary' forces from England, garrisons, and field armies raised in the English-held lands in France. There was an obvious interdependence amongst these three components since the expeditionary forces provided a potential influx of 'new blood' to contribute to the other two, while field armies were often raised from garrisons. The English leaders in the fifteenth century don't seem to have needed to hire mercenaries since they could raise all the soldiers they needed from the British Isles. Some men from Flanders and the German states could be found in the English armies. Some of these came from states traditionally supportive of English ambitions in France, others came to fight under renowned English leaders such as Henry V and a few individuals and small groups just because the English hired fighting men. One example of these men was a Danish man-at-arms, Andrew Ogard, who fought at Verneuil in the Duke of Bedford's retinue. He can be traced as part of Bedford's household from 1422 to at least 1430.[47] But overall, the numbers were always very small.

Since the English tactical system seemed to be so successful, the English commanders were reluctant to develop it. The 'standard' ratio of types of soldier recorded in the indentures was three archers to one man at arms. Once the enemy had broadly arrow-resistant armour and/or advanced on foot to avoid the disorder brought about by wounded horses, success often depended on the men-at-arms being able to resist greater numbers of enemy men-at-arms. From the 1420s onwards this ratio often shifted to include a higher proportion of archers.[48] The reasons for this were nothing to do with the continuing military value of the archers, but with the reluctance of men who were wealthy enough to serve as men-at-arms to take part in the French wars, and the fact that it was cheaper to hire archers because their pay was less. The consequence of this was that the English battle lines could be fragile, particularly against cavalry. There is little if any evidence that the English armies in France came to resemble those used in the Wars of the Roses, where billmen consolidated the battle line so that the proportion of archers to billmen and men-at-arms combined was nearer to one to one.

France

The popular view of French armies in the Hundred Years War is that they were made up of a large number of nobles, knights and men-at-arms who regularly showed great courage but had trouble obeying orders. While there is some truth in this, Agincourt being the classic example of this stereotype, it doesn't tell the whole story. The French commanders were often men with considerable military experience and common sense, who were perfectly capable of planning for battle in ways that gave them a good chance of victory, as the Agincourt plan mentioned above makes clear and as will also become clear in the account of the Battle of Verneuil. At Agincourt the commanders had trouble getting their noble colleagues to do what was necessary to maximise the chance of success. But the other problem the French had was that even when they had made sound preparations and were competently implementing them, the English armies often had trouble recognising when they were beaten, as the battles at Valmont in 1416 and at Verneuil demonstrate.

In all three kingdoms the kings could issue a summons to their healthy male subjects to come to muster points with their arms to repel invasions. In France this was known as the '*arrière-ban*', a summons issued on many occasions in the Hundred Years War to resist the English. These were usually regional summons to face a particular threat in the same way as the English kings would call out the men of particular counties. One such summons made in 1369 requires the men living in both towns and the countryside to assemble 'duly armed and mounted, and those that cannot reasonably procure mounts shall be adequately armed, each according to his rank and ability ...'[49] Twenty years later, one of Charles VI's advisors wrote an allegory discussing military practice as a guide to the young king who had just come of age. In this he advocated relying more on selected professional soldiers who would have greater skill and discipline than on forces raised through the *arrière-ban*. He contrasts these professionals with 'a large crowd of your subjects, some of whom will have come voluntarily, others through the *arrière-ban*, but all of whom will lack discipline, like men coming to a fair'.[50] As the fighting in Normandy and northern France in the 1420s would show, the author is unduly pessimistic about the effectiveness of men summoned under the *arrière-ban*, particularly when they are defending their own neighbourhood. Henry, using his title of Duke of Normandy, first issued this feudal summons to the landholders of Normandy in 1418. After his death in 1422, John, Duke of Bedford, acting as Regent of France, continued to use the *arrière-ban* as a way of raising effective bodies of Norman troops to fight alongside English soldiers in defence of the English-ruled Duchy of Normandy.[51]

The French kings of the fourteenth century reacted quickly to the assaults of the English under Edward III and the ravages of the Black Death to try to ensure a ready supply of competent fighting men. In 1351 John II, later captured in the Battle of Poitiers, issued a royal ordnance concerning the pay, equipment and organisation of the royal army. Much of it is concerned with the organisation of cavalry, ordering that men-at-arms be brought together in companies of at least twenty-five, but varying in size depending on the noble status of the leader. A royal officer such as the Constable or Master of the Crossbowmen put these larger companies together from small groups or individual men-at-arms at the muster point. The royal officer appointed a knight to lead the company and, in an attempt to ensure discipline in the army, made the express instruction that 'those of this company be expressly ordered, on our behalf, to obey and follow the said knight …'[52] The ordnance also included instructions for the recording of the horses used by the men-at-arms and declared that the Crown would provide a replacement for any lost while campaigning. The leader of each company was left with the responsibility of checking that his men were appropriately equipped. Only the last section of the ordnance was concerned with infantry. These should be grouped together in companies of twenty-five or thirty under a captain who received double pay. As with the cavalry this captain was responsible for checking that his men were properly equipped, and for creating a small pennant to act as a rallying point for the company. The ordnances list only two types of infantry levy; crossbowmen and men with shields. It is possible that the men with shields were pavise carriers to protect the crossbowman in the field, rather than men carrying shields and either a pole or edged weapon. Pavises were very necessary given the vulnerability of crossbowmen to enemy missile shot if used in field armies. The French had already learnt this at Crécy when the unfortunate Genoese crossbowmen were dispersed by showers of warbow arrows from the English and Welsh archers.

The ordnances of the French kings issued later in the fourteenth century continued to talk mainly of the use and organisation of men-at-arms. One issued in 1374, which shows that desertion was also a problem for the French kings, talked in terms of the men-at-arms being organised in units of about 100 men. Again it states that royal officers will organise these units and designate leaders when necessary.

While these ordnances are much more interested in the terms of service and organisation of mounted men-at-arms, a reflection of this being a particular strength of French military resources rather than an expression of an attitude that only noble and gentry fighting men counted, they should not be taken as showing that the French kings did not understand warfare. Large bodies of French men-at-arms fought on foot at Poitiers in an effort to neutralise the destructive power of the archers, showing that the French understood the dangers of attacking stalwart infantry in a good defensive position on horseback. Yet they also appreciated that armoured cavalry remained a battle winner in the right conditions.

Although France could support large numbers of men-at-arms, both noble and non-noble, who could fight on horse and on foot, the French kings also made sporadic efforts to raise bodies of effective infantry who could act as missile troops as well as take their place in the line of battle as men-at-arms. In the 1360s and 1370s Charles V took advantage of the Treaty of Brétigny with Edward III to develop French military resources by encouraging the towns and cities to raise bodies of archers and crossbowmen. Unfortunately, in the following more peaceful decades these men do not seem to have maintained their skills. It is difficult to know how many bowmen, most of whom would be crossbowmen, were in the army defeated at Agincourt. French pay records relating to 1415 show companies with a ratio of one bowman to two men-at-arms at best but a good number consisted solely of men-at-arms.[53] Evidence from other campaigns suggest that at times in the late fourteenth and early fifteenth centuries, French armies included companies that were half archer, half men-at-arms, but they never seemed to rival the effectiveness of the English and Welsh archers.[54] The French shortage of missile troops was finally solved in Charles VII's military reforms in the 1440s, which led to his kingdom being able to raise powerful balanced forces of cavalry, infantry, missile troops and artillery, with a notable recognition of the effectiveness of gunpowder weapons. However, after 1418 it is likely that quite a number of ordinary men in Maine, Anjou, the Île-de-France and other areas of regular conflict became experienced soldiers either in the retinues of local leaders fighting the English or as part-time soldiers in defence of their neighbourhoods.

The French military leaders in the fifteenth century clearly understood the significance of archery on the battlefield, how could they not given their experiences in the previous century? Their efforts to recruit bodies of archers relied in large part on hiring mercenaries. There are several mentions in the records of companies of Genoese crossbowmen being employed in France in the decade after Agincourt. The Scots, long-time allies of the French through the Auld Alliance, were often seen as mercenaries rather than allies, since the French kings were responsible for their pay. Charles VII clearly put them in the despised category of mercenary on occasion because of their tendency to live off the land when he could not afford to pay them. But he also recognised their loyalty and military value because he made considerable efforts politically and financially to get as many Scottish troops as he could. The Scots seem to have been longbowmen, but whether their bows matched the power of those used by the English and Welsh archers is uncertain. The big question is what sort of bowstaves did they have access to? By the beginning of the fifteenth century England had well-established trade links to northern Europe and with the Italians to obtain supplies of good-quality yew bowstaves.[55] But there is much less evidence of any such trade supporting the Scottish archers of this time.

The ordnances of John II noted above show that the French took much more interest in raising bodies of men accustomed to use the crossbow than the English did. The virtues of the crossbow for use in the defence of garrisons were appreciated in both countries. By the beginning of the fifteenth century it was more powerful than a military longbow: the shooting arc followed by the bolt of crossbow was flatter than that followed by an arrow from a military longbow (except at ranges of 60yd or less) and so it was more likely to strike armour at a penetrating angle; and it required less training to become competent in its use than did a military longbow. Whether these powerful crossbows, spanned with the aid of a small winch, outranged the military longbow is doubtful. But the great disadvantage of the crossbow was that it was much slower to shoot than a military longbow, which meant that crossbowmen were never able to have a major influence on the battlefield during the Hundred Years War.

While the French raised bodies of well-trained crossbowmen both from town militias, particularly those in the north of the country, and by hiring them from the Italians, especially from Genoa, they were unable to develop a tactical system that used them effectively in the field. In part this was a matter of rate of shot. Even when protected by pavises, crossbowmen were likely to be overwhelmed by an arrowstorm launched by the English and Welsh archers.

The French kings often employed considerable bodies of mercenary troops in their armies. The employment of mercenaries was a complicated matter. They come in two types: general fighting men and specialists. The general fighting men often came from kingdoms which had a feeling of enmity towards the English for various reasons, such as the Navarese in the fourteenth century and the Scots in the fifteenth century. The importance of the Scots was that they provided good-quality infantry in numbers that seemed to be unavailable from within France. The specialist troops were hired to fill perceived gaps in the military skills that were available to the French kings from their own subjects. Genoese crossbowmen were employed in both the fourteenth and fifteenth centuries because they were reckoned to be among the best in Europe. The Lombard heavy cavalry employed in the 1420s were employed for the same reasons. The need for this latter group is more surprising given that the French could always raise good numbers of armoured cavalry. The explanation was twofold. Firstly, the Lombards had the best armour of the time for both men and horses, which made them broadly impervious to war-bow archery. Secondly, their employment, along with that of Castilian and Scottish men-at-arms, probably reflected the French leaders' level of confidence in the morale of French men-at-arms after Agincourt and other reverses. In the first quarter of the fifteenth century the French kings employed mercenaries on such a scale that many of their armies were more foreign than French. This was less true of the garrisons that held castles, towns and their surrounding areas because the mercenaries had a tendency to live off the land as the French king was always struggling to find money to pay them.

The Scots supplied a whole army, albeit not an official royal army of Scotland but one raised by Scottish magnates, particularly the Douglases and their connections. The French and the Scots negotiated treaties that allowed the French fairly free access to Scotland to recruit armies and arrange their transport to France. These have not survived although they were referred to in the negotiations held in 1423, which raised the army that fought at Verneuil.[56] There is evidence that the French tried to do the same in negotiations with Castile, but that they only succeeded in getting smaller numbers of troops with knightly or noble commanders.[57] Northern Italy provided a wide range of troops, including the crossbowmen and heavy cavalry already mentioned. Genoa and Milan were important recruiting centres for the French envoys. Since warfare in Italy was largely a commercial activity dominated by the *Condottieri*, mercenary captains who led ready-made armies on contracts agreed with the various states in the Italian peninsula, there were plenty of companies available for the French to hire. Some might be hired from the Italian state itself, like the Genoese crossbowmen, others with the sanction of the north Italian rulers. The Duke of Milan certainly allowed French recruiters to work in his lands, probably feeling that it was a good way to rid them of underemployed mercenary companies.[58]

One of the drawbacks of employing mercenaries has already been noted; they tended to live off the land they were hired to defend. While this was a notorious problem with mercenaries, Charles was being disingenuous when he made disparaging comments about them, since native French armies regularly behaved the same way as the French kings were always very tardy with pay. But this leads to the main problem with mercenaries; they were expensive and had to be paid fairly punctually, certainly much more frequently than native troops who seem to have been more resigned to pay being owed. An associated problem with mercenaries, which seems to have been much more damaging in the fourteenth century than in the fifteenth century, was how to get rid of them when you either no longer needed them or could no longer afford them. In the fourteenth century the general mercenary troops that had been employed by both sides started to live off the land in large companies when peace was declared. Their numbers were such that they presented real problems to the French when they tried to restore peace. This was much less apparent in the fifteenth century, in part because there were probably a lower proportion of mercenaries employed. The Scots, for example, officially thought of themselves as allies, as even Charles VII saw them some of the time. In the fifteenth century peace and order was disrupted by underemployed native troops, whether English or French, who could be more easily drawn back into employment in the campaigning seasons.

Scotland

Military practice in Scotland in the fourteenth and fifteenth centuries differed from that in both England and France in that the Scots did not develop paid, contracted armies for 'domestic' use.[59] The armies used in the name of the King of Scotland to rebuff English incursions, raid northern England and contain their troublesome Highland subjects were largely raised on the old feudal principle that able men served at their own expense for forty days both inside and outside Scotland. This did not mean that they were all inexperienced, poorly equipped amateurs, as their successes in these centuries proved. However, by the end of the fourteenth century the 'bond of retinue' had become important. These seem to have been largely superseded by 'bonds of alliance' and 'bonds of manrent' by the late fifteenth century.[60] 'Bonds of retinue' differed from the English indentures used to raise armies in that they seem to have been made between magnates and lesser nobles as a way of the magnate building up his retinue and binding his lesser tenants to him in return for money rather than land. They were very similar to 'money fiefs', found in very small numbers in England and larger numbers in France, whereby the king gave a man an annual payment on the understanding that he would serve the king in war. Clearly the magnate might have used the retinue built up in this way in any of the national wars against the English, but it would also have given him standing when he was engaged in disputes with other magnates. Retinues raised with these bonds would have been at the heart of the army which fought the great Battle of Harlaw against the Lord of the Isles. Possibly the use of money rather than land as the payment for the support of lesser nobles and gentry became important in Scotland because of the relative shortage of good land.

By the end of the fourteenth century, family groupings had become apparent as a mechanism for raising military retinues as true feudalism decayed.[61] These were the clans in the Highlands and the kins in the Lowlands. There is very little evidence of significant numbers of Highlanders being present in the 'Army of Scotland' in France, but it is likely that companies raised through Lowland kins were present.

The 'Army of Scotland' that served in France between about 1419 and 1424 was in some ways just a very large retinue raised at the request of Charles, the Dauphin, later Charles VII of France. He paid the leaders of the Scots for specified numbers of soldiers. These may not have been specified in contractual agreements issued to the captains in Scotland before they raised their men, but the numbers were certainly recorded once the army was in France in accounting records of pay issued to the Scottish commanders. While it is reasonable to assume that such monies were used to pay the Scottish troops, to some extent at least, these men also tended to live off the land that they were hired to protect. Money was at the core of why so many Scots were prepared to fight in France. There may have been traditional ill feeling towards the English; certainly the Earl of Douglas had a long history of fighting them, although even he would trim to meet the need of the times. Some ordinary soldiers may have followed their leaders out of a sense of duty to their kin chief or landlord. But there is no doubt that many of them, just like their enemies in the English armies, fought because it seemed worthwhile. The chances of pay and booty outweighed the risks. The Earl of Douglas himself was hired for the price of being made Duke of Touraine and Lieutenant General of France.

Discipline

Discipline in the armies and garrisons of Burgundy, England, France and Scotland in the first quarter of the fifteenth century is a complex matter. English armies were the only ones fighting in their enemies' lands for most of the wars. But as is noted in more detail elsewhere, once Henry V had declared that the purpose of his war in France was to recover his just inheritance, particularly the Duchy of Normandy, the English troops were expected to behave as though they were defending their own land, not seizing the enemy's lands. This attitude, that the English were defending their just landholdings in France and so should treat the inhabitants justly within their own Norman and French laws, became more important after the Treaty of Troyes in 1420. So, both the English and French armies should have treated the civilians with respect for the same reason; they were not enemies. Of course this did not happen because when one side moved into lands at least nominally under the control and protection of the other they pillaged; not necessarily out of malice but often out of financial need, both to feed and support themselves and their comrades and to supplement their pay. Bedford made determined efforts to deal with deserters, who were often a source of this type of disorder. Brigandage and irregular resistance by mainly French people exacerbated the abuse and mistreatment of civilians. Charles the Dauphin also recognised these problems, and made sporadic efforts to contain brigandage in the areas he controlled. His efforts seem to have been less successful than those made by Bedford's administration.

The other group within which discipline, or lack of it, could have serious consequences was the commanders, particularly when an army was preparing for battle and in the battle itself. The French performance at Agincourt gives clear evidence of the consequences of the reluctance on the part of noble leaders to obey orders (or perhaps requests) from their nominal commanders in battle. Sir John de la Pole's defeat at La Brossonière in 1423 demonstrates the strategic and political consequences when a commander disobeyed his orders at a strategic level. But other commanders, such as the Earl of Salisbury, carried out their roles very successfully and had sufficient understanding of the broad strategic purpose of a campaign to enable them to extend their role to great effect. Salisbury also had a keen understanding of the discipline necessary to give him the best chance of success in battle. His preparations in the final stages of the expedition that resulted in the Battle of Cravant in 1423 are an excellent example of this. He had been dispatched by Bedford, the Regent of France, to help the Burgundians raise the siege of Cravant. He met up with the Burgundian army that he was helping in this (the events of the battle suggest that in reality the English were the main part of the combined army in effectiveness at least) at Auxerre, about 12 miles from the enemy at Cravant. In the council of war held on his arrival he made every effort to ensure that the two allies would work well together in the battle to come. It is most likely that it was on his insistence that a set of ordinances of war were issued to the combined army. Among the English, sets of ordinances of war can be found from as early as Richard II's reign (although these are believed to be based on earlier sets from Edward III's time),[62] and are another sign of the professionalisation of warfare among the English. It is worth looking at these ordinances of war because there is no clear evidence that the French, Burgundians or Scots issued similar ordinances to help maintain discipline. Certainly the ordinances issued by the French kings noted above were more general being concerned with mustering, checking appropriateness of arms, establishing units and their captains and establishing the overall commanders rather than detailed disciplinary rules found in the English ones. The ordinances issued in Auxerre made a clear statement that the English and Burgundian forces joined in one indivisible army. Recognising that soldiers of different nationalities rarely get on even when close allies, the men were ordered to live in harmony with each other and a marshal from each nation was appointed to oversee this. Importantly, given the number of occasions in fifteenth-century warfare when opponents had a very limited idea of where each other was, a scouting force of 120 men-at-arms, half Burgundian and half English, was established with orders to set out the following day to assess the French positions. The men were to carry two days' food, and back-up supplies were organised. English tactical practice was enforced by articles that required each archer to have a stake to set for his defence and that everyone was to dismount when near the enemy and the horses were to be taken well to the rear. Finally, no one was to leave the march or the battle line without permission and no prisoners were to be taken until the victory was certain. This last proviso was very important because of the disruption that could be caused to a battle line if men got embroiled in securing ransom-worthy prisoners. Nothing was unexpected in these ordinances given the circumstances of fifteenth-century warfare, but the very fact that they were issued showed experienced commanders (almost certainly Salisbury following English practice in this case) knew the value of spelling out such practical details.

The events of the Battle of Verneuil demonstrated the importance of good discipline at both levels: discipline among individual soldiers and retinues and the discipline among the various major commanders in each army.

6

Arms and armour at the time of the Battle of Verneuil

ll three kingdoms used the same types of arms and armour; it was just that each favoured the use of some particular types more than others. This came from each of three kingdoms having different types of soldier as the core of their armies. Archers, for example, were raised by English, Scottish, French, Gascon and Burgundian captains, but the most sought after were the English and Welsh. Why? They certainly had more experience and had lived in a country which had actively encouraged military archery for at least three generations by the time of Verneuil. But England and Wales were not the only countries which developed some tradition of hand bow archery. William Wallace had archers from Ettrick Forest at the Battle of Falkirk, although it was their absence rather than their presence that had an effect on the outcome of the battle. The Counts of Foix in Aquitaine used archers, both local recruits and English hirelings, in their wars with their noble rivals in the area from about 1360 onwards. The Burgundian army throughout the fifteenth century included archers, perhaps initially in imitation of their English allies. The Burgundians were both enthusiastic hirers of English and Welsh archers and employers of 'home grown' archers. So the question remains, why were the English and Welsh the dominant archers on the battlefield for two centuries? While they were not invincible, indeed they were on the losing side in a number of battles, they were never defeated by archers of another nation. But, while we always think of the English and Welsh as longbow archers, the English at least also used crossbows to a limited degree. Unlike the practice in Continental European armies, there is no evidence that they used them in field armies, but only in garrisons.

Men from all three kingdoms wore plate armour, but again the proportion of men using part or full plate armour varied in the three kingdoms. There were two significant stages in the development of plate armour that happened around the beginning of the fifteenth century which have great importance for the Battle of Verneuil. These were the manufacture of full suits of plate armour and advances in iron and steel production. Taken together, they meant that a man wearing the best quality plate armour could be reasonably confident that war-bow arrows presented no fatal threat until they were shot at point-blank range (about 40–60yd) or found one of the gaps in a suit of plate armour necessary to allow movement. Protecting these openings in a suit of armour was a challenge to armourers which they met with increasing success in the fifteenth century. Just as the English tactical system was unique in military history, so the western European development of full suits of rigid plate armour is not found in any other culture.[63] In the Moslem world, India, China and Japan, robust helmets, chainmail, scale armour and relatively small plates that overlapped or reinforced chainmail were the norm. All of these cultures had sufficient metallurgical skills to make effective plate armour if they wished, it was just that they seemed to prize the flexibility of their style of armour over the arguably higher level of protection offered by full plate armour. Why western Europe military culture developed suits of full plate armour which were extravagantly expensive in their use of materials and skilled time is difficult to explain for certain. The Classical Greek tradition favoured rigid breast and back plates while the Roman tradition went for smaller overlapping plates or even scales. It is likely that the use of powerful crossbows in Continental European warfare and the use of the English and Welsh longbow were a powerful stimulus for this development. Advances in iron and steel production in the late fourteenth century made the development of full suits of plate armour worthwhile because they made it likely that the plate would be more or less impervious to missiles. It was in north Italy where 'a certain sophistication in manufacturing techniques is apparent by 1400 when higher quality iron and steel were produced by new carburising processes and the use of the blast furnace'.[64] These technological improvements, particularly surface hardening, enabled armourers to improve the impenetrability of their products without necessarily increasing the weight of the suit of armour. This was a significant improvement to field armours, which were tiring to wear while engaging in demanding physical activity like advancing across a rough battlefield or hand-to-hand fighting. If men wearing armour designed for fighting on horseback were fighting on foot, they would find this more tiring than if they had been wearing a foot armour, because a mounted man would tend to wear heavier leg protection. This would have a noticeable effect on the way they walked and on their sustained agility. This may explain in part the behaviour of the Lombards in the Battle of Cravant (see the account of this battle below). Also, most plate armours, whether designed to be worn on foot or horseback, restricted how deeply the wearer could breathe, which in turn affected the wearer's stamina.[65] In addition to these technological developments, by the second decade of the fifteenth century the armourers of north Italy had come to the final stage of the development of the various pieces of a full body armour, and the way they fitted together. The developments of the rest of the century were aimed at improving the functionality and appearance of the armour.[66] This armour had been developed to meet the needs of the professional mercenary soldiers in Italy. They had concentrated on ensuring that a mounted man could charge in battle with confidence that he was unlikely to be fatally wounded by the opposing mercenaries. As a result the shoulder pieces or pauldrons were large and asymmetrical (the left being larger than the right to remove the need for a shield) to protect a common weak point in most earlier armours, and the helmet (known as an armet) was shaped like the bow of a ship to deflect arrowstrikes and other blows as the owner charged. These developments led to armour from north Italy being the most sought after for perhaps two generations until the German armourers caught up with the technology. It also meant that mercenaries from north Italy who were equipped with this armour were much sought after, as the account of the Battle of Verneuil below will show.

In the fifteenth century, the design and shape of armour, particularly the pieces protecting the body and the head, developed to improve the protection it offered. Two major helmet types developed: the bascinet, a close-fitting helmet often tapering to a point at the top of the head to provide glancing surfaces; and the sallet, which looked a bit like a smooth, steel baseball cap worn back to front with a tail to protect the back of the neck. Both types were used with or without visors.

A fundamental problem with good suits of plate armour was that, to be as comfortable to wear and effective as possible, the armour had to fit the wearer well. In other words they were made to measure. This made the suits very expensive and time-consuming to obtain. If the armour was made to measure this presented the owner with a major problem – he couldn't change shape much. This problem is made clear by the armours of Henry VIII in the collection of the Royal Armouries, which show that he gained weight as he aged. As a result it was difficult for anyone other than the original owner of the armour to wear the suit without alterations, which might include modifying or replacing some parts. But armour was like modern men's suits: not all are made to measure. There are records of merchants carrying bales of armour and numbers of helmets of differing styles to England, France and Spain. This armour was not designed to make full suits but provide a good level of protection for men who could not afford bespoke armour. Since armour needed to fit well to be comfortable and effective, this had an effect on its value as booty.

Plate armour was worn with various types of soft or flexible protection, and many fighting men wore very little plate – maybe only a helmet. In the main, men who had little if any plate armour couldn't afford it and would hope to get some as booty. However, some men, what proportion we cannot know, deliberately relied on the more flexible forms of protection because they were lighter, less draining of stamina and relatively effective. These soft, flexible armours included gambesons, chainmail, and brigandines. The gambeson (commonly known as an aketon or actoun in Scotland) was usually made of linen, quilted and padded in vertical strips, commonly long enough to reach the wearer's thighs. The quilting was usually stuffed with folded linen, woollen fibres or other cheap frayed cloth. When sleeves were part of the gambeson they were separate pieces laced to eyelets in the armholes of the gambeson. The impenetrability of the gambeson depended on how tightly folded the stuffing was but it was an efficient protection much favoured by the English and Welsh archers and Scottish fighting men. Shorter versions were worn under plate armour to cushion the wearer. Chainmail was no longer worn on its own by this time in western Europe but was used with plate armour to protect the spaces necessary for limbs to be able to move freely and often the undersides of arms and backs of legs. The brigandine was like a gambeson with much less padding, having small, overlapping plates like scales sewn onto the garment. These scales were often covered with at least one layer of fabric, sometimes quite showy material. A brigandine was quite heavy, less flexible than a gambeson, but provided better protection. The point has already been made that it is possible that the development of war-bow archery, with its advantages of range, penetration and relatively rapid shooting, encouraged the development of full suits of plate armour, rather than flexible armour such as mail with plates worn to protect particularly vulnerable areas. Even good mail worn over a gambeson will not reliably keep out war-bow arrows if they are fitted with the appropriate head. This last point is key; there was an 'arms race' between medieval English arrowsmiths who continued to develop types of military arrowhead between the thirteenth and sixteenth centuries to penetrate armour, while the armourers improved the arrow resistance of their products. At the beginning of the period the specialist military arrowheads in use were types whose development can be traced back to Viking times. These included long needle-pointed bodkins that would go through an individual ring in chainmail and quite probably penetrate the gambeson worn underneath. However, as the wearing of armour plates over the mail became more common in the fourteenth century, this type of arrowhead became obsolete. It just bent against plate. While this may not have been a problem for the English archers fighting the Scots in the 1330s, because the great majority of the Scottish soldiers would have no plate at all, it was a problem fighting the knights and nobles of France in the following decades. As a result, shorter, more triangular heads were developed with bigger sockets for the heavier arrowshafts required as bows gained in draw weight. Edward III's administration made a significant contribution to this development in 1368 when it issued orders to the sheriffs of twenty-six English counties for a large number of arrows. These orders were very specific about the quality of the arrows necessary, not only requiring that seasoned wood be used for the shafts, but saying that the arrows were to be 'fitted with steel heads to the pattern of the iron head which shall be delivered to him (the sheriff) on the king's behalf'.[67] These orders were not the first time that military arrowheads made of steel were mentioned in royal orders, but it is the first time that all the heads were to be steel. This, and the supplying of a design pattern, shows that the royal administration wanted a standard, good-quality military arrow with the capability to penetrate plate. However, recent tests suggest that the arrowheads developed later in the fifteenth century to penetrate plate armour may, paradoxically, have been less effective at penetrating gambesons and brigandines.[68]

The types of hand-to-hand weapon used in all three kingdoms were much the same. Every fighting man carried at least one knife, ranging from the specialised misericord through to an everyday eating knife. The misericord, later known as the rondel dagger, had one purpose in war – finishing off an armoured knight. They had long, stiff, slim blades, not uncommonly 12in (30cm) long, and were designed to fit through the gaps in armour. The handles of these daggers often had flat ends to allow them to be driven through mail and padded jackets by a hammer blow from the hand. These were perhaps more commonly owned by wealthier fighting men, although they would be popular battlefield booty. By the fifteenth century they were worn by better-off citizens, aping the military style. The bollock dagger, so named from the shape of its handle, has been found widely in England and parts of northern Europe, and was used by ordinary men. Many bollock daggers found in England are single-edged with blades up to about 13in (335mm) long.[69] They would serve well as fighting knives, although less effective for subduing an armoured man than a rondel dagger, and should be regarded as part of a man's personal property in peace and war.

Ownership of a sword was almost as widespread among the soldiery of all classes as was ownership of knives and daggers. These varied widely in type and quality depending on the standing of the owner. As a result of the long run of relative military success for the English and Welsh soldiers from 1415 onwards, many of the ordinary archers and men-at-arms probably owned better quality swords than might be expected for men of their social status. From the thirteenth century onwards, knightly swords came in two broad types, the great (or war) sword and the arming sword. The blade of the great sword was about 48in (122cm) long with a grip long enough to allow it to be used two-handed as well as one-handed. Most surviving examples are well enough balanced to allow effective one-handed use. Originally, the great sword had a blade for both cut and thrust, but by the second half of the fourteenth century the blade shape changed noticeably. It was longer, narrower and stiffer, and its manufacturing probably placed greater demands on the skills of the swordsmith than had the earlier type. It is generally considered to have been developed in response to the increasing use of plate armour, which not only provided protection against the arrows of the upstart English archers, but also slashing blows from swords. This new blade shape shows that sword fighting techniques were changing to incorporate more thrusting moves to attack weak points in armour. In the first half of the fifteenth century, if Talhoffer's manual is any guide, these swords could be used 'half sword', with one hand holding the blade halfway down, so that the point could be thrust into the weak points of the armour with force at close quarters.[70] It is difficult to know how attractive great swords would be as booty for the ordinary archer and soldier of the various nations fighting in France at this time because of their specialised design, which required special training to use effectively. The arming sword was smaller, the blade being about 28–32in (71–81cm) long, and was worn as a secondary weapon by most fighting men and as a dress weapon marking social status.[71] This is not to denigrate its real utility as a one-handed fighting sword for both cut and thrust. Most arming swords were light and well balanced so that they could be used in a fast, agile style of fighting which would contrast with the popular image of medieval battles, namely lines of armoured men bludgeoning each other with heavy weapons.[72] The archers and other ordinary infantrymen would often use arming swords. Lightly armoured men such as archers could take on more heavily armoured men-at-arms with the arming sword because it was easy to manipulate. They also used the more brutal falchion, which had a short, wide, heavy blade with a curved edge and straight back and was used for hacking blows. Besides the inevitable buffeting effect of being hit by a brawny archer using a falchion, the blow could distort or crack individual plates in a suit of armour.

This was also the period when the use of the shield declined, whereas the use of the buckler continued. It has been suggested that this decline came about because of the improvements in the quality of armour and the move to using two-handed weapons like the poleaxe and the great sword.[73] This was despite the undoubted value of a shield against an arrowstorm of war-bow arrows.

Otherwise, the hand weapons used by the men of the various nations involved in the fighting in France in the first three decades of the fifteenth century varied acording to the type of fighting they were trained for, their financial and social status, and to some degree which nation they came from.

Finally, in this general summary of the arms and armour used by the men fighting in the wars in France in the first quarter of the fifteenth century, there is the matter of training. Nobles and knights were well trained in use of arms; being an effective fighting man was still one of their major roles in society. Since English armies were made up of paid soldiers it is reasonable to expect that they all had some level of skill with their weapons. Similarly, the French urban militias would have practised. The Scottish soldiers also seem to have had some skill. The legal requirements for ordinary English and Welsh men to practise archery have been noted above. But the question remains, how did all these men gain their weapon skills? For the ordinary men of all three nations there is almost no evidence. No doubt experienced soldiers led the practice but they have left almost no trace. There are tantalising references in the Register of Freemen of York to two men who may have played a part in this training. In 1298 Robert of Werdale, who was described as an archer, was enrolled in the register, and in 1384–85 Adam Whytt, a buckler player, was enrolled.[74] To be eligible to be a Freeman in York, these men would have become established in the city by following their trade in their own right for a number of years. They would also be reasonably prosperous since there were fees to pay to be registered. In short, they would have been respectable citizens of York, not just rough, skilled fighting men. They are the only two men on the register who might have been instructors in fighting arts. However, for men who were prepared to pay for training there were manuals of fighting and no doubt masters of arms to train them.[75] In noble households the training was led by experienced members of the household. Some of these may have had access to one of these fighting manuals. But the fact that these manuals were written at all suggests very strongly that there were professional teachers of fighting skills. The earliest manual (Royal Armouries Ms.I.33) dates to around 1300 and was created in south Germany. This German tradition continued when Liechtenaur created his manual somewhere between about 1350 and 1389, when his work was incorporated in another manual compiled by Dobringer. In about 1410 Fiori de Liberi produced the first surviving Italian manual. Evidence of an English tradition of fighting manuals is found in two fifteenth-century manuscripts on swordplay. The existence of theses manuals shows that the medieval warrior was interested in developing his skills; medieval battles were not just two lines of meatheads battering each other. As Liechtenaur put it, 'above all things you should learn to strike correctly if you want to strike strongly'.[76] While it would be a mistake to suggest that the majority of the professional fighting men in the wars in France during the early fifteenth century had access to a fighting manual, it is not unreasonable to suggest that many benefited from training or demonstrations by men with skill and experience, some of whom had access to such a manual.

England

Our picture of arms and armour in medieval England is dominated by images of archery. The English war-bow was about 6ft (1.83m) long, made from a self stave, that is a naturally occurring stave with no gluing or laminating. This bow was used with a long draw; the largest group of the arrows found on the *Mary Rose* suggest a draw of about 30in (*c.*760mm).[77] Modern replicas of these bows made from similar woods to those available to the medieval bowyers have a draw weight up to maybe 170lb. These bows were able to launch heavy arrows (about 2¼ oz or 64g min) up to about 270yd (*c.*247m) if the performance of modern replicas is any guide.[78] We have very little archaeological evidence from the medieval period in general for the bows or arrow shafts, although a good range of arrowheads have survived. The main find of bows and arrows was made in the wreck of the *Mary Rose*, which sank in 1545. The date of this find means that these bows and arrows come at the end of over two centuries of development driven by real experience of using the war-bow in battle. As a result the performance of the modern replica bows which are made according to the evidence from the *Mary Rose* may well be better than the majority of bows in use at Crécy and Poitiers but not necessarily of those in use at Agincourt and Verneuil. From the mid-fourteenth century onwards, French, Breton and Burgundian allies of the English kings often bought war-bows in England rather than developing a local bow-making industry. One example of this practice contemporary with the Battle of Verneuil was when Hugh de Lannoy, the Burgundian captain of Meaux, along with four other men, whose names sound French or in one case Italian, were given a licence to ship a number of bows from England without paying duty.[79] Why import rather than make locally?

1. English bowyers had about a century of experience of making war-bows. Their understanding of what wood could do and the efficient design of war-bows would have been unrivalled.
2. England had already established an international timber trade to supply good quality bowstaves to the bowyers.

Despite these two points, there is no doubt that local bowyers in western Continental Europe made longbows and war-bows.

English and Welsh archers in the fifteenth century were expected to turn up at the muster properly and completely equipped, so the English royal administration only had to supply replacement bows. Significant efforts were made to ensure that supplies of these, all of excellent quality, were available for the military archers.[80] As a result there was probably very little variation in the bows the archers used, and no incentive for them to spend money on buying a bow. It is quite possible that some military archers may have had their bows altered to suit them by a local bowyer. Indeed, some of the archers would have the skill to do this themselves. There are occasional references to bowyers being part of a retinue or garrison.

The skill to use these heavy bows effectively does not come easily and the men of England and Wales practised from childhood to develop it. In part they did it because they wanted to but from 1363 onwards they did it because the law said that they should practise archery. There is one question that remains very difficult to answer: is it that only the English and Welsh developed the ability to use this weapon effectively before the fifteenth century? Even after the military reforms of Charles VII in the 1440s, there is no evidence of French archers defeating the English and Welsh archers. The French left the English to their 'old' technology and made greater use of gunpowder weapons than the English did, particularly those that could be used in the field rather than purely for sieges or defending fortifications.

The development of arms and armour in England followed the western European traditions as the effigies in many parish churches showing knights and nobles in armour make clear. English armourers of the fourteenth and fifteenth centuries could not compete with their Continental rivals for quality and design of armour but they produced perfectly serviceable plate. 'Soft' armour rather than plate armour became well developed in England, possibly because of the dominance of the archer in English military thinking. It is also probable that since the English knights and men-at-arms expected to be fighting on foot, they wore lighter armours in general, probably with less plate on the legs than was the practice with some of their enemies, particularly the north Italian mercenaries employed by the French. The archers needed to wear protection which allowed their arms and bodies the easy movement necessary to draw a heavy war-bow. These movements are different from those made in hand-to-hand fighting, particularly the way the shoulders and back have to work (a sort of backward curving motion which can be seen in illustrations in many western European medieval manuscripts). As a result the archers tended to wear gambesons, or to a lesser degree brigandines, because these had a degree of flexibility. They would have had limited arm protection, since whatever they used would have to be close-fitting so that it didn't interfere with the bowstring. This meant that the best protected archers probably wore a sallet, a brigandine which would be sleeveless and short enough to allow the movement necessary and chainmail sleeves and leggings. As with everything else concerning military equipment in the English armies of this time, except for the war-bow, the type and quality of hand weapons owned and used by the individual soldiers depended on their wealth, social status and military experience.

While all the knights and men-at-arms would own and carry a sword and dagger into battle, many had a preference for some other weapon as their primary means of attack. Because they expected to fight on foot some may have used the great sword, but English knights and men-at-arms often preferred the poleaxe. By the beginning of the fifteenth century, this weapon seemed to have a standard length of about 5ft (1.5m), including the head.[81] (The halberd was a parallel development but commonly less 'stylish' than the poleaxe, often up to about 9ft (2¾m) long overall, and was widely used by European infantry.) The head of a poleaxe had an axe blade on one side and a hammer head on the other which was spiked like a big meat tenderiser, and a spike on the top. The head often had long, iron fastening strips which provided the wooden haft with some protection against cutting blows. A modern author described this weapon as '... to all intents and purposes a can opener, each blade, spike and face designed to crush and pierce armour plate'.[82] This was a devastating close quarters weapon which was used with both hands, the user relying on his armour, skill and ferocity for survival. Shorter battle axes and battle hammers designed for one-handed use, which could be used mounted or on foot, were also used, often with a shield. How much the English knights and men-at-arms used lances or spears on foot is not clear. The English and Welsh archers demonstrated in most battles that they were good close quarters infantry when necessary. Indeed, they seemed to think that this was as much their job as shooting arrows, and enthusiastically took part in close fighting. They did this for a number of reasons: professionalism, loyalty to their comrades, the chance to take ransom-worthy prisoners or other booty and, in many of the battles, survival. Victory was the only way to ensure this; although there is evidence of archers being captured and ransomed, their prospects were very uncertain in defeat. Every archer would have at least one knife, most likely a bollock dagger, and many would have an arming sword or a falchion. Some muster records show that a sword was regarded as part of the basic equipment of an archer, that he must have to be accepted at muster by the late 1420s at least.[83] Many may have used a buckler with their sword, showing skills in the traditional English fighting art of sword and buckler play. The buckler is a small shield 6 to 18in (15 to 45cm) in diameter, held in one hand by a grip made behind the central boss. In addition archers may have used weapons that could be hung in their belts like axes and maces.

Scotland

Scotland had its own traditions in arms and armour. These were influenced both by native traditions in the Gaelic areas of the country, particularly those described in chronicles, histories and other accounts written in medieval Scotland and in the sixteenth and seventeenth centuries, and Continental traditions imported from England and from France as part of the Auld Alliance.[84] However, the development of arms and armour in Scotland was restricted by the relative poverty and lack of surplus income throughout the medieval period in comparison with England and France. By the start of the fifteenth century, soft armour was the Scottish standard for nobles, knights, chieftains and elite soldiers (Gallowglasses in Irish and West Highland military affairs). This comprised a long-sleeved knee-length aketon made of linen or leather vertically stitched into long, stuffed strips. A full-length mail shirt might be worn over this by the better-off warriors. If grave slabs are any guide, the head was protected by an open-faced bascinet with a chainmail cowl attached to reinforce the protection on the neck and shoulders. It is difficult to know how much reinforced protection for arms and legs was worn. Chainmail leggings or metal splints on forearms and lower legs, if used at all, were more likely among men from the lowlands than among those from the west and the Highlands. Members of the royal family and the high nobility used suits of plate armour by the beginning of the fifteenth century, which were usually imported from Europe. Alexander Stewart, the Wolf of Badenoch, who died in 1405, is shown in full armour on his tomb in Dunkeld Cathedral, while Archibald Douglas, 4th Earl of Douglas, was allegedly wearing armour three years in the making at the Battle of Homildon Hill.[85] At this battle Douglas was wounded five times, including losing an eye and a testicle, which shows that even very good armour (allowing for some exaggeration over the manufacturing time) was not impenetrable in the press of a medieval battle. Ordinary fighting men wore just an aketon, sometimes coated with pitch or covered in leather, and simple open-faced helmets. In 1385 Jean de Vienne, Admiral of France, reported to the French royal council after an expedition to Scotland that he had seen the whole of the Scottish military array and that there were no more than 500 men-at-arms equipped to the standard expected in France. The rest of the men (he thought about 30,000) he considered to be poorly armed and trained and not to be relied on once the enemy was sighted.[86] This comment shows three things. One is the relative poverty of Scotland reflected in the arms and armour that its people could afford. Secondly, since we can assume that a good number of the men he dismissed wore aketons, he was ignorant of how effective a good one could be. Thirdly, by showing his knightly disdain for many of the Scots, he showed no understanding of their fighting spirit, particularly when facing the English. It is probable that over twenty years later, when the Scots were preparing to send men to fight in France, there were more men with better armour because of the profits made from some substantial cross-border raids in the intervening years. But it would remain the case that a good number of the Scottish men-at-arms would be more lightly armoured than their opponents.

The weapons used varied not only with the wealth and status of the individual, but which tradition he belonged to. As with the English, every man carried a knife. In the Lowlands these might be bollock daggers, but specialised 'anti-armour' daggers like the rondel dagger seem to have been rarer, no doubt because there was less need for them in most Scottish warfare. In general, Scottish fighting knives were single-edged and the blade could be as long as 18in (46cm). Men from the west of Scotland (possibly including Galloway, which had a long tradition of being different from the rest of southern Scotland, in part because Gaelic survived there longer than in other parts of southern Scotland) and the Highlands used both one- and two-handed swords, axes of varying sizes, spears, and bows and arrows. The men from the rest of Scotland at this time were less likely to be using two-handed weapons, although the knights and nobles who followed the European tradition of arms probably used the great sword. Arming swords, small battle axes and maces would have been used by the better-off soldiers of all types, or infantrymen who had gained battlefield booty. Spears were common among all classes, almost always for use as hand weapons in the schiltron rather than as javelins. There was some tradition of military archery but it is difficult to know now how widespread it was across Scotland.

France

The use of plate armour developed rapidly in France in the fourteenth century for a number of reasons. There was a large number of men-at-arms including many nobles and knights who had sufficient resources to keep up with developments in military equipment. It is likely that, since

France was a much richer kingdom than England or Scotland, there were more men who had excellent imported armours made to more up-to-date standards than could be found in the other two kingdoms. But such men would still be a minority. French nobles, knights and men-at-arms not only fought the English, and amongst themselves in the Orléanist/Armagnac struggles, but also took part in major international adventures like the ill-starred 'crusade' that ended at the Battle of Nicopolis in 1396. The French knew from bitter experience the dangers the war-bow posed to them and were determined to nullify it if possible by improving their personal protection. Because they hoped to fight on horseback more than English knights and men-at-arms did, and because of their expectation that they would be facing the war-bow, French knights and men-at-arms may have tended to carry shields more than their opponents. In turn, this would have meant that they were less likely to use poleaxes.

The arms and armour of the non-noble troops are less well described. It is reasonable to assume that the urban militias had gambesons and open helmets at least, and that whatever their main weapon, they carried daggers and possibly swords. It has been noted above that an important role for these militias was providing practised missile troops – most commonly, but not exclusively, crossbowmen. These militias had two major roles; they could defend their own walled towns and cities, and they could provide missile troops in field armies.

Other nations

Men from other nations served in these wars, mainly as part of mercenary companies, although some individuals served, maybe bringing some retainers for support. These individuals can be found in both the French and English armies, but most commonly were men-at-arms from Flanders and the Rhineland serving the English king. While there were never large numbers of these men, they were drawn by the prestige of serving such a renowned soldier as Henry V. They were also drawn by the opportunity to earn pay and booty. The French armies included many mercenaries, mainly from Spain, northern Italy and Scotland. With the exception of the Scots, whose arms and armour have been discussed above, these men wore both plate armour and soft armour according to their status, very much within the military traditions of western Europe. It is quite possible that the Spanish troops may have worn less plate, reflecting their experience of fighting the Moors.

The most advanced mercenary troops in terms of equipment were the armoured horsemen from Lombardy. They benefited from the rapid technical advances made by the north Italian armourers noted above and wore high-quality full plate armour with similar quality protection for their horses. Sometimes a north Italian captain would be hired with a number of men-at-arms, but on a number of occasions it is recorded that these men were hired in 'lances'. The Italian lance at this time was made up of three men: a man-at-arms wearing full armour and often riding an armoured horse, a valet who wore light armour and fought as a light cavalryman, and a page who was primarily non-combatant.[87]

7

Henry V and the conquest of Normandy

When Henry V came to the throne in 1413 the contrast between his reign and his father's could not be more marked. Henry had a confidence and clarity of purpose which his father seems to have lost once he became king. Without compromising royal authority, Henry showed some favour to nobles who had lost out in his father's time, and made two gestures which showed his confidence as king. He reburied Richard II with due honours in Westminster Abbey and took Edmund Mortimer, who had a good claim to the throne, into his court circle. Then he restated the claims his great grandfather, Edward III, had made to the duchies of Normandy and Aquitaine and prepared to pursue them vigorously. Both Henry IV and Richard II had much preferred peace with France and had neglected these claims. Such was Henry's determination that before the end of 1415 he had won his great victory at Agincourt, an event that resounded through men's minds in England, France and elsewhere in western Christendom. In political and military terms, what did it actually achieve? It established Henry's reputation as perhaps the foremost military leader of his time in western Europe. It re-established the reputation of the English fighting man, particularly demonstrating once again that the English and Welsh archers could turn a battle. But the strategic importance of Henry's capture of Harfleur was greater. Situated on one side of the Seine estuary, it gave the English another bridgehead into northern France, and opened the invasion route to Rouen, capital of the Duchy of Normandy and, more menacingly for the French, a possible approach to Paris. From an English, domestic point of view the capture of Harfleur removed from French control one of the most important bases used to harass English shipping in the Channel.

Despite the shock felt in France after the defeat, and the ensuing search for explanations and scapegoats, the French made serious efforts to rebuff the English in 1416, focussing particularly on the recovery of Harfleur. They took the initiative by establishing a headquarters at Honfleur, just across the estuary of the Seine from Harfleur, and began to organise a major naval campaign. They built up a strong fleet, which included a powerful mercenary force from Genoa consisting of eight carracks, a similar number of galleys and 600 crossbowmen.[88] The carracks were larger and higher than anything that the French or English had in their fleets, giving a considerable advantage to the French fleet if it came to a fight. Naval tactics at this time were straightforward – get alongside the enemy ship, try to gain some advantage with missile weapons so that the men-at-arms could board and effectively fight a land battle. The companies of fighting men that served in English ships had proportionately fewer archers than land forces did. But they still tended to have twice as many archers as men-at-arms. The prowess of the English and Welsh archers gave the English fleets an advantage, which the very size of the Genoese carracks would go some way to neutralise. Importantly the Genoese crossbowmen had a long-established reputation in warfare in the fourteenth and fifteenth centuries, and could be a potent counter to the English archers.

The French royal administration was not only hiring naval forces to reinforce their efforts against the resurgent English. Soon after the disaster at Agincourt they began actively hiring mercenaries to fight on land. In 1415–16 they seem to have been looking for auxiliaries to assist French forces, rather than hiring whole armies as happened for a few years after 1418. An embassy was sent to Genoa in the winter of 1415–16 to recruit crossbowmen. The embassy was successful, and hired at least 660 crossbowmen who joined the campaign to regain Harfleur in the summer of 1416.[89] These men were in addition to the men who were on the Genoese fleet and were expected to form part of the land forces besieging Harfleur. The French also hired companies of Spanish troops, mainly from Castile. These men seem to have been both crossbowmen and men-at-arms.

The French approach to the campaigns of 1416 showed that they had remembered the lessons of Edward III's campaigns in the previous century. They could make campaigning in France unprofitable and dangerous for the English by improving the fortifications of towns, cities and castles and use them to control Normandy. This strategy had limited the effectiveness (and profitability) of the English campaigns from the 1360s to the 1380s, which had been based on the chevauchée. However, as will become clear, times had changed because gunpowder weapons were now effective against walls, giving an advantage to those attacking fortifications over those defending them. More importantly, Henry V was a very different character to his great-grandfather. Henry soon showed that he understood that the conquest of Normandy, which was his main territorial focus, would depend on dogged reduction of fortified places to control land rather than raids to seize booty and terrorise the population. He had learnt the importance of winning the support of the population to gain control of the land in his five years of campaigning in Wales against Owain Glyndŵr. He had learnt the need for a calculated approach to the war in France when he considered the gamble of the march from Harfleur to Calais in the previous year. While the victory at Agincourt led to him and the English archers winning their fearsome reputation, it could so easily have finished his ambitions in France if the battle had gone the other way. The French leaders seem to have planned to recover the territorial losses of the previous year without having to hazard another major land battle against the English, since they had little confidence in the outcome. They used their powerful fleet to take control of the Channel, making a number of attacks on the south coast of England, including raiding the Isle of Wight and Southampton, and blockading Portsmouth. These activities covered the real French effort, which was an attempt to retake Harfleur. Henry had ensured that the defences of Harfleur were thoroughly and quickly rebuilt and he put a substantial garrison in place. He also encouraged English settlers to repopulate the town. But when the French and Genoese fleet blockaded Harfleur on the seaward side the large English garrison began to suffer a serious shortage of supplies.

At the same time as they were taking control of the Channel and blockading Harfleur by sea, the French under the Count of Armagnac, Constable of France; Louis de Loigny, a Marshal of France; and the

Count of Narbonne, who became one of the more effective French commanders, attempted to blockade the landward side as well. The aim was to hinder foraging and plundering expeditions by the garrison, rather than establish a close siege, which would be much more hazardous. In early 1416 the English garrison of Harfleur comprised about 900 men-at-arms and 1,500 archers under the Earl of Dorset. While this large garrison kept the town secure, its very size left Dorset with the problem of how to keep it adequately supplied, given the blockades. A success against the French at nearby Montvilliers encouraged Dorset to undertake more ambitious military adventures. In March he set off north-east from Harfleur with a mixed force of about 1,000 mounted men on a substantial foraging raid. He went as far as Cany, about 35 miles (56km) away, before turning back. Armagnac sent out scouts, more than Dorset seems to have done, and discovered the English army as it made its way back towards Harfleur, no doubt laden with booty and foraged supplies. He drew up his army of between 3,000 and 4,000 men at Valmont about 25 miles from Harfleur, blocking the English path. Dorset drew up his men in a rather attenuated line to try to avoid being outflanked, which meant that the French were able to break up the line with a series of mounted charges that killed maybe 160 of the English.[90] However, the cavalry went on to plunder Dorset's wagon train and horse lines rather than turn to attack his rear, which gave him and his men time to reform in a nearby hedged enclosure. Armagnac was loath to attack the English now that darkness was beginning to fall and they were in a defendable position. He may well have felt that having battered them and captured both their horses and their booty he could wait for them either to surrender or cut them up as they retreated. Some negotiations took place at this point but Dorset would not surrender and Armagnac wouldn't let the English just march back to Harfleur, so they came to nothing. At this point Armagnac slipped up, he didn't maintain sufficient guards to stop the English escaping in the darkness. When he discovered their escape, he sent a force under Louis de Loigny to find them and keep track of them until Armagnac could come up with the rest of the French forces. De Loigny was not meant to engage the English. However, when he found the English trudging back along the beach nearing Harfleur, he forgot this instruction. He attacked in enthusiastic disorder, his men rushing down the cliff slopes towards the English, who calmly slaughtered the French as they arrived piecemeal. The English were able to loot the bodies before driving off the rest of Armagnac's forces with the aid of the Harfleur garrison. Despite significant losses, Dorset's men won a notable little victory through their courage, discipline and determination, but it is unlikely that it had significant effect on the situation in Harfleur. Armagnac's 'Fabian' policy was not appreciated by the French, who wanted to avenge Agincourt and capture ransomable prisoners.[91] But he achieved his strategic aims since the garrison's opportunities to forage were still restricted and the naval blockade meant that it was in ever more straitened circumstances. Moreover, if Henry was to relieve Harfleur, he would be forced to do it on French terms. He would have to attack the formidable Franco-Genoese fleet. So the English in Harfleur had to hang on through the spring and into the summer while Henry gathered a fleet together.

The fleet gathered at two bases, Winchelsea and Southampton, and was ready to sail to the rendezvous at Beachy Head by the end of July. The archers and men-at-arms who made up the fighting power of the fleets at this time also seem to have collected at these two ports before formal muster. An order sent to the Sheriff of Southampton in July 1416 instructed him to make a proclamation '… that all captains and leaders of men-at-arms, hobelars and archers who are to sail with the king on his present expedition shall be with him at Southampton … and shall take their wages due for the expedition when they shall be on board the ships'.[92] The simple expedient of paying the men the first instalment of their wages on board ship severely restricted the opportunity for them to cheat Henry by taking wages at the time of muster and deserting before the campaign got underway. However, Henry was unable to lead the fleet to the relief of Harfleur in person, as he seems to have originally intended, because he had been engaged in peace negotiations since the late spring with the encouragement of the Emperor Sigismund. Indeed, on the same day that the fleet set out across the Channel to Harfleur, Henry signed the Treaty of Canterbury with the emperor. Henry was fortunate to have a very competent and reliable deputy in his brother John, Duke of Bedford, to lead the fleet. Duke John and the part of the fleet preparing at Southampton had been delayed by ships of the Franco-Genoese fleet blockading Southampton. However, by 14 August the fleet had assembled off Beachy Head and set sail for the Seine estuary and Harfleur. They enjoyed good weather and anchored in the Seine estuary that same day. Bedford sent small boats to reconnoitre the main Franco-Genoese fleet, which was anchored a little further up the estuary. In the morning he arrayed his fleet and ordered the attack, which simply involved the English fleet sailing up to the anchored Franco-Genoese fleet, battering into the gaps between the enemy ships, grappling and attacking them, rather like trying to storm a fort. Some reports suggest that some English ships managed to get round one end of the opposing line, but this is not certain. The battle was prolonged, with Genoese carracks giving the English particular difficulties because of their greater height, but eventually the English triumphed, in no small part because the longbowmen could outshoot the opposing archers, who were predominantly crossbowmen. The English captured four of the carracks, which boosted the English fleet in the future. The English lost about 700 men killed and had many wounded, including Bedford himself, while the French and Genoese lost over twice as many and about 400 prisoners.[93]

While this notable victory relieved Harfleur and damaged French naval power significantly, it didn't give England control of the Channel. In June of the following year the Earl of Huntingdon won another hard-fought victory over a Franco-Genoese fleet at the mouth of the Seine. He captured another four Genoese carracks, the French Admiral and 'alle the tresour that they alle shulde have to wages with ffore a quarter off a year'.[94] After this victory the English seem to have gained naval dominance in the Channel.

In 1416 Henry pursued his goals in France in two ways. There were the preparations for the military activities which, under the leadership of his brother John, brought relief to Harfleur. At the same time, he put his personal efforts into a sustained diplomatic effort, particularly negotiations with Emperor Sigismund, which, while they may not have led to widespread peace in western Europe, did lead to the Treaty of Canterbury wherein Henry and Sigismund agreed an alliance. The first step of this alliance was an attempt to open negotiations with John the Fearless, Duke of Burgundy, but he was suspicious of their aims. In the end Henry managed to reconcile Sigismund and John, who had disputes over John's eastern borders and his holdings in Flanders. But Henry and John's negotiations came to nothing; a contemporary writer described John in unflattering terms: 'the duke detained our king all this time with evasions and ambiguities … in the end he would be found a double dealer, one person in public and another in private'.[95] However, it seems likely that both Henry and John ended these meetings with a fairly clear understanding of each other's immediate aims, and so had the confidence to pursue their own agendas without too much concern about coming into conflict with each other.[96] Henry proved to be more than a charismatic leader of men in battle. In his campaigns from 1417 to his death in 1422, he demonstrated a strategic sense of what was achievable in France. He had to counter the general French strategy which they had used successfully against his great-grandfather, Edward III. The French were relying on castles and fortified towns to provide shelter for the population, to keep supplies of victuals and goods secure from English foragers and finally, to be bases for raids on English-held areas. This meant that chevauchées, the great plundering expeditions much favoured by English military leaders in the fourteenth century, became both militarily ineffective and unprofitable. But Henry was not interested in grandiose plundering raids that were strategically pointless, since, as his victory at Agincourt had demonstrated, even if these raids provoked the French into a battle, winning such a battle did not bring them to negotiate seriously. His strategy was more realistic; he set out to recover what he viewed as the English lands in northern France. He started his (re)conquest of Normandy, by attacking the major administrative centres such as Caen and Rouen as well as subduing military strong points. Caen was the first to be taken. Henry had a good artillery train by the standards of the day and he used it skilfully to make practicable breaches. The troops of his brother the Duke of Clarence broke in first on the east side of the city and so distracted the defenders, which enabled Henry's men to break in as well. Given that the city fell by storm, the fact that it was not violently sacked shows the control Henry had over his men. There is no doubt many inhabitants, particularly the men, were killed in the storming, but the aftermath did not degenerate into rapine and pillaging. Henry was uncompromising in his treatment of the population of Caen. He required all those who wished to remain in the city to take an immediate oath of fealty to him. He expelled all those who wouldn't and, as at Harfleur, many of the 'non-productive' inhabitants; that is women, children, the elderly and the poor.[97]

Meanwhile, the forces of the French Crown, which for convenience could be called the Armagnacs, were distracted by the activities of John the Fearless, Duke of Burgundy. He advanced as far as Corbeil, about 115 miles east of Paris, which he besieged unsuccessfully. He was very careful as to how much pressure he put on the Armagnacs. His differences with the other senior Valois dukes have been outlined above, but he claimed that he was loyal to Charles VI and so was not prepared to make any explicit alliance with Henry. Indeed, his military activities in 1416 and 1417 can seem half-hearted, but it is likely that this was a matter of calculation in that he wanted to gain some territorial advantage and maintain political pressure on the Armagnacs without doing enough to allow the English to gain from his endeavours. He was unrealistic, if not dishonest, in this, since his military activities, including the seizure of Amiens, Beauvais and Reims, were bound to distract the Armagnacs, and so help Henry. In 1417, the Armagnacs, despite being the party of the legal King of France, struggled to raise the money necessary to support their forces. They were so short of money that they had to allow the garrison of Paris to ravage the surrounding country in lieu of wages.[98]

As Henry gained control of more of Normandy, the Duke of Brittany and the leaders in Maine and Anjou became more alarmed. They sent fruitless requests for assistance to King Charles VI in Paris, effectively to the Armagnac lords who led the government since Charles was suffering from bouts of insanity at the time. But, since the Armagnacs couldn't even pay the wages of the city garrison, they certainly weren't able to send any help to other areas. As a result the leaders of Brittany, Maine and Anjou made truces with Henry. This suited him very well since it allowed him to establish a winter siege of Falaise in December 1417. This was significant for a number of reasons. Firstly, to establish an effective siege at all in the early fifteenth century the leader of the besiegers needed to be confident that he was not going to be suddenly threatened or attacked by a substantial relieving force. If he was, there would be every likelihood that he would have to abandon his cumbersome siege train should he be forced to abandon the siege. Henry knew that the Armagnacs could do nothing, and was confident that the local population was quiet enough to present no threat. Secondly, it showed that he knew the English had such control over the Channel that adequate supplies could be sent from England to sustain the besiegers, if they could not get enough locally. It was another sign of the increasing professionalisation of Henry's army in that the soldiers could be relied on to undertake the dangerous work of a siege in the winter, and of Henry's powers of leadership.[99] Finally, it made clear to the French in Normandy that there was no point in resisting Henry since he was implacably determined to regain what he seems by this point to have regarded as his rightful inheritance, the Duchy of Normandy. Henry didn't waste his men's lives in dramatic assaults; he patiently relied on his artillery to breach the walls, so that the town surrendered at the beginning of January and the castle a month later.

In 1418 the Armagnacs continued their efforts against the Duke of Burgundy, with limited success, before they ran out of money again. But this problem, shortage of money to pay the soldiers, did not only affect the French 'Royalist' forces. The Burgundian forces regularly lived off the land. Perhaps the commanders justified this because they felt that they were passing through territory which sympathised with the Armagnac party. They certainly couldn't claim that they were in lands where the population had come to terms with the English, since the Burgundians were careful to avoid any danger of a confrontation with Henry's men. At the beginning of this year even the English garrisons in the south of Normandy and Anjou were living off the land. Once he was aware of this, Henry sent clear orders that it had to stop. The English forces, while they undoubtedly didn't behave perfectly in their relations with the French population at large, were the only forces in northern France whose leaders made sincere, and probably largely successful, attempts to curb pillaging by the soldiers. Henry seems to have made clear that this was a war to recover lands that rightfully belonged to the English king, so the inhabitants were to be treated fairly. No doubt he also made the pragmatic decision that if he could provide basic security for the population of the areas he conquered, in contrast to what the French king had been able to provide, they might well become better reconciled to his rule. Over time, this policy seems to have had some success, as will become clear in the account of the rule of his brother John, Duke of Bedford, as Regent of France after Henry's death. However, in 1418, brigandage became a problem not only in the areas of northern France held by Henry but in the areas around Paris disputed by the Burgundians and the Armagnacs. The English forces not only had to deal with this banditry within their borders, they also had to deal with guerrilla warfare 'carried on by refugees and adventurous noblemen along the marches'.[100] Some of these noblemen gained some support from the Armagnacs and later the Dauphin, others carried out raids with their own men.

Whatever happened at a local level in the way of French resistance, 1418 saw Henry confirm his claim to Normandy in one emphatic act: the siege and taking of Rouen. He decided to lead the siege himself. Given his military reputation it made sense, since his presence would buoy up the English troops and challenge Charles VI of France, or more realistically his queen and her supporters, to save the city or appear defeated. Since the stakes were so high Henry made careful preparation, collecting together a wide range of equipment and reinforcements from England. He was confident in his own military abilities and those of his men so that when an uprising broke out in Paris which led to John the Fearless, Duke of Burgundy, taking control of the French royal capital, he had no second thoughts about pressing on with preparations for the siege. He may have had an idea that the uprising had little or nothing to do with his plans since it seems to have been caused by a combination of the citizens of Paris getting tired of the behaviour of the Armagnac lords and their retainers, and the political scheming of Duke John. It led to two months of bloodletting as the citizens of Paris and Burgundian supporters massacred the supporters of the Duke of Armagnac. The duke himself was taken prisoner and murdered by the citizens of Paris. John, Duke of Burgundy entered Paris on 14 July 1418 and took control of Charles VI. This gave him the mantle of royal approval, although King Charles was no more than a symbol for much of the time at this point in his life. Queen Isabelle and her supporters immediately allied themselves with the Duke of Burgundy. However, Charles, the Dauphin of France, escaped capture by the Burgundians and took refuge south of the Loire, and so provided a rallying point for the Armagnac party. Duke John no longer needed Henry V as an ally since he had achieved most of his political ambitions.[101] In his new role of protector of the King of France he became an active opponent of Henry, sending troops to garrison Rouen and defend the Seine crossings in the area. Henry planned to cross the Seine at Pont-de-l'Arche, but with the albeit temporary ending of the Armagnac/Burgundy conflict the French had a more unified sense of purpose, and they strongly defended the crossings of the Seine around Rouen. Henry's brother the Duke of Clarence led the drive to capture Pont-de-l'Arche with a force that included fresh troops from England brought over by the Duke of Exeter.[102] After several fruitless attempts to storm Pont-de-l'Arche, Henry decided on an alternative plan. The Seine is broad around Pont-de-l'Arche, with a number of islands in it. Using boats that they either seized in the area or brought with them, an English force crossed to one of the larger islands. According to Burne, who visited the area in the 1950s, this left them within about 170yd of the French-held northern bank of the river.[103] This would have been an easy shot for the archers in the English army, who were able to provide devastating covering fire to enable a small force of men-at-arms to establish a bridgehead on the French-held bank. Now Henry was able to make rapid progress by attacking Pont-de-l'Arche from both sides. He also set up two pontoon bridges to circumvent the bridge. The French forces retreated and the town surrendered.

Henry moved on to establish a tight siege around Rouen by the end of July. He was stretching the military resources of his kingdom thin, since his subordinates were also besieging Cherbourg, Domfront and Avranches at the same time, so his siege train at Rouen was not as substantial as he wished at the beginning of the siege. He prevented the French from sending supplies by boat to Rouen by blocking the Seine upstream in the direction of Paris by stretching chains across it. The city had to rely on its stores to hold out.

Once the siege had started, Duke John of Burgundy began negotiations with the Dauphin Charles, but these two devious and suspicious men were unable to come to any agreement. The Dauphin then approached Henry to see if they could become allies against Burgundy. Henry was quite prepared to agree to this if the Dauphin agreed to the partition of France. He wouldn't do this, so the siege dragged on into the winter. A humane side to Henry's implacability was shown when he allowed his men to pass some of their food over to the thousands of poor people driven out of Rouen by the garrison in an attempt to save supplies. Most of these unfortunates remained trapped between the city walls and the siege lines. They were mainly women, children and the elderly, and many died in the harsh winter conditions. Despite his sincere religious devotion, and his concern for the wellbeing of non-combatants evidenced in his military ordinances, the fate of these people doesn't seem to have had any effect on the way Henry prosecuted the siege.

The inhabitants of Rouen seem to have been able to send a number of messages to Paris begging for help. The Duke of Burgundy led a French army to Pontoise, which is about 20 miles from Paris and about 56 miles from Rouen, where he stopped. He was unwilling to go further from Paris for fear of the resurgent Armagnacs retaking control of the capital. At the end of December, with no sign of relief, the citizens persuaded the determined garrison to negotiate with Henry.

When Rouen finally surrendered in January 1419, Henry didn't behave triumphantly, entering the city with banners and pageantry; instead he just went to the cathedral in dignified fashion to give thanks to God for His favour. Then, in line with his declared belief that he was just recovering his own duchy, he arranged for supplies to be brought into the city, which was in dire straits after the siege. The other side of this policy was that the citizens of Rouen were treated differently in the aftermath of the siege than were those of Harfleur and Caen earlier in Henry's campaigns. They had to pay a huge fine of 300,000 ecus to Henry as a penalty for their resistance. This again shows Henry's hard-headed pragmatism. The city survived to become the capital of English-held Normandy and felt relieved to be spared a sack, and Henry got a large sum of money to help with the costs of war. He also allowed any citizen who would swear fealty to remain (likely to be a higher proportion of the population than was the case at Caen because the balance of power in Normandy was much more in Henry's favour than it was in 1417), and decreed that the city would enjoy the privileges it had before the reign of Philip IV. One group who may have felt hard done by were the ordinary soldiers who, after all the hard and dangerous work of a siege, were deprived of their chance to profit from booty. However, at least they would have received their pay.

The fall of Rouen had a serious impact on the major towns and cities in Normandy which were still held by Armagnac supporters, since Vernon, Mantes, Dieppe, Gournay, Eu and Honfleur all surrendered in February 1419. Henry racked up the pressure on the French king's party, which meant Burgundy and the queen – they had custody of the king, whose periods of lucidity were few by this time. He sent the Earl of Huntingdon and the Captal de Buch to take Pontoise. They achieved this with a night escalade of the walls by a small party who opened the gates to Huntingdon's main force. The horrors that could befall a town taken by storm are made clear in the words of *A Parisian Journal*: 'the ones that can escape are lucky for no Saracen ever did worse to Christians than they are doing.' Refugees straggled into Paris over the following week to escape the 'cruel, bloody English'.[104] Henry also sent his brother Clarence on what amounted to a chevauchée up to the walls of Paris. Allowing for exaggeration in the account of the fall of Pontoise, since the author of this journal tended towards colourful reports of events, this and Clarence's *chevauchée* towards Paris showed that Henry could be very ruthless when necessary. Besides the strategic value of terror on the inhabitants of Paris, he may have considered the approaches to Paris less deserving of gentle handling since they were outside his Duchy of Normandy.

Henry's greatest practical problem in 1419 was that his Duchy of Normandy didn't have a secure southern border. The Loire was a possibility, but to achieve that would require the English to take over Maine and part of Anjou, a step beyond Henry's ambitions at the time. As a result the English were engaged in endemic border warfare, trying to establish a firm march, which they could control from fortified towns and castles.

By the early summer of 1419 the Armagnacs were left with little choice but to rely on diplomacy to make any improvements in their situation. They had been negotiating in Scotland since 1418 in an attempt to raise large numbers of troops in the spirit of the 'Auld Alliance'. Even before these negotiations came to any conclusion, companies of Scottish soldiers were fighting in France. These negotiations showed clearly the divisions in the French camp between the king's party, dominated by the Duke of Burgundy, and the Armagnac party, which had Charles the Dauphin as its figurehead.

Their inability to do anything to save Rouen from Henry seems to have shocked all the French leaders into serious negotiations with Henry and each other. The dukes of Armagnac and Burgundy agreed truces with Henry – separately of course, given their mutual hatred. The Duke of Burgundy, probably with the support of Queen Isabelle of France, entered into more substantial negotiations with Henry. He again proposed the partition of France and his marriage to Catherine, the daughter of Charles VI.

The marriage was agreed, although there was much haggling over the dowry, but the partition of France again proved to be much more of a problem. The willingness of both Burgundy, and apparently the queen, to ignore the opinions and interests of the Dauphin in the detail of these negotiations is significant politically, and somewhat surprising on practical grounds. Charles the Dauphin wasn't sitting idling his time away. He was concentrating on trying to keep control of France south of the Loire. To this end he managed to collect together forces at Parthenay, about 45 miles south of the Loire, and at Bourges, which was about 67 miles south of Orléans and soon became his capital. These forces meant that he could counter any Burgundian forces that moved west from the duchy, and any English forces that pushed up from Aquitaine.[105] But he did nothing active to stir up the military situation. The Dauphin's main successes at this time came as part of the diplomatic efforts being made by all parties at this time. If he was going to be left out of negotiations with the English, then he determined to find his own allies to maintain his position in France free from English and Burgundian control. He approached countries such as Castile and Scotland who had long-standing enmities with England. He negotiated with the Duke of Brittany, who was nominally at least his father's subject, but who in fact dithered between treaties with the English and the French. He also contacted more distant states including Savoy, Milan and Genoa who if nothing else could provide good-quality mercenary troops so long as he could find the money to pay them. The Castilians' enmity for the English went back to the fourteenth century, when both the Black Prince and John of Gaunt had participated in disputes over the succession to the Castilian throne. Their main value to the Dauphin was their powerful fleet, although mercenary companies from Castile and other parts of Spain joined his army. The Scots, in response to desperate pleas from the Dauphin, made the greatest contribution to improving his position. In 1419, an agreement was reached with Albany's government in Scotland to dispatch 6,000 men under the earls of Buchan and Wigton to France, an army which was probably vital to the survival of the Armagnac cause.

The arrival of significant numbers of Scottish soldiers in France presented a real problem for Henry's strategy in France. He had known for some time that negotiations between the Dauphin and Scotland could present him with a problem. The process of negotiating for these men, actually raising them and getting the Castilian fleet to Scotland to transport them took months. Henry ordered that twelve ships and some balingers (small, shallow draught trading ships, either sail- or oar-powered) set out from south-west England to intercept the Castilian fleet. When this force finally found the Castilian fleet off La Rochelle it was grossly inadequate to take on over forty large, well-armed ships and was brushed aside. This highlighted Henry's naval problems. Control of the Channel, which he had in large measure after the naval victories of 1416 and 1417, was vital to his success in France. But the continual shuffling of men and supplies back and forth over the Channel kept both royal ships and a good number of civilian ships employed. At the same time the usual English mercantile endeavours to Continental Europe had to be maintained if England was to have any chance of prosperity. All this meant that finding an adequate force of ships to interrupt sea communication between Scotland and France was very difficult if not impossible. If he couldn't rely on finding enough ships to defeat these transport fleets from Scotland, another option was to try to deny them good ports in France. He could do this either by blockading La Rochelle or, by capturing it. Blockading the port in sufficient strength to resist the experienced and well-equipped Castilian fleet was just not possible. He had too few royal ships and the English merchant fleet was already overstretched, supplying the army in France and maintaining English trade. Capturing La Rochelle would require an English army to cross miles of hostile territory whether the expedition set out from Normandy or English-held Aquitaine in the south. After this long march the English would more than likely have to settle down for a siege. Even if the English could raise the necessary forces for this expedition it would be a foolhardy adventure, even for someone of Henry's military prowess. Moreover, Henry could not rely on the Duke of Burgundy to leave English interests in Normandy undisturbed if he set out on this adventure to La Rochelle. When news of the arrival of the Scottish army in France reached Henry, he could not have known how important the Scots' efforts against the English would become to the French over the next five years. He may well have felt, with some justification, that he and his English soldiers could handle any army they might meet in France, a view held by many in Continental Europe. However, by 1420 there were signs that Henry was taking the Scottish forces in France seriously and that he had found a policy which gave him a better chance of managing them than a potentially risky military adventure. He used diplomacy!

But this is getting ahead of events and it is timely to return to 1419 and the Duke of Burgundy, who had a serious problem. He couldn't agree to Henry V's demands for the partition of France. His hold on Paris, which he perceived as a key part of his control of France through King Charles and Queen Isabelle, was threatened by English advances and by pressure from the newly reinforced Armagnacs. As a result he restarted negotiations with the Dauphin Charles. Neither party trusted the other, so careful arrangements were made for a personal meeting between Duke John and Charles, finding a way for both to feel that their personal safety was guaranteed. They met in September on the bridge over the River Yonne at Montereau. This allowed both to approach from their own territory, and leave a substantial guard at their respective ends of the bridge. The number of attendants each brought to the meeting was restricted. When the two men met, the Dauphin Charles seems to have cast aside diplomacy, for John the Fearless was killed by Charles's attendants as he knelt before him. There is academic debate about how far the Dauphin was involved in the plan to kill the Duke, but it is difficult to believe it surprised him when it happened. At the simplest level, it was revenge for the murder in 1407 of the Duke of Orléans by the Duke of Burgundy. It removed any likelihood of the Burgundians and the Armagnacs combining to repel the English for over a decade.[106] It may have been an attempt by Charles and his advisors to remove a man who in their view was a bad counsellor to the king and queen. Whatever the thinking, the immediate consequence was to harden the divisions within France. Philip, the new Duke of Burgundy, openly allied with Henry. The assassination at Montereau also seems to have changed Henry's thinking. Earlier in 1419, when he had been negotiating for the partition of France, he had only wanted sovereignty over Normandy and Aquitaine, and marriage with Catherine, Charles VI's daughter. In the negotiations with Charles VI and Queen Isabelle in 1420, which led to the Treaty of Troyes, he negotiated for the Crown of France. Henry made much of the murder, declaring that it showed that the Dauphin Charles was unfit to succeed to the throne of France. The Dauphin was explicitly excluded from these negotiations by a proclamation issued at

Troyes in early 1420 in the name of Charles VI of France. It is unlikely that he was in any mental condition to have any real understanding of the significance of this proclamation. Queen Isabelle and Philip, Duke of Burgundy were almost certainly the main agents behind it. The proclamation directly charged the Dauphin with the murder of the Duke of Burgundy at Montereau. It called on all Frenchmen to disregard his orders and any claims he made to lands in the kingdom of France. It also declared him to be unworthy to be heir to the French Crown.[107] This cleared the way for the Treaty of Troyes to be negotiated. Henry was not a man to rely solely on peace negotiations; he knew that if he did not keep pressure on the French a treaty might never be agreed. This consideration applied as much to the party around the king and queen of France, where the slippery Philip, Duke of Burgundy, was the prime mover, as it did with regard to the irreconcilable French of the Dauphin's party.

Normandy was consolidated in a series of small sieges so that Dreux, Ivry and the famous Château Gaillard all fell to the English. Meanwhile, the Earl of Salisbury as the King's Lieutenant in Lower Normandy was active in Maine between Alencon and Le Mans as part of the efforts to establish a secure march in the south. He captured Ballon, about 20 miles north of Le Mans, among other places, and besieged Fresnay-le-Vicomte in late February.[108] This stimulated the French into a determined effort to relieve Fresnay. They assembled a substantial force, which included a good number of Scots, under Marshal de Rieux at Le Mans. The Franco-Scottish force seemed confident that Salisbury was either unaware of their preparations or unable to do anything about it because he had too small a force to pursue the siege and bar their advance. They were wrong. Salisbury dispatched the Earl of Huntingdon with a force to stop them. Since he had noticeably fewer men than de Rieux, he gained good information about the approach of the enemy and laid a very successful ambush. The Franco-Scottish force was scattered, Marshal de Rieux captured and, in a piece of surprising good fortune, the Scottish war chest was captured as well.[109] As a result, Fresnay fell and Salisbury continued his efforts to secure the exposed southern border of Normandy. But these military successes were completely overshadowed when the Treaty of Troyes was agreed.

8

Henry V: Regent of France

The Treaty of Troyes agreed in May 1420 was Henry V's crowning achievement in France. With this treaty, Henry achieved all his declared war aims and more. It is a mark of his reputation in France that the treaty made him heir to the French throne. While this may have appeared to be a gesture of despair by Queen Isabeau and Philip of Burgundy, it was a realistic policy from the French point of view. Who else could bring peace to France?

The main points of the Treaty of Troyes were:[110]

Henry V was recognised as Charles VI's heir.
Henry V was to be Regent of France while Charles was ill.
Henry would marry Catherine, daughter of Charles VI.

Henry undertook to bring the lands under the Dauphin's control back under the control of the French king.

When both kingdoms were ruled by one person, they would remain as separate sovereignties, with their own institutions, administrations and legal practices.

Henry would continue to rule Normandy and Aquitaine in Charles VI's lifetime. On his death they would become part of the kingdom of France again.

When did Henry decide that he should be King of France? As late as 1418, Henry had declared that he was only interested in recovering Normandy and retaining Aquitaine; he did not restate his great grandfather's claim to the French throne. There is no reason to believe that he was disingenuous in this, so why did he change his mind? One could speculate that given his fierce religious devotion he viewed his success in France as God-given, and now God was giving him the throne as well. There is no evidence of Henry thinking this way since there was a chain of practical considerations that led him to this position. Until the treaty there was no legal justification for his conquests, since neither the dukes of Burgundy, the Armagnac party nor those behind Charles VI in the 1420 negotiations, were prepared to divide France by granting Henry Normandy and Aquitaine free of homage to the French king. Therefore Henry found himself accepting the indivisibility of France, and becoming another one of the nobles struggling to govern the whole country.[111] At this time he had no need to fear an alliance between the Dauphin and Philip the Good, Duke of Burgundy, because of the murder at Montereau, but he seems to have been concerned to avoid having to deal with an alliance between Burgundy and the French king. The real flaw in the treaty was that it provided no legal grounds for the disinheritance of the Dauphin. Despite rumours that Charles the Dauphin was illegitimate, neither Henry, nor those controlling Charles VI, ever declared that he was. The obvious reason for this was that Queen Isabeau could not allow it. In practical terms, the Dauphin presented a real problem because he controlled perhaps half of France, concentrated in the wealthy lands south of the Loire, so materially he was potentially more powerful than his father. Even supporters and subjects of the Duke of Burgundy were divided over the issue of fealty. There were some who felt that their highest fealty was to the kingdom of France represented by Charles VI and the Dauphin, and that Henry V remained a usurper. There were others who showed consistent loyalty to the English throughout the 1420s; meanwhile Philip their duke followed a more devious path.

The terms of the treaty also attracted a mixed response in England. Positive reactions included the enthusiastic celebrations of both the treaty and Henry and Catherine's marriage. Since the English now controlled most of the major ports on the north coast of France and had agreed positive treaty links with both Burgundy and Brittany, commercial activities prospered. England had naval control of the Channel which greatly reduced the likelihood of French or Breton piracy. It also brought a level of security from French raids to the south coast of England unknown for about fifty years. More negative responses can be found in the reports of parliamentary proceedings. While there is no doubt about the fundamental loyalty of the English to their king, in contrast to the situation in France, theirs was not an unquestioning loyalty. Parliament, and particularly the Commons, felt that it had a duty to safeguard the interests of the English at large, by which the Commons often meant the commercial interests and taxpayers of England. Records of the proceedings of Parliament at this time show that there was concern that when one man was king of both England and France, despite the terms of the treaty, this could lead to the integration of the kingdoms. Also there was well-founded concern that the commitment to continuing war in France would require financing, in part at least, by England. This was particularly unappealing since under the terms of the treaty this war of conquest aimed to restore the kingdom of the King of France, not provide foreign lands under English rule. Another real concern voiced by the Commons was that the royal administration was too focussed on affairs in France and the South of England. They petitioned the Regent of England, Humphrey, Duke of Gloucester, and Henry himself for more protection for English ships sailing in the North Sea because of the depredations of the Scots. The petition claimed that the Scots were taking troops to France and wool to Flanders (in competition with the English wool trade) in captured English ships.[112] This petition was unsuccessful since its concerns did not measure highly against Henry's larger interests.

Military activity in 1420 didn't stop with the signing of the treaty. The Dauphin was at the centre of the strongest group of opponents, but there were also local resistors in Normandy, one of the most effective being Jacques d'Harcourt, Sire of Tancarville. These local resistors were motivated by various factors: hatred of the English, patriotism, loyalty to the Dauphin, loss of estates and office because of the wars, and opportunism expressed by brigandage. While Henry's presence in France tended to daunt the French, it may also have led to overconfidence among the English and Burgundian forces. This enabled French forces to defeat raids by the English and Burgundians on occasion. One such happened at Senlis only 32 miles from Paris where Henry was staying at the time. After taking a mere two-day honeymoon, Henry set out with his wife, his father-in-law and the Duke of Burgundy to take (or recapture in the terms of the treaty) Sens, Montereau and Melun. These towns lay south or south-east of Paris, and by gaining control of them Henry hoped to consolidate both the security of Paris for his father-in-law, and communications with Burgundy. Sens and Montereau fell quickly but Melun, which was the nearest to Paris, was a very different proposition. Henry besieged Melun at the head of an Anglo-Burgundian force, and he was kept at bay for over four months. The commander of the garrison of Melun, the Sire of Barbazan, was a brave, resourceful and determined opponent for Henry. At one point, after mine and counter mine had met to form a large underground chamber, Henry and Barbazan are reputed to have had a joust on horseback. Henry had a house built for his wife among the siege works, where he is reported to have had his musicians play for her at dawn and dusk.[113] Aware that there were Scots in the garrison, Henry presented the captive James I of Scotland to summon them to surrender, but to no effect.

Melun held out until mid-November before surrendering, by which time Henry's patience was non-existent. He had twenty Scots from the garrison hanged as traitors to their king and nearly executed the garrison commander for the same reason since his king Charles VI had also been present. Victory allowed the two kings, Henry and Charles, to make a triumphant return to Paris. This campaign was more than a demonstration of common purpose by the kings of France and England. It highlights another of the major military problems which the English, with some Burgundian support, had to deal with in the next few years. It was necessary to clear Armagnac forces out of their bases in wide areas around Paris so that they couldn't threaten the stability of the Anglo-French government set up by the treaty. Picardy was another area of serious resistance to both Henry's and Philip of Burgundy's aspirations. In a response to these troubles Clarence wasted the efforts and energies of the English forces by making a chevauchée southwards towards the forest of Orléans. No doubt this was entertaining and profitable for the soldiers who took part, and could be justified in that it distracted or discouraged the Armagnac forces. But in reality it was a demonstration of Clarence's lack of vision about the needs and nature of the campaigning necessary to establish English Normandy. In this he was not alone. As will become clear, some other English commanders were more attracted by the excitement of raiding than they were by the slog of establishing secure borders and besieging enemy strongholds.

The counts of Aumale and Narbonne, leading largely French forces with some Spaniards, were active on the Dauphin's behalf in the same area. The Scots seem to have been fairly quiet. Although the Armagnac French were reluctant to risk a major set-piece battle with the English in general and Henry in particular, they had no intention of sitting quietly while Henry established himself within the terms of the Treaty of Troyes. Although the Dauphin was not a military man in any sense, he was clever, had good advisors and supporters, and tough, competent allies in the Scots. His forces also had one great advantage over the English and Burgundians; their lines of communication within the land of France were more direct and much less vulnerable to interruption.

At the same time, Henry was beginning serious diplomatic efforts to resolve the 'Scottish problem'. Henry returned to England early in 1421 after a three-year absence. He wanted to present his queen to his English subjects and, perhaps more importantly, present himself to them to remind them of their hero king. While England was still broadly loyal to Henry, there were grumblings about his long absence in France and the tax burden the English people were carrying to meet the cost of the French wars. Henry and Catherine received a spectacular welcome, particularly in London. This was followed up by an equally impressive coronation of Catherine as Queen of England. But this sense of joy and time of splendour lasted for only a month.

The Battle of Baugé

Henry left Thomas, Duke of Clarence as his lieutenant in France. Whatever their relationship had been in their father's reign, when they had been rivals for his affection, they seem to have become closer in adulthood. Clarence was Henry's heir since he was Henry's eldest brother. Henry probably felt that Clarence's experience in the French Wars as one of his lieutenants fitted him for the job, although he had little choice really, since Clarence was second in the kingdom. But Henry was mistaken in his estimation of Clarence, since without his elder bother's guiding hand, he proved to have weak military judgement. In March 1421 Clarence collected together maybe 4,000 men by taking men from the garrisons in Normandy to augment a small field army he had already.

He set out towards Anjou, in an expedition that may have been designed to distract a Franco-Scottish invasion of southern Normandy, or it may have been just another chevauchée. Whatever his plan, he had limited success and was rebuffed at Angers when he tried to attack the city. The Dauphin's army in the area was larger than Clarence's, including at least 4,000 Scots under the earls of Buchan and Wigtown, and maybe 1,500 French troops under the Constable Lafayette. It seems that they benefited from better intelligence about their enemy's whereabouts than did Clarence. This was no doubt a combination of the local population being more forthcoming, since the English were invaders, and more successful scouting. Once they knew where the English were they moved their army to a position threatening the route back to Normandy. In general the Scottish armies in France seem to have been pugnacious, so this may have been a deliberate attempt to seek a battle.

Clarence seems to have been uncertain what to do next for he stayed at Beaufort for another day, while part of his army, mainly the archers, foraged for supplies.[114] He may have been hoping to get news of where the enemy forces were, his army may have needed to forage for supplies and loot, or he may just have stopped in frustration wondering what the honourable course of action was. Whatever the reason, some enemy scouts were captured by the foragers and sent back to the English camp for interrogation. Once Clarence realised how close the Franco-Scottish army was, he decided to attack without delay. The experienced Earl of Huntingdon tried to persuade the duke to wait for the rest of his army, but to no avail. This was folly, since Clarence had at best a third of his army to hand; the rest were scattered in foraging bands. More significantly, he lacked archers, since they made up the bulk of the foragers while the 'better born' men-at-arms remained at the camp around their royal commander. He came upon the Franco-Scottish army who were camped at Baugé on the opposite side of the River Couasnon. The author of *A Parisian Journal*, who is not a reliable military correspondent, reports that the French had deliberately posted a few hundred men in clear view, wearing bright armour and with their banners flying bravely in the breeze, to lure Clarence on into an impetuous attack.[115] The English attempted to cross the bridge but were prevented by a body of Scottish infantry and archers. The *Scotichronicon* makes it clear that the threat posed by these men was more to the horses of the English knights than to the armoured men themselves, reporting that '… leaving their horses behind, the duke and his men gained a passage on foot'.[116] After forcing the bridge, and quite possibly crossing a shallow part of the river as well, the English regrouped, while the Scots retreated in good order to the town of Baugé. Clarence then led his men in no great order in a spirited mounted attack on the main Franco-Scottish force, which had used the time bought by the Scottish infantry to prepare. He was outnumbered at least three to one and was probably attacking uphill, so the inevitable happened. Not only was his force put to flight after a stiff fight, but he and many others were killed, while more were captured. At this point events become less clear. It is likely that the majority of the victorious Franco-Scottish army pursued the remnants of Clarence's force as daylight began to fade. The Earl of Salisbury brought up the archers and drove off those French and Scots that had remained on the battlefield and recovered Clarence's body. But he was in a difficult position, potentially at the mercy of a force at least twice as strong as his own, and with very few men-at-arms to support his archers. However, Salisbury, one of the greatest English commanders who served in France in the fifteenth century, made an orderly retreat back to Normandy by a mixture of guile and good fortune. In this he was aided both by the quality of his own men, since by this time many of the archers would have been experienced professional soldiers, and by the carelessness of Lafayette and Buchan, who seem to have made poor efforts at scouting in their pursuit.

The Battle of Baugé had a significance out of all proportion to the size of the forces involved. An English army led by King Henry's lieutenant in France had been defeated. The King's Lieutenant, who was an English royal duke and heir to the throne, was killed, and five other major nobles killed or captured. Pope Martin V is reported to have said *'vere Scoti Anglorum tiriaca sunt'* – verily the Scots are an antidote to the English.[117] Duke Jean VI of Brittany settled on alliance with France as a result of the battle, although his loyalty was flexible and remade his alliance with the English in 1423. The Scottish commanders, the earls of Buchan and Wigton, begged the Dauphin to join them and invade Normandy, writing 'with God's help all is yours'.[118] But Charles vacillated. Meanwhile, Salisbury reorganised the defences of Normandy. He made serious efforts to restrict desertion by English troops by ordering that no one could embark for England without a specific licence and enforcing discipline among the English garrisons more strictly. Ever practical, he attempted to pay the men their due wages, and so remove a real grievance among the soldiers that led them to desert or live off the Normans and French they were meant to protect. These efforts to restore morale among the English troops meant that he was ready to face whatever threat the Scots and French presented. In May, after wasting a few weeks through relative inaction after the victory, the Armagnacs moved to attack Chartres in a push towards Paris against the Burgundians. They may have encouraged sedition in Paris itself since by June the Duke of Exeter, the English governor of the city, had managed largely to lose control of the city to the populace. However, this seems to have been a matter of upsetting the Burgundian supporters rather than any upsurge of pro-Armagnac feeling. Meanwhile, Salisbury didn't feel that he could risk battle since he had to strip out many of the garrison troops just to make a show of holding the marches of Normandy. In an effort to consolidate English morale and restore the finances of his army he led a chevauchée south towards Angers in late May and early June. He was successful returning with 'the fareste and gretteste prey of bestes as alle the seiden that saw hem'.[119] He then settled back to watching the borders of Normandy. The French and Scots gained confidence from the victory, as Newhall puts it: '… the moral effect of this encounter was enormous. The death or capture of an English duke and five earls broke the spell of Agincourt.'[120] While Henry's military reputation was untarnished, the myth of English invincibility which arose from Agincourt was not re-established until the Battle of Verneuil three years later. The French and Scots took no immediate advantage in military terms from the victory in the Normandy area because of Charles's vacillation. The strategic target he eventually set himself by his drive towards Chartres and ultimately Paris was sound. The reputation of the Scottish forces among their hosts was enhanced. Grant argues that 'had Clarence been victorious, the English would have crossed the Loire and possibly conquered central France'.[121] That is, the victory at Baugé marked a turning point in the war, since the English were turned back from Orléans and the Loire, with the result that southern Normandy and Maine remained the area where the opposing armies manoeuvred and raided.[122] This view cannot be sustained; even Henry, had he lived longer, would have found his resources stretched to dominate France south of the Loire. But there can be no doubt that the victory at Baugé bought a significant respite for the Armagnacs.

The Scots gained greatly from their victory, and it really was their victory since, although some French nobles tried to belittle their contribution, they had taken the majority of the noble prisoners. It was Buchan and his fellow captains who wrote to the Dauphin after the battle sending him Clarence's standard. Charles's arguably misdirected campaign has been recounted above, but he was more effective in his determination to honour the Scots. He corrected his nobles who had mocked the Scots as 'mutton guzzlers and wine sacks' and he honoured the leading Scots, particularly Buchan, who was made Constable of France and Wigton, who was made Count de Longueville.[123] However, granting this important honour to a foreigner did not go down well with the French nobility who felt that their 'rights' to preferment were being usurped. This tension between the French nobility and the Scottish commanders caused problems later.

Popular English opinion of Baugé as recorded in the following decades is consistent – it was Clarence's fault. *The Brut*, a chronicle in English compiled before 1450 in its earliest versions, declared that Clarence was killed because 'he would not be governed'.[124] Another account shows the popular opinion of the English archers saying that Clarence was defeated because 'they wolde nott take with hem archers, but thought to have doo with the ffrenshmen them selfe wythoute hem. And yet when he was slayne, the archers came and rescued the body of the Duke which the wolde have carried with hem, God have mercy a pon his soule, he was a valiant man'.[125]

Henry V's return to France and his final months

Henry took over two months after news of the defeat at Baugé reached him to make his return to France. He must have felt that the situation in France did not merit his immediate return, and so he stayed in England attending to his kingdom. In his estimation, the major issue was to pacify the grumblers in the country at large and the Commons of Parliament in particular, who were very unhappy about the cost of the wars in France.

Adam Usk, a contemporary observer whose chronicle ends abruptly in mid-1421, expresses this unhappiness writing, '... the lord king is now fleecing anyone with money, rich or poor, throughout the realm, in readiness for his return to France'.[126]

Henry was reasonably successful and returned to France in early June with reinforcements and a full war chest. Besides these very necessary funds Henry also brought substantial reinforcements with him, which enabled him to pursue the war in France with vigour. Salisbury wrote assuring him that things were secure in Normandy, especially after his successful raid towards Angers. This meant that Henry was able to go to Paris to sort out the mess that his governor Exeter had got into.

Exeter seems to have had little understanding of how to manage the population of Paris who had strong opinions about most things, particularly their rights as citizens of the capital of France. He seems to have done little to restore confidence in the English cause after Baugé. Finally he had to retire to the Bastille for his own safety when he provoked the population to outright riot and disorder by arresting the Sire of L'Isle Adam for plotting to betray Paris to the Armagnacs. This seems incredible, since L'Isle Adam, a Burgundian, was consistently loyal to his duke's interests, and it is very difficult to see how betraying Paris to the Armagnacs served these interests. Whatever was behind the arrest, L'Isle Adam was not finally cleared until autumn 1423, and his reputation with the English may have been permanently damaged. Henry removed Exeter and restored order in the capital before mustering a substantial force of perhaps 6,000 men to relieve Chartres.[127] He set out on a long march towards the Loire at Orléans. Charles abandoned his siege at Chartres as soon as Henry's intentions became apparent. Henry completed his sweep to the Loire, recapturing the places that had fallen to the Armagnacs in Charles's advance on Chartres. Although the Dauphin was back on the southern side of the Loire, Henry made a provocative march to Sens and then on towards Meaux. In setting out on this two-month-long demonstration, Henry undoubtedly wanted to provoke the Dauphin and his military counsellors into a pitched battle. In the aftermath of Baugé they had been concentrating on pushing the Burgundians back so the route of Henry's march was calculated to bring him near to them. But nothing of the sort came of it. Henry's reputation was such that they were very wary of engaging with an English army under his leadership at all. Also, disease and extreme shortage of supplies meant that both Henry's army and the French forces at Vendôme were seriously weakened. Henry understood that he could not make an attempt to advance to the Loire and attack Orléans with a view to gaining territory at this time, because he still didn't have sufficient control of the lands south and east of Paris. He showed this in the route he took to emphasise English power after his brother's death, and in his actions once he reached Meaux. The city was strategically much more important than the failure of Clarence's chevauchée, since it was one of Charles's major strongholds east of Paris. Forces based in and around it could potentially threaten Burgundian access to Paris, and the eastern borders of English-held territory. Henry felt that going south-east to address the concerns of the Parisians by investing Meaux was sensible because he knew that Salisbury had stabilised the situation on the southern borders of Normandy. But stability on the Norman marches did not mean peace: low-level warfare persisted with first one side then the other gaining some territory or some other small advantage.

So, while Salisbury had been making his raid into Maine in June, the French retook Bec in Normandy. Having made the raid to boost English morale, Salisbury then concentrated on trying to keep Armagnac raiding forces at bay. Before he left Paris, Henry sent the Earl of Suffolk to support Salisbury in Lower Normandy against persistent Armagnac attacks, particularly the area around Avranches and Coutances. As the year wore on, the Armagnacs concentrated more on Normandy than elsewhere, probably because Henry wasn't anywhere near since he was marching east towards Meaux. In late September Aumale was organising raids into Maine and Normandy, and in December he besieged and took Ballon about 20 miles north of Le Mans. However, he could make no further progress northwards towards the main English-held lands because he had to fall back, both to counter an English attack on Dangeau about 63 miles east of Le Mans and to avoid the risk of having an English force behind him threatening his line of retreat.

The effect of the Battle of Baugé on Anglo-Scottish relations is very puzzling. After this blow to English ambitions in France, in which the Scots played a noteworthy part, it is possible that the Scottish government gained confidence in their dealings with Henry. This was important to Murdoch, 2nd Duke of Albany, who had succeeded his father as Governor of Scotland while King James was detained in England, since he was both much less popular in Scotland and less politically able than his father had been. Henry had been following a subtle policy over Anglo-Scottish relations for some time, and this had begun to make real progress by 1420, when he issued a number of safe conducts to Scottish nobles who wished to meet their king in England (or even in France) in the second half of the year. These became more frequent in 1421 as negotiations for James' return to Scotland became more substantive.[128] One of the most surprising developments happened two months after Baugé. Archibald, Earl of Douglas, the Tyneman, swore to serve Henry with 200 men-at-arms and 200 archers against all except James, King of Scotland. Douglas was to join Henry's armies in Easter 1422. But Douglas had put himself in a very difficult position by making this oath.

His son, the Earl of Wigtown, and son-in-law, the Earl of Buchan, were leaders of the Scottish army in France, so he appeared to be setting himself up to fight his family. As it happened Douglas was lucky that Henry died around the time he was meant to act upon his oath. The other strange thing about this oath was that it was made at all. Douglas had been an implacable enemy of the English for twenty years or more, but he also had a reputation for being an even more determined pursuer of his own interests. It seems likely that in 1421, Douglas was deeply uneasy about the way that the Stewart dukes of Albany were establishing a governing dynasty while King James was a prisoner in England, and the way that this might affect his own interests. Also, he may have decided that Henry was soon going to ransom James and that it would be better for Douglas interests at large if he became an early supporter of the new king. All this activity around James of Scotland shows that Henry was taking a wide strategic view of how to manage the Scots in France. He seems to have been working towards the release of James, in the hope of having an ally on the Scottish throne.

As Henry restored English fortunes around Paris and marched towards the Loire, the Scots seem to have consolidated the Dauphin's hold on the lands between his base at Bourges and Orléans itself, most likely in fighting against the Burgundians. In October Henry settled down to besiege the formidable fortified town of Meaux, about 30 miles east of Paris. Meaux was a very difficult proposition for the attacker. Its walls were protected on three sides by a loop of the River Marne, and it had a large garrison under the leadership of a long-standing Armagnac, the

Bastard of Vaurus. He and his men had established a fearful reputation for banditry and cruelty throughout the surrounding area as far as Paris itself. Henry undertook this siege at what would generally be considered the wrong time of the year because of complaints from the citizens of Paris made either to himself or his 'ally' Charles VI of France. This grim, bloody winter siege is often held up as one of Henry's great achievements, because it went against the military wisdom of the time. He was able to keep his forces in place and adequately supplied until the town finally surrendered in May 1422. He refused to be distracted by any activities of the French and Scots. Their most serious effort was in January 1422 when the Scots took Avranches and Salisbury needed reinforcements to retake it.

This short-term success by the Scots showed up one of the major problems that bedevilled the English commanders in these years of significant success for the English. Many of their men were hired on fixed-term indentures, often of no more than six months, which meant that the English leaders had to shuffle troops about to fill gaps created by men completing their period of service. This could be a particular problem in the winter, when English troop numbers were lower. Armagnac forces were able to take advantage of these shortfalls in the numbers of troops opposing them. The paid-off men did not necessarily go back to England, but often provided a pool of experienced men who could be re-employed at short notice when funds allowed or circumstances demanded. But while they waited for new employment opportunities, these military men sometimes threatened the peace and good order of the English-held lands in northern France. Meanwhile, Henry's focus on the siege never faltered and he found time to keep up diplomatic contacts with Genoa and the Emperor Sigismund. At the same time he was able to rely on his captains on the northern borders of Normandy to rebuff the irreconcilable Dauphinist Jacques d'Harcourt in this area. After the reports of Henry's implacable siege of Meaux reached him, the ever vacillating Duke of Brittany decided to honour the terms of the Treaty of Troyes and began to move back into the English and Burgundian camp.

The Bastard of Vaurus and his men held the town of Meaux for five months despite Henry's best efforts, only retreating to the Market, the island citadel of the town, after the English defeated a carefully planned attempt at reinforcement. Here they held out for another two months until May 1422. Whatever else can be said about the Bastard of Vaurus and his men, and they had earned a dire reputation before Henry's siege, they were brave and determined. It is a mark of Henry's effect on the morale of the Armagnacs that no serious attempt at relief was made; the one defeated in March 1422 was more a chivalric gesture of defiance than a serious attempt at relief. As the siege went on the defenders would have known that their chances of mercy were ebbing away. When Meaux finally fell Henry acted within the laws of war but gave no mercy. The Bastard of Vaurus and three of his senior colleagues were executed for their behaviour before the siege, Henry also executing all of the gunners because they had been particularly successful in killing a number of English nobles and knights. The rest of the garrison and some of their leaders were imprisoned; these latter included two leading churchmen, the Bishop of Meaux and the Abbot of Saint Faro. Henry demonstrated that no one, clerical or lay, was outside his reach if they defied him. Besides the potential earnings from ransoms from all these prisoners, there was also a rich haul of booty to reward the men who actually fought the siege.

This was, however, a very costly victory. English soldiers had died from disease and battle, and the seven-month siege had eaten into Henry's war chest. And barely two months after the fall of Meaux, Henry was dead. While it is not clear exactly what killed him, it seems likely that he contracted dysentery at the siege, and refused to rest enough to give himself a chance of recovery. After the conclusion of the siege Henry returned to Paris and was reunited with Catherine and his baby son. His brother John had also come to France, bringing about 1,000 men to replace casualties and men whose indenture had expired. Henry was unable to rest for long since the Dauphin was leading a powerful force north-east towards Cosne on the borders of Burgundy. The Dauphin again showed that he was much keener to fight Duke Philip and his Burgundians than to face the English under Henry. Philip of Burgundy called up his own army and asked for assistance from Henry. The Burgundian army at this time may not have been a match for the forces that the Armagnacs could raise, particularly when the Scots were present. Philip also would have wanted the English to be present to make success before Cosne so much more certain. Henry seems to have been only too willing to help Philip despite his weak health, and rushed to support him with a substantial force.

However, Henry soon became too weak to continue the march and had to turn back, leaving John, Duke of Bedford, to lead the army to the meeting point with Philip. The Dauphin had established a siege of Cosne, and had agreed with Philip that they should meet in battle by a set date, the *journée* in contemporary chivalric terms, or Cosne would surrender. Originally this was a chivalric custom whereby two knights agreed to resolve the matter by battle before sunset on an agreed day. However, it had become a pragmatic solution allowing the defenders to make a sincere effort at resistance but to leave with honour and their lives in recognition of the hopelessness of their situation. It was a popular arrangement with the ordinary fighting men who achieved their captain's aims without having to risk a sustained siege or bloody storming.

In this case, when the combined Anglo-Burgundian army arrived at Cosne on the agreed day there was no sign of the Dauphin and his French army. This did the Dauphin's reputation no good at all. But the Dauphin did not have to worry about damage to his reputation because Henry died at Vincennes on 31 August 1422.

Henry's death brought new hope to the Armagnacs; the one English commander they truly feared was gone. At the same time, the morale of the English, Normans and Burgundians took a blow. Was this a great chance for Charles the Dauphin to re-establish his reputation and regain ground? His supporters in Lower Normandy thought so and made an attempt on Fresnay-le-Vicomte. However, they were unsuccessful and were then mauled as they retreated by the Anglo-Norman forces. More significant was an attack from Maine into southern Normandy led by the counts of Aumale and Narbonne, two of the Dauphin's most experienced and effective commanders. After some sustained raiding they turned for home. On their way back Anglo-Norman forces attacked them but Aumale and Narbonne defeated them and so returned to Maine in triumph. But these activities had no effect on the overall situation in France and Henry's great achievements.

9

The legacy of Henry V

Henry V's legacy can be considered from two points of view: that held by the English and that by the French at large and the Armagnacs in particular. These points of view were not always contradictory, whatever was happening on the ground in France. Firstly, the English point of view. Henry died holding more land in France than any king of England had since Henry II. In addition he left a strong alliance with Philip, Duke of Burgundy, who gave Henry military and political support in France. After the Treaty of Troyes, the calculating Philip could work with Henry more openly in his military activities, since both could be seen as supporting Charles VI to regain control of France. While the Treaty of Troyes granted everything Henry wanted on paper, two major blocks to implementing it existed in Henry's lifetime: the Dauphin, Charles, who was disinherited by it, and the hostility many French men and women had to any treaty which seemed to give away French sovereignty to an English king. Henry's marriage to Catherine of Valois provided a solution to both these problems, since it could be expected to produce heirs for both kingdoms. Indeed, this happened with the birth of Prince Henry in December 1421. All Henry V had to do was outlive the ageing, mad Charles VI and he would have been in a remarkably powerful position. But he didn't. He actually died two months before Charles, leaving his baby son as heir to both thrones. When Charles VI died it clarified the Dauphin's position in many people's eyes; he was no longer just the disinherited Dauphin in rebellion against his father, he was Charles VII of France.

Henry tried to ensure his legacy by leaving a will with codicils and spoken instructions as to how his lands should be governed after his death. His will made his youngest brother, Duke Humphrey of Gloucester, guardian of his son. Nothing in Henry's will or instructions made Humphrey Regent in England, although Duke John of Bedford, Henry's oldest surviving brother, was explicitly made regent for the English-held lands in France. Philip, Duke of Burgundy seems to have been declared Regent of France because of Charles VI's incapacity. However, this soon lapsed with the death of Charles VI. In the event, Duke Humphrey made a claim to be Regent of England because he had been granted guardianship of the young Henry VI and because he felt he should have parity with his brother Bedford. Parliament rejected his claim, if on no other grounds than the conventional laws of inheritance, which made the Duke of Bedford heir to the throne if anything befell the young king.

It was not just as simple a matter as Bedford being older than Gloucester. The highly ambitious Henry Beaufort, Bishop of Winchester, had stoked the opposition in Parliament to Gloucester's ambitions, since he opposed much of Gloucester's policy towards France and wanted to make space for a major role for himself. Parliament was concerned that the two kingdoms should be kept separate as prescribed in the Treaty of Troyes. Parliament, Beaufort and the royal brothers reached a compromise that respected both traditional inheritance rules and the Treaty of Troyes. Bedford was regent in France; he was also protector, defender and chief councillor of England, but only when he was in England. This ensured the separation of the two kingdoms. Gloucester held Bedford's English roles when he was in France. A council was also appointed to assist with the government of England. Bedford accepted this arrangement because he felt it fairly represented Henry's wishes. Gloucester was not so content.

As regards Scotland, Henry had also been working towards an ambitious solution. He had been engaged in serious negotiations for King James to return to Scotland. As part of this negotiation, there were serious efforts to forbid the raising of Scottish troops to fight in France which would have solved a military problem in France, and put Charles the Dauphin in even greater difficulties. Links to the English Royal Family were cemented in 1424 when James married Joan Beaufort, a second cousin of Henry's. This match seems to have been of James and Joan's making and the romance had begun before Henry's death.

Henry's legacy in England was ambiguous. There is no doubt that there was popular pride in English achievements in France, which was reflected in the spectacular celebrations of Henry's victories and Catherine's coronation. But his continuous need for money had become a cause for discontent among the English (and Welsh). Adam Usk, writing about the Parliament held after the victory at Agincourt, noted that it granted a tax of a fifteenth of the value of property both for the current year and the following year. It also granted Henry taxes at prescribed rates on most types of merchandise for life. Adam felt that 'this was no more than he deserved as a recognition of his achievements'.[129] But by 1421 Adam's view had changed and after describing Henry's exactions as 'fleecing' he went on to write: 'No wonder then that the unbearable impositions being demanded from the people to this end (the financing of the war in France) are accompanied by dark – though private – mutterings and curses and by the hatred of such exactions'.[130] This part of Henry's legacy, a strong resentment amongst English taxpayers about paying for the defence of English-held parts of France and an equally strongly held view that taxes should be raised in France to pay for this, bequeathed real problems to his successors. The need to raise taxes in France, often in areas suffering directly from damaging raids, made difficulties for Henry's successors in France, particularly his brother John, Duke of Bedford.

Henry's sustained campaigns in France encouraged the development of a professional military class among the English. There had always been professional soldiers in England since before the Norman Conquest, and the whole theory of feudal society had been that knights were supported by their landholdings to allow them to be professional soldiers. But there were signs that this had been no more than a theory since Edward I's reign at least, when his demands for military service made some of the men eligible for knighthood reluctant to take it up. This reluctance became more widespread in the reigns of his successors. Since Henry's campaigns were continuous from 1415, albeit with varying numbers of men involved at different times, this led to the development of what

Anne Curry has called England's first standing army.[131] For many years, this part of Henry's legacy enabled the English forces to achieve greater things in France than their numbers and resources might have led us to expect. Longer term it may have fuelled the unrest that became the Wars of the Roses because there was a considerable number of men from all levels of English society who became detached from that society by their sustained military service abroad. When Charles VII eventually recovered control of France except for Calais in the 1450s, these men were left with a real sense of homelessness and purposelessness. The network of garrisons in northern France which provided control and security in English-held France was only possible because of this professionalisation of English military service. Henry established this to protect what he saw as his subjects in France, and these professional soldiers achieved this with varying success until the fall of English Normandy. Since Henry believed that Normandy was his duchy by right without owing fealty to the French king he had begun to issue summons for feudal service to the landholders of Normandy, so they joined the English forces defending Normandy. The majority of these would be Norman French, although the proportion of English landholders increased the longer Normandy was an English-ruled duchy. This remained a key part of the English military system until the loss of Normandy.[132] Finally, it is well worth noting that what Henry achieved in France in terms of lands under English control and the extent of English political power in France, he achieved in barely seven years. It took the French thirty years to recover control. A number of historians have suggested that Henry was overambitious and unrealistic in his aims of establishing a joint kingdom of England and France. Given the inequality in size and resources of all kinds between England and France this is a fair observation. Even in his lifetime there were mutterings in England about the taxes raised to fight the French wars. This was the real bind that the English rulers were in. As far as the majority of the English with any sort of local standing and power were concerned, if the wars were successful, they were expected to bring wealth to England and to be self-supporting from the resources of France. This wealth could come from booty of all sorts including landholdings and taxation from France, something which long-term might antagonise the French subjects of England and so make the wars drag on. If the wars were less successful, the expenditure on them would be resented in England, leading Parliament to refuse to grant taxes and thereby come into dispute with the king. Who knows? If Henry had not died relatively young then it raises fascinating historical 'what if' questions; but these are often unanswerable.

From the French point of view, Henry V's death took a talismanic figure from the wars. The English mourned the loss of a great soldier king who they believed was unbeatable. The French were cheered by his death because they too had felt he was unbeatable. Another boost for the French came in October 1422, barely two months after Henry's death, when the ailing Charles VI died. In theory, under the Treaty of Troyes the infant Henry VI was now king of both England and France, but Charles's death gave the Dauphin the opportunity to consolidate his position. He was no longer the leader of the Armagnac party acting against the interests of the anointed King of France; he was Charles VII of France. Although his formal coronation would have to wait eight years, he was now the sole leader of the French. This placed Philip, Duke of Burgundy, in a much more complicated situation. While Charles VI was alive Philip could be Regent of France because of Charles's madness, and so could support Henry V and the English under the terms of the Treaty of Troyes. But on the succession of Charles VII he was in a more difficult position. Supporters of the Treaty of Troyes would expect him to support the infant Henry VI of England and the Duke of Bedford as Regent.

Opponents of the treaty would regard him as a rebel against the French king, Charles VII, if he maintained his support for the English. But he had two reasons for legitimately opposing Charles VII. Firstly, the Treaty of Troyes had disinherited Charles when he was still Dauphin and, secondly, Charles as Dauphin had been closely involved in the murder of Philip's father at Montereau in 1419. This second reason was almost certainly more important in Philip's mind. He regarded himself as the premier duke of France, who was in serious dispute with the alleged King of France, but he did not regard himself as at war with France. Many of his military activities against the Armagnac party of Charles VII were driven by a desire to advance Burgundy's interests, and none of them could be regarded as all out-war against France in the way that the English waged war in France.[133]

Henry's death also made the direction of the war much less certain for the English because there were serious differences of opinion between his brothers and uncle. John, Duke of Bedford and his uncle, Henry Beaufort, Bishop of Winchester, recognised that the alliance with the Duke of Burgundy was necessary for the Henrician legacy based on the terms of the Treaty of Troyes to have any realistic chance of success. There were also economic benefits to this alliance because of the Duke of Burgundy's power and influence in Flanders, the market for much of the English wool produced each year. But Humphrey, Duke of Gloucester seems to have been suspicious of Philip of Burgundy, questioning both his loyalty as an ally and the motives for many of his actions. Duke Humphrey appears to have believed that England could achieve its ends by war alone. While he was not a stupid man as his interest in books and the arts showed, he took a rather simplistic, bellicose approach to the French wars, as did his dead brother Clarence. Philip of Burgundy on the other hand was a deep thinking, devious man who approached the hazards of war in a much more calculating way. This difference was at the heart of Duke Humphrey's distrust of the Duke of Burgundy. This distrust was fuelled by three specific incidents at this time. The Duke of Burgundy's request for English help to rescue Cosne had led to Henry not taking the rest which might have preserved his life. The expedition proved to be unnecessary, since the Dauphin had not attended the *journée* at Cosne, which probably made Humphrey feel that Burgundy was being militarily feeble and that he should have solved the problem himself. In addition Philip of Burgundy did not attend either Henry V's or Charles VI's funerals. The belligerent Humphrey saw these as signs of self-interested double-dealing. But as would become apparent later, Humphrey also put self-interest above the maintenance of his young nephew's interests on occasion. Any significance Philip's equivocations around the time of Henry's death may have had was actually soon outweighed when he renewed his oath to the Treaty of Troyes and betrothed Anne, probably his favourite sister, to the Duke of Bedford later in 1422. It needs to be said that Duke Humphrey wasn't alone in distrusting Philip of Burgundy; many French people were uncomfortable with any treaties or policies which increased his power and influence in Paris and north-eastern France.

In contrast to his younger brother Humphrey, John, Duke of Bedford was more like Henry in that he saw that political actions were necessary as much as military efforts if the English cause was to succeed in France.

The clearest demonstration of this came in June 1423, when he married Anne, sister of Philip, Duke of Burgundy, in a formidable gesture of consolidation for the alliance between the English and the Burgundians. But even this gesture of friendship was flawed in the eyes of Humphrey and his supporters. The marriage of Bedford and Anne of Burgundy was part of a Triple Alliance whereby Philip of Burgundy consolidated his position among the French by marrying his elder sister Margaret to Arthur de Richemont, brother of Duke Jean of Brittany. Richemont used the English title Earl of Richmond, as had his father who died in 1399. Arthur de Richemont had not been allowed to inherit the title and its revenues, which understandably coloured Arthur's opinion of the English, since he proved to be an implacable foe. While Philip of Burgundy could 'spin' this marriage as helping to cement Brittany's favour to the Anglo-Burgundian alliance, others could see it as keeping his options open with regard to Charles VII's court. Richemont became a significant figure in Charles's court from around this time and loyally ensured that Philip of Burgundy's interests were served. Bedford's marriage was particularly important to the English because Anne's close relationship with her brother, meant that she was able to ensure that any misunderstandings between her husband and her brother were kept to a minimum. Also, she was popular with the French people, particularly in the key cities of Rouen and Paris. But this marriage was perhaps the last of the efforts made to solve the real problem faced by the English and Burgundians in late 1422; how to stabilise the situation in France after the death of Henry.

The true nature of Bedford's predicament was that he was trying to maintain something that always was a barely realistic position; that the King of England was also King of France. As has already been noted, *if* Henry V had lived longer, his abilities and reputation *may* have enabled this to become a reality. His marriage to Catherine of France and the children from this marriage all added to the possibility of Henry's success in this great project. But Henry was dead, and his son, who truly symbolised the joining of the two kingships, was an infant. Bedford as regent in France loyally and very competently attempted to maintain his brother's legacy, but the basic problem was that the English were in France. While people in England enjoyed the idea of military glory, and sufficient numbers were prepared to risk military activity, they did not do it for nothing. They expected to make financial gains from war in France. From Bedford's point of view this raised the danger of Henry VI's English subjects looting his French subjects! In addition, while the English Parliament might accept Englishmen fighting in France, it was very reluctant to approve taxation to pay these fighting men. Since the Treaty of Troyes made it clear that each of the joint kingdoms was going to be governed according to its own laws and traditions, there was a strong feeling in England that this included each kingdom financing any armies necessary to maintain security. While Normandy proved to be quite willing to raise taxes to support the largely English army and garrisons that fought to maintain its security, these taxes could not pay for a large enough field army to subdue Charles of France. In addition, Bedford, as Governor of Normandy and the conquered lands in northern France by the terms of the Treaty of Troyes, was keen that the inhabitants of these areas should accept his regime as the legitimate government. A large, formally established army of occupation made up of foreigners (English and Welsh) would not achieve this aim.[134] So for all these reasons, Bedford was always left trying to achieve too much with too few troops.

Meanwhile the war went on. The Dauphin's forces, led by Ambroise de Lore and Jean, Sire of Coulances, took advantage of the unsettled times after Henry's death and raided as far as Bernay, only 39 miles south-west of the Norman capital of Rouen. The Anglo-Norman garrison of Bernay abandoned the town as the French approached. The French retreated with their booty, and inflicted a heavy defeat on the forces sent after them. Although this attack was typical of the raiding that went on, its successful outcome for the French led to fantastical rumours. Bedford had been captured; either Henry VI or Philip of Burgundy had been killed. More real was an attempted plot to betray Paris to Charles's supporters. Soon after this plot was uncovered, more treachery led to Meulan being reoccupied by Armagnac forces. This was a very useful acquisition for Charles since it allowed his supporters to disrupt the river traffic supplying Paris and to disturb the eastern marches of Normandy. Anything that caused unease and discomfort to the people of Paris and its surrounding area presented the English and Burgundians with major problems in their efforts to win popular acceptance of their rule of large parts of France.

Charles rounded off what had been a good few weeks for him and his supporters by being declared king at the end of October 1422, six days after his father's death. Bedford showed energy and determination in his military efforts to maintain the security of Normandy and the other areas of northern France held by the English. All soldiers were ordered to return to their captains, and a levy of the Norman subjects was ordered to assemble in arms at Domfront. In general, the Normans, who appear to have been pragmatic people who celebrated their differences from the rest of France, were supportive of their English overlords. They provided useful military forces, both as garrisons and field forces to repel raids. Then Bedford began to prepare for the next year's campaigns. Assemblies of the Norman Estates General and of the Norman clergy granted him taxes for the defence of Normandy. Reinforcements were requested from England, the first 1,500 men of whom (75 per cent archers) arrived in May 1423. Meanwhile in Paris, in the aftermath of the plot to betray the city to Charles, people suspected of supporting him were rounded up and an oath of allegiance to Bedford, as Regent of France, was required from all the inhabitants of the city.

Charles VII spent late 1422 in negotiations to obtain a formidable force of allies and mercenaries to both stiffen his French forces and get specialist forces for a serious military effort in the following year. The Scottish army in France was to be significantly reinforced, providing Charles with tough infantry including a significant number of archers. The Castilians supplied both a fleet and some troops. They, like the Scots, had a long-standing enmity towards the English dating back to the time of the Black Prince, and so were only too willing to join the French against their old enemy. However, for many Castilian soldiers and particularly the sailors, traditional enmity did not override the need for payment. The Lombard mercenaries complimented the Scots well, since they tended to comprise well-armoured cavalry and skilled crossbowmen. As will become clear in the account of the Battle of Cravant, Charles, his nobles and subjects had a very two-faced attitude to all these mercenaries. Their attitude seems to have been '… that they were a necessary evil endured for lack of an alternative rather than warmly welcomed as friends'.[135] With hindsight, this seems a particularly harsh attitude in the case of the Scots, who certainly expected to be paid as the collapse of some expeditions for lack of pay proved, but who also fought hard against their 'auld inemie' with mixed success and great loss.

The next stage of Bedford's activities to stabilise the English position in Normandy and the other lands conquered by Henry was to reduce the acts of violence visited on the population of Normandy as far as possible. Some of this violence arose from the nature of border warfare, raid and counter-raid made by garrisons on both sides. The raids had a number of interlocking motives. Some were attempts to gain specific military advantage; it was surprising how often a town or castle was taken unawares, either by an escalade (sneakily climbing over the walls at night), treachery or even just rapidly stormed before an effective defence could be mounted. Sometimes raiding was just low-level, small-scale warfare designed to wear down and demoralise. Finally, garrisons quite often threatened the local people they were meant to protect to get them to pay appatis. This, as the name suggest, was a French system whereby garrisons were paid in money and kind by the neighbourhoods they protected, often in lieu of wages from the Crown. But it very easily degenerated into extortion by garrisons on opposing sides and even by competing garrisons allegedly on the same side. Bedford made regular serious efforts to stop this by enforcing discipline and by trying to keep pay arrears to a level that the soldiers would tolerate.

Charles was less scrupulous towards his subjects at this time out of necessity because he had more of a struggle than Bedford to find enough money to wage war. One of the main reasons for Charles's continued financial problems at this time was that '... the transition from feudal to national taxation was not yet complete by 1420 in France, while England had had a system of national taxation since the late thirteenth century'.[136] More formal military violence was added to these low-level raids through the mounting of chevauchées. These large-scale raids could enable the attackers to accumulate substantial booty including livestock, if contemporary accounts can be relied upon, and also to seize ransom-worthy prisoners. Chevauchées could be much riskier activities than some of those who led them realised; after all, Clarence was mounting one when he met his death. But the events of 1421 show how chevauchées could not only bring profit but also great boosts to morale. The Battle of Baugé was the greatest success that the French and Scots had won since the disaster of Agincourt, while Salisbury made a successful chevauchée towards Angers in the aftermath to remind the English and Normans that, properly led, they had nothing to fear from the enemy. Finally, the population of Normandy and the surrounding areas were faced with some level of brigandage. Some French historians in the late nineteenth and early twentieth centuries have portrayed this as a resistance movement, in an anachronistic expression of national pride, at a time when France was still smarting after defeat in the Franco-Prussian War. There is some truth in this; there were brigands who might more correctly be called partisans, but it is easy to overestimate the number who had patriotic reasons for their actions in comparison with those who simply took advantage of disturbed times.

Bandits or Resistance fighters

Once Henry V began his serious effort to recover Normandy in 1417, somewhere that he soon declared was part of his historic inheritance, the English approach to the war had to change. A war of raiding and looting would win nothing except booty – attractive to the soldiers themselves who wanted to profit from their dangers; it would not do anything towards helping Henry achieve his ambitions. His determination to recover England's historic lands in France meant that he needed to win over the people as well as gain control of lands by military conquest. As a result he enforced firm discipline on his soldiers and engaged in a strategic war, grinding out control over the Duchy of Normandy in a series of successful major sieges. After the fall of Caen in 1417 and Rouen in 1419 Henry allowed those French men and women who would swear allegiance to him to retain their property in the cities. Those who refused to swear were exiled and their property redistributed to English settlers and loyal French people.

This policy served several purposes. It exploited the independent identity that many inhabitants of Normandy seemed to have cherished, the idea that they were Normans first and Frenchmen second. While it is impossible to estimate how many inhabitants of Normandy felt this way, there can be no doubt that there were a good number who preferred a strong Duke of Normandy to an ineffectual King of France who kept demanding taxes. It also gave the impression that Henry was a fair man who recognised that not every citizen of a city that resisted him was a diehard Armagnac, and so it served people's self-interest to take the oath and keep their property. The result of this policy of divide *to* rule was the potential weakening of the resistance in other towns and cities that might be preparing to resist Henry, since there was a strong opinion that there could be only one outcome when besieged by him – an English victory.

By giving French citizens a way to retain their property after the English capture of these major cities, Henry was making a significant effort towards the restoration of the local economy, which, given the size and wealth of Caen and Rouen, was important to the whole economy of Normandy. But the negative side of this policy was that it polarised allegiances; there were those who saw themselves as Normans, or were just pragmatic, and there were those who were loyal Armagnacs, displaced by the invader. These latter provided some of the most effective military leaders against the English, the cousins Jacques d'Harcourt and Jean d'Harcourt, Count of Aumale, for example, who both refused to swear the oath after the fall of Rouen. This hardening of allegiances led to an increase in the viciousness of the partisan activity and brigandage which took place in northern France.

Brigandage was not new to Normandy or indeed France in general, it did not just spring up as men were displaced and brutalised by Henry V's invasion. The lawlessness and armed activity that was part of the Armagnac/Burgundian feud had already encouraged it. Some of this lawlessness arose from the casual way both sides raised armed forces and then didn't pay them; one example of this was the company of Gascons who established themselves at Montargis, east of Orléans, in 1411. An even more startling sign of the problem of brigandage was when, from monies being levied to resist Henry V's invasion in 1415, some was very specifically earmarked to be used 'for clearing the kingdom of robbers and the men of the free companies'.[137] The brigands who troubled the English administration of northern France consisted of two main categories: those who lived in the towns and fortifications who claimed allegiance to the Armagnacs and later Charles VII, and those who are often described as living in the woods. These were a mixed bag as has been noted above. They included plain outlaws, those who had been displaced by war and some who may have deliberately gone into the woods to harass the hated English. These 'irregulars' could be effective in larger activities than merely making roads unsafe. On a number of occasions, small towns were taken by escalade or treachery by ill-defined groups of Armagnacs who held them until either the English turned up to recover the town or Armagnac forces arrived to consolidate their gain. These combined forces of formal garrisons and irregulars had their greatest triumph against the Anglo-Burgundian areas of France in 1421 when they so disrupted communications to Paris that commerce was damaged, food supplies were restricted and the plight of the citizens worsened to such a degree that 'you found people dead of the dreadful poverty that they suffered because of the scarcity and famine caused by the accursed war which increased constantly becoming worse every day'.[138]

Throughout the 1420s the English administration seems to have seen these brigands as belonging to one of two categories; those who were simply described as brigands and robbers in the court records and those who committed more sophisticated misdeeds and were labelled something along the lines of 'traitors, brigands, enemies and adversaries'. The first category included Englishmen on occasion, no doubt deserters, and the second true resistance fighters working against English and Burgundian interests. Traitors also included those who had taken an oath of allegiance to Henry and so maintained their property and position, but who had later worked against the English. At the start of his Regency, Bedford tried using clemency against the brigands, issuing general amnesties in 1422 and 1423. But later, particularly after his victory in the Battle of Verneuil shattered French hopes of any recovery after Henry V's death, he relied more on police actions and judicial penalties to contain the brigands.

Another part of the 'informal' resistance to the English and Burgundians were the spies and couriers who tried to encourage disaffection and treachery, which sometimes led to towns and fortresses changing hands. Waurin makes mention of several such agents, the majority of whom were women. It is impossible to know now the extent to which women took a prominent part in the Armagnac informal resistance. They may have deliberately taken part in some of the major attempts to destabilise the English and Burgundian holdings because they might be expected to get past the guards more easily. As Joan of Arc's activities a few years later showed, there is no reason to believe that the women of war-torn France were inclined to just sit meekly at home, so it is reasonable to accept that they were a regular part of this informal resistance. Of course it may be that the generally reliable Waurin emphasised the role of Armagnac women out of shock or admiration at such unseemly behaviour. But bandits and irregular fighters remained part of Henry's legacy as long as the English-held land in northern France.

1423: The Regent of France versus the King of France

At the start of 1423 Bedford was in a position where he could begin to develop Henry V's legacy, in the interests of the King of France, his nephew Henry VI of England. He had established his regency and stabilised the situation in Normandy and the rest of northern France under the sway of the English and the Burgundians in the previous year. He began by moving to repress three main centres of activity against Norman and English interests elsewhere in northern France. Firstly, he set out to recover Meulan in January 1423, which would relieve pressure on Paris. The French attempted to relieve Meulan, but the relieving force, made up of both Scots and French and led by the Constable of France, the Earl of Buchan, fell apart because of lack of pay. Some French chroniclers record that this relieving army was also hampered by serious disputes between Buchan and his French subordinates. These disputes may have arisen from the short-sighted resentment that some Frenchmen felt against the Scots in general and their leaders in particular, because of the titles and estates Charles lavished on them. This sort of discord between French and Scottish commanders led to more disastrous results in the following year. Both of these explanations for the Franco-Scottish failure seem likely and the result was that Bedford took Meulan in March 1423, showing that he was just as capable of leading the English and Norman forces in a successful winter siege as Henry had been. But he had two much more difficult sieges than that at Meulan to undertake, if he was to be successful in his efforts to bring a significant improvement in the level of stability in Normandy. Even before he had taken Meulan, Bedford ordered preparations for the siege of the fortified island monastery of Mont St Michel on the western marches of Normandy. This would be popular with the Normans because the French garrison at Mont St Michel mounted regular raids. The first step was for the English to fortify Tombelaine, another tidal island in the bay of St Michel. They did this in the spring of 1423, and installed a garrison to try to contain the raids from Mont St Michel. Meanwhile, on the eastern marches Bedford ordered the siege of Le Crotoy in May/June 1423. Le Crotoy was at the mouth of the River Somme, roughly midway between Dieppe and Boulogne. The irreconcilable Norman French nobleman, Jacques d'Harcourt, held it with a large well-resourced garrison and had conducted regular raids both into Normandy and the parts of Flanders controlled by the Duke of Burgundy. It also provided a base for what would later be called privateers. Because of its situation the siege of Le Crotoy was a combined operation between the Earl of Suffolk, Admiral of Normandy and Sir Ralph Bouteiller, the bailli or civilian administrator of Caux, the region of Normandy that probably suffered most from d'Harcourt's raids. Bedford, in recognition of the importance of the siege both militarily and politically, made sure that the forces undertaking it were properly resourced. He ordered three large new guns to be made at Rouen and sent a substantial force made up of men from various garrisons in Normandy to pursue the siege. The siege started well for the English when they forced d'Harcourt to pull back from his outlying forts and settle down for a determined defence of Le Crotoy itself.

By early summer 1423 Bedford had good reason to feel that military matters were going well. Also he had confidence that most of the Norman population was prepared to accept English rule because he had showed fairness and justice in his rule of the Duchy. He had made serious efforts to control the English soldiery and by including Normans in the government of their Duchy made his rule seem less foreign to the population at large. So he was able to go to Troyes and celebrate his marriage to Anne of Burgundy. Although this was a political marriage, it seems to have been a success in that both parties appear to have been genuinely fond of each other. Bedford valued his young wife's ability to win over his French and Norman subjects and she had a vital role in keeping her devious brother Philip sufficiently committed to the English cause. It was easy for Anne to support her husband's regency of the English realm in France because he was efficient, thoughtful and fair-minded, winning good opinions from many writers of the time.

The Battle of Cravant

Charles VII and his advisors knew that in 1423 they could not just sit by and watch Bedford and his commanders reduce their loyalist footholds in northern France, particularly after the fiasco at Cosne in the previous year. But they were still reluctant to have a direct confrontation with the English. So they decided to follow the same strategy as the previous year, and try to divert the English from their efforts in Normandy, Picardy and the area of Paris, by attacking Burgundy. This was a sound idea at a strategic level showing that Charles recognised both the importance of Burgundians to the English efforts and that, regardless of what Duke Philip might do, some Burgundians were unhappy about being allies of the traditional enemy of France. There is some evidence of popular dissent to the pro-English policy of the Duke of Burgundy. The inhabitants of La Ferté-Milon let Armagnac forces into the walled town. The largely English garrison was able to withdraw to the castle, where they mounted a stout resistance. La Ferté-Milon is about 55 miles north-east of Paris and was in an area important for two reasons: It was a major communications route between the English and Burgundians and was significant to Philip's ducal interests as the route from Burgundy to his lands in Flanders. Lord de L'Isle Adam, a Burgundian nobleman with considerable military experience, who at this point was generally fighting under English command, quickly and brutally recaptured the town with a relieving force.[139] Although they had been unable to hold La Ferté-Milon, this episode may have encouraged Charles and his advisors in their main strategy.

As a result of his diplomatic activities late in 1422, Charles was able to put a strong army into the field for this expedition. The largest contingent was the Scots, tough infantry with an increasing number of archers, whose morale would have been boosted by memories of Baugé.

There seem to have been a good number of French, probably mainly armoured knights and men-at-arms, and some Aragonese. Some of these men from both kingdoms were routiers, mercenary companies who tended to live off the land unless very closely controlled. There were also some Lombards who were potentially significant since they were well-armoured cavalry whose state-of-the-art plate armour for both man and horse made them fairly impervious to English archery. This heterogenous force was led by Sir John Stewart of Darnley, who was the most senior Scot in France at the time, with the Count of Vendôme as second-in-command. But before the Scottish soldiers would undertake any campaigning they demanded their arrears of pay. Charles scraped together the equivalent of two months' pay for them, which allowed the campaign to start.[140] They were ordered to besiege Cravant, the seizure of which would have similar consequences tobthat of La Ferté-Milon; it would allow the Armagnacs to disrupt communications between the heartland of the Duchy of Burgundy with both Paris and Flanders. While the Armagnac leaders seem to have been confident that they could handle any response from the Burgundians, their big uncertainty was how fast would the Duke of Bedford react.

Unlike Charles, but like Henry before him, Bedford was sufficiently well informed and confident in his understanding of the military and political situation in France to react effectively to threats such as the one to Cravant. Thomas, Earl of Salisbury was engaged in a surprisingly drawn-out siege of Montaiguillon south-east of Paris. Bedford sent him reinforcements fresh from England under Lord Willoughby, and ordered him to relieve Cravant. He left a small force to maintain the siege and set out towards Auxerre, where he would meet a Burgundian force gathered to join him in the relief of Cravant. The Burgundians reached Auxerre first and gave Salisbury and his English soldiers an enthusiastic ceremonial welcome when they reached the city on 29 July. Matters were pressing since Cravant had not been well stocked for a siege and the garrison was in desperate straits by this time. The Burgundians seem to have been pleased to accept Salisbury as the commander of a combined force; no doubt this had been agreed in negotiations beforehand, although there is no record of this. There could have been no reasonable objection to this since Salisbury was arguably the best soldier in France at the time. The allies held a council of war in Auxerre

Cathedral on the evening of the 29th, wherein it was agreed that the two contingents were to fight as one. After issuing a broad order requiring the men of both contingents to live amiably with each other, the council appointed a marshal from each nationality to keep order and enforce discipline. Even for a leader like Salisbury who seems to have inspired great loyalty and respect among his men, it would have been necessary to have an active marshal to contain the English archers in particular, who had no great respect for any foreign soldiers. A number of the other decisions made were simply sensible military orders. The archers were to cut themselves a pointed stake each; every man was to carry food for two days; each contingent was to provide sixty men-at-arms for scouting (something even experienced commanders seem to have been careless about in these wars). There were two orders aimed at ensuring steadiness in the battle line, which echoed the English ordinances of war issued since the second half of the fourteenth century. When the army neared the enemy and was preparing to fight, all horses were to be sent well to the rear. This reflected the English tactical system wherein men-at-arms fought on foot and so committed the Burgundians to the same approach on this occasion. The other order was no prisoners were to be taken until victory was ensured. This stopped men being distracted from the fight in hand by the taking and securing prisoners for ransom.[141] So as far as the English and Burgundians were concerned, they had made solid preparations for the relief of Cravant. The next day they set out along the valley of the River Yonne to find the French army and relieve Cravant. After a fairly short march in the summer heat the French army was located and Salisbury called a halt. The pace of the march may have been slowed by the Burgundian contingent, including carts carrying between thirty and forty veuglaires (what would later be called fowlers by the English) manned by the men of Auxerre.[142] Surprisingly perhaps, given his reputation for decisive action, Salisbury did nothing else that day. He may have been hoping that Cosne would repeat itself and the French army would creep away; or, and this seems quite likely given what happened the next day, Salisbury sent his scouts out to check the lie of the land on the final approach to Cravant, looking at both banks of the Yonne. The next day it was apparent that the French army was still in the field and not only outnumbered the Anglo-Burgundian forces but was in an advantageous position to block their advance.

Salisbury decided to backtrack towards Auxerre a short distance, to a convenient crossing point on the Yonne. He then marched towards Cravant on the opposite bank. When he reached the town he found the French army drawn up on the river bank blocking his approach. He now paused and began to draw up his army to face the task ahead, making an opposed river crossing. English armies of the period were particularly good at this, since the English and Welsh longbowmen could provide a debilitating covering fire for the men-at-arms, and on this occasion they would be helped by the gunpowder artillery of the Burgundians. It is likely that Salisbury had planned for this assault across the river, having had plenty of time to scout the riverbanks. Fortunately it was high summer so the river was relatively low and slow flowing.

The veuglaires seem to have been used in the early stages of the battle to unsettle the Franco-Scottish forces defending the opposite riverbank. Cravant was unique among the battles fought by the English in France because it was the only one which began with an archery and gunpowder artillery barrage. It is also unusual among the battles fought by the armies of the Valois dukes of Burgundy in the fifteenth century, because it was one of only two battles involving their forces which began that way.[143] When he was ready Salisbury led the attack, in Waurin's words: '[they] advanced suddenly with the ardour of rash courage, and the archers began to shoot all together, and the men-at-arms to go with alacrity into the water'.[144] The Scots' archers on the opposite bank were unable to resist the arrowshot from the English and Welsh archers. The Burgundian veuglaires may have ceased firing at this point if the fall of shot was considered to be too unpredictable. Also, while veuglaires were faster to reload than many guns of the time, they were hardly rapid-fire weapons. Salisbury was able to storm the bank and attack the men-at-arms in the French army. At the same time the English right wing under Lord Willoughby attempted to force the bridge on the road to Cravant. As soon as the Burgundians saw the English advance they also charged into the river to join in the assault on the enemy. While Salisbury and the English and Burgundian men-at-arms led the assault on the French side of the river, it is clear from later events in the battle that the English archers followed them across the river and continued to shoot. It is difficult to know how the multinational French army had been arrayed. Stewart and Vendôme either stuck to the traditional

Scottish tactics of fighting on foot and so had largely dismounted their horsemen, or, seeing Salisbury's preparations to cross the river, copied the English tactics and deployed the men-at-arms on foot as heavy infantry supported by the good numbers of Scottish archers in their army. A less likely possibility is that they had relaxed their guard after being misled about Salisbury's intentions because he declined battle on the previous day and he seemed to be taking a long time making his preparations for battle. The Scots infantry were stalwart as usual and resisted Willoughby's assault on the bridge for some time. However, those that faced Salisbury in company with the French men-at-arms were unable to stop his attack across the river, probably because they had very little armour to resist the arrows showered upon them. Once Salisbury had forced the opposition back, the archers who also crossed the river began to shoot into the flank of the men holding the bridge and the riverbank nearer to the town. Their arrows discomfited the Lombards by piercing their leg armour and finding other weaknesses in the side or back of the harness. The heavily armoured Italians were clearly caught on foot and in their efforts to escape from the English arrows ran for their horses. The author of the *Livre de Trahison* records that, 'One could hear the Scots in the bad French which they were commonly known to speak, swearing ...' at the retreating men.[145] This is probably reliable since this author seems to have been in the Burgundian forces at Cravant. If Stewart and Vendôme had deliberately dismounted the Italians to use them as heavy infantry in line with English (and Scottish) tactical practice, it was a notable mistake.

The Italians were unused to fighting on foot; this was not their role in warfare in the Italian peninsula. Stewart and Vendôme deprived themselves of a powerful mounted force in high-quality armour, which could have been used in an attempt to push Salisbury's men back into the river. However the French army was ordered, it was soon falling apart under the English and Burgundian attack. Once Willoughby forced the bridge the disordered French army was in serious trouble, its main escape route now lay close to the walls of Cravant, where the garrison, despite being weakened from having little or no food for some time, had sallied out. The result was a crushing defeat with heavy casualties and a good number of prisoners, including Stewart and Vendôme.[146] Looking back at the Battle of Cravant, it seems to have been a disaster for the French. Their patiently and expensively collected army had been destroyed. Their strategically sensible attack on the Duchy of Burgundy and its communication lines had failed completely. And finally it brought no relief to the strongholds like Le Crotoy and Montaiguillon besieged by the English. The citizens of Paris certainly saw it as something to be celebrated, with 'great bonfires and dancing ...' as the author of *A Parisian Journal* notes with pious distaste.[147] It is probable that these celebrations reflected the pro-Burgundian feelings that were well established in the city rather than any outburst of pro-English feeling. But Charles and the French seem to have seen it differently.

Charles himself made light of the defeat in a startling letter to the Citizens of Lyons, writing, 'Anyway at the said siege there were very few nobles of our realm, almost none in fact, but only Scots, Spaniards and other foreigners who normally live off the land so the harm done was not so great.'[148] While he was in part being accurate in this sentiment – both the Scots and the Spaniards were prone to live off the land, particularly since their pay was usually very overdue – French chroniclers suggest that this was an outright lie, and that a good number of Frenchmen were killed or captured. Also, the fact that Charles appears to have paid 148 ecus (around £24 sterling) to ransom twenty Scottish archers from the English, who were prepared to hang them, suggest that his real views of the Scots in particular were different.[149] But Charles may have been successful in this playing down of events because in the eyes of many of the French it was the presence of the English in Normandy and the Paris area that was the real affront. Great dukes of France like the Duke of Burgundy were often semi-independent of the French king, and warring with the Royalist party was normal behaviour in medieval France, perhaps seen as no more than a family row. But it was a family row that French chroniclers lamented for the damage it did to France. More important for the success of Charles's attempts to ignore the defeat at Cravant in late summer 1423 was the behaviour of one of the English commanders in southern Normandy. Sir John de la Pole, the brother of the Earl of Suffolk, was the English commander at Avranches and he had been ordered to press the siege of Mont St Michel as part of Bedford's strategy to reduce the 'nuisance' garrisons that were making life uncomfortable by raiding the lands of his Norman subjects. De la Pole had been given sufficient men to achieve this, largely drawn from the English garrisons at

Caen and towns in the Cotentin peninsula. The Norman Estates General had granted money to pay for these soldiers among others, believing that they were going to contain or capture the French stronghold. However, when he heard news of the victory at Cravant he decided that he should go on a chevauchée into Anjou. This would be much more exciting and potentially profitable than settling down for a prolonged, difficult siege. It also happened to be directly contrary to his orders from Bedford. He collected a small army, around 1,500 men from his 'besieging' forces and from the garrisons of Avranches, St Lô and other centres in southern Normandy, and set out southwards. He raided as far as Angers, which was too strong for him to threaten, and so, laden with booty, he turned for home. Unfortunately for him Jean d'Harcourt, the Count of Aumale, was at Tours with an army, prepared to follow up the successful attack made on Ivry by local irregular troops. Aumale showed his quality as a commander by gaining a good idea of where the English force was from local informants and scouts, and marching quickly north-west to cut them off from the safety of Normandy. De la Pole, on the other hand, seems to have been very careless of the enemy, no doubt believing that they were unable or unwilling to interfere with an English force of this size. Waurin, a Burgundian gentleman who fought alongside the English on a number of occasions, has left us an account of what happened next. At La Brossonière, near La Gravelle west of Laval, de la Pole was proved wrong, since, '[the English] knew nothing of their enemies until they were in the fields about half a league [about 1½ miles] from their position when they perceived them'. Aumale, who had a mixed force of experienced fighting men and local levies, was prepared for the fight, while the English were in marching order and encumbered by their booty.

Despite being both outnumbered and unprepared, the English dismounted and got ready to fight in their usual manner. Waurin described the battle as follows: '… there was a very hard struggle. Notwithstanding which if the English could have got their backs against any sort of hedge, the French would never have got the better of them without great loss; but the said English, not knowing of the approach of their enemies, were so taken by surprise, that with great difficulty they found time to put themselves in order and chose a place for a vigorous defence.'[150] The English force was destroyed and de la Pole, with the few others who survived the fight, was taken prisoner. If Waurin is right about how close the English got to the French before they saw them, they might have had as little as ten to fifteen minutes to prepare for the fight before Aumale's horsemen were on them, while his infantry would have joined the assault at least twenty minutes later. While Waurin offers an explanation for the defeat, which was entirely de la Pole's fault, he clearly had a high opinion of the toughness and competence of the English men-at-arms and archers from his remarks on how the French would have had a much harder job if the English had been able to take up a better defensive position. De la Pole's expedition bore an uncanny resemblance to Clarence's disastrous chevauchée two years earlier, covering much of the same ground and doing a similar amount of damage to the English cause.

Aumale celebrated his victory by raiding as far as St Lô and Avranches, which he besieged, knowing that the garrisons had been seriously weakened to make up the force he crushed at La Brossonière. When he heard that an English relieving force was approaching, he abandoned his siege of Avranches and returned in triumph to French-held areas. This success brought respite to Mont St Michel, ensured that the French hung on to Ivry and most importantly boosted morale among the French people within and without the lands ruled by Charles. He was able to make sure that people living south of the Loire heard much of Aumale's victory over the feared English and very little of the disaster at Cravant. As events at Verneuil in the following year suggest, this relatively small-scale success left Aumale with the strong feeling that a powerful cavalry assault could negate the English tactical system if they had insufficient cover like hedges or stakes. This tactical insight was neither new nor wrong and it was the guiding principle behind the way that the French and Scottish commanders undertook their manoeuvres leading up to the Battle of Verneuil in the following year.

Bedford acted fast to restore the situation. He appointed Lord Scales as captain general of the Seine towns and Alençon in November 1423. Scales supervised the whole of the Seine valley from Paris to Rouen, maintaining what amounted to a military police role preventing French irregulars from raiding across the river and attempting to prevent banditry in general. This was a key part of what would now be called a campaign for the hearts and minds of the population. The Estates of Normandy made their displeasure over de la Pole's folly clear, and this was expressed in the writs issued in Henry VI's name (but in reality at Bedford's behest) for the collection of part of a grant agreed by the Estates. Not only does the statement of the purpose of this grant include the recovery of Mont St Michel and Ivry, but 'the extirpation of the brigands who, in divers places of our said duchy, have committed in times past and do commit, many evil deeds, thefts and robberies ...'[151]

The appointment of Lord Scales allowed Bedford to concentrate on making the southern borders of Normandy more secure. Despite Bedford's broadly successful attempts to secure English Normandy and the lands approaching Paris, there was a broad border area between the English and Burgundian-dominated areas and the areas loyal to Charles where draining tit-for-tat fighting continued. *A Parisian Journal* comments, 'At that time the English would sometimes take one place from the Armagnacs in the morning and lose two in the evening. So this war accursed by God went on.'[152] This sentiment of war weariness is no surprise after nearly two decades of disruption caused initially by the internal aristocratic disputes in France and then by the English invasion.

While events in France were the most significant in the complicated struggle involving England, France and Scotland in 1422–23, it would be a mistake to ignore the developments in relations between England and Scotland 'at home'. By September 1423 agreement had been reached for the release of James so that he could return to rule Scotland. The Earl of Douglas seems to have been heavily involved in the negotiations, while appearing to have a substantial involvement in the Scottish army in France through his heir, the Earl of Wigtown, and his son-in-law the Earl of Buchan. Potentially, the release of James could be expected to lead to the recall of the Scottish army in France, a major strategic gain for the English, but events turned out very differently.

The winter of 1423–24 was not peaceful. At a strategic level there were preparations which with hindsight suggest that 'both sides prepared for a great trial of strength on the Norman frontiers'.[153] It is certain that both sides wanted to recover their strength after the events of 1423, and that the French leaders and Aumale in particular seem to have thought that they had a plan based on experience which would enable them to defeat the English. It is important to remember that if the French did repeat Baugé and not only defeat the English, but also kill or capture Bedford and Salisbury, then the English hold on northern France would be parlous.

At a more local level, Sir Thomas Rempston and the Duke of Luxembourg played cat and mouse with French forces under La Hire and Poton de Xaintrailles in the north-east of France, taking and losing castles. The most serious episode was when the French surprised the Burgundian-held town and castle of Compiègne in late 1423. This was a blow because its loss interrupted the communication routes from Paris to the north and to Flanders. The recovery of Compiègne needed an Anglo-Burgundian force led by the regent himself, and was not achieved until April 1424. How much Bedford and the English soldiers involvement in this was a sign of the relative incompetence of the Burgundian forces, and how much it was a sign of Bedford being more practically committed to the Anglo-Burgundian alliance than his brother-in-law Philip of Burgundy is unclear. Later events suggest that both interpretations are valid. The drawn-out siege of Le Crotoy was also coming to a conclusion. After d'Harcourt managed to escape from the siege, the defenders had agreed that if the English held the field outside the city in March 1424 they would surrender. Le Crotoy was too far north for the French to be able to mount any significant relief, so in March Sir Ralph Bouteiller held the field with his small besieging force and gained the city. Substantial English reinforcements arrived a few weeks later to secure Le Crotoy.

While the English, and to a lesser degree the Burgundians, had been largely successful in consolidating their position in Normandy and north-eastern France, Charles and the Armagnacs seem to have felt that events elsewhere in the autumn of 1423 had gone their way as they made their preparations to press the war in 1424. They had made much of the victory at La Brossonière and used it to cancel out the bad news of their larger-scale defeat at Cravant. They also took heart from their success in a relatively neglected battle at La Bussière in Eastern France against the Burgundians. In this battle five or six hundred heavily armoured Lombard cavalry, led by their experienced commanders Theode de Valpargue and Bourne Quaqueren, broke a Burgundian army under the Marshal of Burgundy.[154] This showed that when the Italian cavalry was used properly, as a shock weapon, they were battle winners. As a result of these two battles there seems to have been a high level of confidence in Charles's court about the way to defeat Bedford.

«BATAILLE DE VERNEUIL
le 17 Août 1424
DANS CETTE PLAINE, LORS D'UNE DES BATAILLES
LES PLUS MEURTRIÈRES DE LA GUERRE DE CENT ANS,
TOMBÈRENT POUR LA DÉFENSE DE LA FRANCE
7000 VALEUREUX SOLDATS FRANÇAIS ET ÉCOSSAIS,
DONT
John STEWART
Earl of BUCHAN
CONNÉTABLE DE FRANCE
Archibald DOUGLAS
Duc de TOURAINE
Jehan D'HARCOURT
Comte D'AUMALE »
«L'Auld Alliance n'a pas été écrite sur un parchemin de peau
de brebis mais gravée sur de la peau d'homme, tracée non
par l'encre mais par le sang» Alain CHARTIER XVᵉᵐᵉ s.»
STÈLE INAUGURÉE PAR LA VILLE DE VERNEUIL ET
L'ASSOCIATION «ALLIANCE FRANCE-ÉCOSSE»
LE 18 Juillet 1999

This memorial of the battle was set up in 1999 in the Allée des Écossais. (© of the author)

Street names commemorating the battle. The Allée des Ecossais is roughly
the starting position of the Scots in the battle, while the Impasse de la Bataille
is perhaps where the French cavalry on the right wing of their army started.
(© the author)

View of the battlefield. Looking towards Verneuil from roughly the starting position of the English. They would have seen the church tower. The Grey Tower and the remnants of the town walls are obscured by modern development. (© the author)

Town walls, Verneuil. One of the remnants of the town walls, which would have provided excellent views of the battle. (© the author)

The Grey Tower, Verneuil, constructed in 1204 by Philippe Augustus of France. It would have provided the French garrison of Verneuil with a grandstand view of the battle. (© the author)

A manuscript illustration of the Battle of Verneuil. It is from a fifteenth-century *Chronicle* and is one of the exhibits in the Grey Tower, which is now a museum dedicated to the battle. While it is in no way an accurate picture of the battle, it recalls some of its main features, with French cavalry attacking the English archers and the opposing men-at-arms advancing on each other. (© the author)

The cavalry attack from the wall painting discovered in a house in Verneuil in 1997 and now preserved in the Centre Hospitalier de Verneuil. The mural was probably painted in the sixteenth century and is thought to show Judith and Holofernes in one part, and the Jewish army attacking his besieging Assyrian army in the rest. Local writers (such as E. Cornetto, 'Une victoire sur le temps: la peinture murale dans l'Hotel a'Artus Fillon', *Bulletin Municipal de Verneuil sur Avre*, no. 20, July 1984) have suggested that the attacking cavalry are a remembrance of the opening stages of the Battle of Verneuil a century earlier. (© the author)

These are some of the finds from the battlefield in the Grey Tower. Unfortunately the arms on the harness ornament have not been identified.
(© the author)

Grave slabs from Iona showing traditional Scottish armour worn by men-at-arms, knights and nobles. (© Crown Copyright reproduced courtesy of Historic Scotland. www.historicscotlandimages.gov.uk)

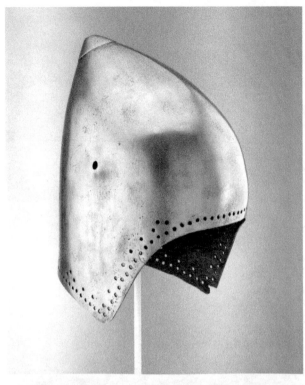

A fifteenth-century bascinet from Dean Castle. This type of helmet can be seen on the men on the grave slabs. It could also have been worn by Scottish knights and nobles at Verneuil, who were armoured in the European tradition. It was probably imported from Europe. (© By permission of East Ayrshire Council/East Ayrshire Leisure)

A helmet from Dean Castle of the type that could have been worn by ordinary soldiers. It is old-fashioned compared with the bascinet. There is no evidence of where it was made. (© By permission of East Ayrshire Council/East Ayrshire Leisure)

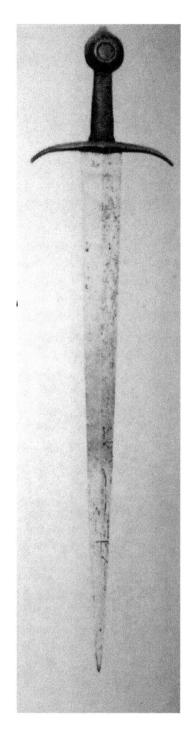
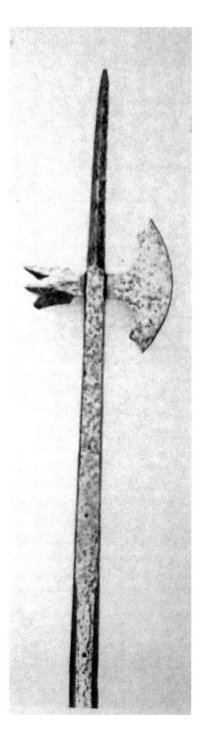

Weapons used at Verneuil. A fifteenth-century arming sword and a poleaxe dating to the first quarter of the fifteenth century. Both from the Wallace Collection. (© the author, with thanks to the Wallace Collection)

Replicas of an English warbow and arrows. The bow was made of Italian yew by P. Bickerstaffe and the arrows by S. Stratton. Both are made to the dimensions of finds from the *Mary Rose*, and can be taken as a good approximations of the bows and arrows used at Verneuil. (© the author)

English armour of the early fifteenth century. This early fifteenth-century wall painting from Hornton, Oxfordshire shows St George on foot killing the dragon. The armour style is late fourteenth–early fifteenth century and gives a reasonable idea of what might have been common wear among the English men-at-arms, although the helmet is old-fashioned for the 1420s. Anne Marshall (www.paintedchurch.org/horntgeo.htm) speculates that the background details of heraldic feathers, red coronets and white fleur-de-lys may be a reference to the marriage of Henry V and Catherine of Valois. Given the popularity of the cult of St George among the English soldiery, including Henry V and John, Duke of Bedford, this painting may well reference the English military successes of the first quarter of the fifteenth century. (© the author)

AAINVS PHI IPPVS HISPANVS DESCOI AB LS   REI AT

Italian armour of the first half of the fifteenth century. A painting of Pippo Spano
by Andrea del Castagno, *c.* 1450, now in the Uffizi Gallery. Pippo Spano was a
renowned *condottiero* (captain of mercenaries) employed by the kings of Hungary
for much of his career. He died in 1426. This armour is typical of north Italian
armours of the period. The large pauldrons (shoulder and armpit protection) were
effective against arrows. A fairly close-fitting bascinet with a rounded visor would
protect the head. (© S.S.P.S.A.E. e per il Polo Museale della città di Firenze)

E. Lutterell delin.   I Vanderbanck Sculp.

KING HENRY THE V.th

Henry V, the Shakespearian hero, portrayed in a Victorian engraving. Were his ambitions in France ever realistic?

Henry VI, disputed King of France from 1422 to 1453.

Charles VII portrayed in
*Les Vigilles de la Mort de
Charles VII*, Lyons, *c.* 1500. To
the French he was Le *Trés
Victorieux*; an unlikely tag in
1421, when he was forced to
withdraw from battle with
Henry V and was repudiated
as heir to the throne by his
father Charles VI.

Battles and Major Sieges 1415–24

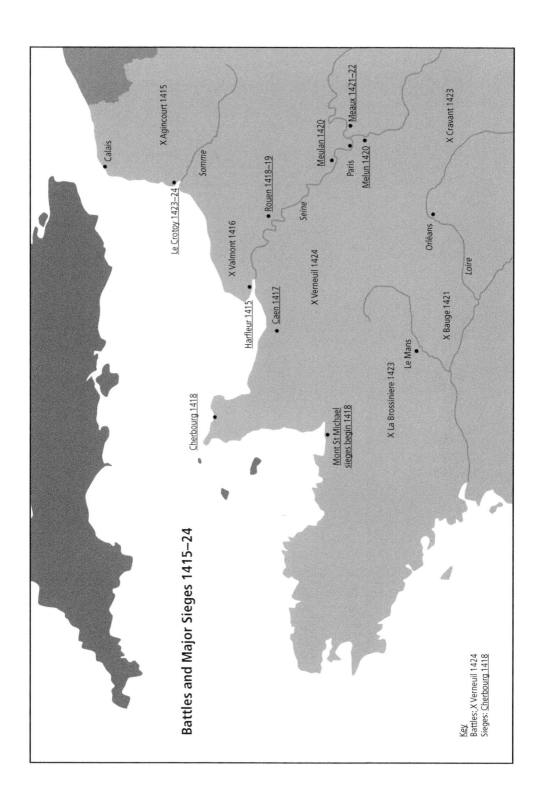

Calais

X Agincourt 1415

Somme

Le Crotoy 1423–24

X Valmont 1416

Harfleur 1415

Caen 1417

Rouen 1418–19

Seine

Meulan 1420

X Verneuil 1424

Paris

Melun 1420

Meaux 1421–22

X Cravant 1423

Orléans

Loire

Cherbourg 1418

Mont St Michael
sieges begin 1418

X La Brossiniere 1423

Le Mans

X Bauge 1421

Key
Battles: X Verneuil 1424
Sieges: Cherbourg 1418

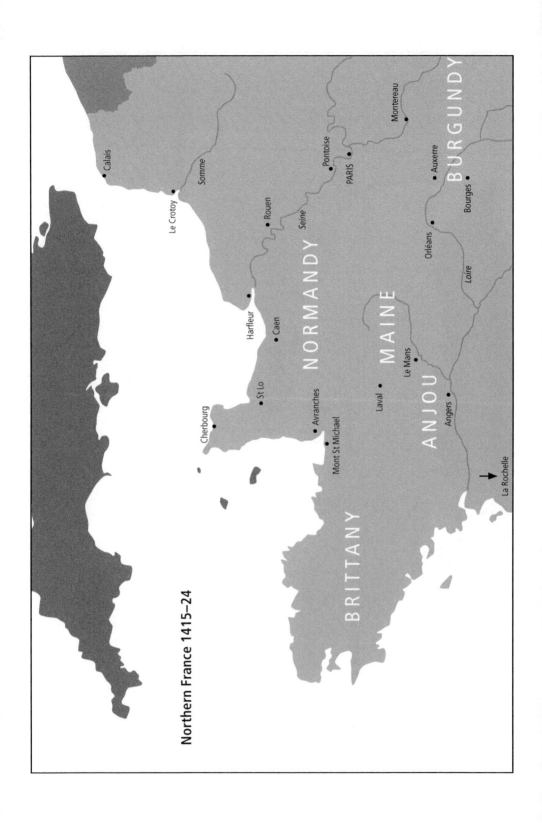

Northern France 1415–24

Calais

Le Crotoy

Somme

Cherbourg

St Lo

Harfleur

Caen

NORMANDY

Avranches

Mont St Michael

BRITTANY

Rouen

Seine

Pontoise

PARIS

Montereau

Auxerre

BURGUNDY

Bourges

Orléans

Loire

MAINE

Laval

Le Mans

ANJOU

Angers

La Rochelle

II

The road to Verneuil

However he publicly interpreted it, the defeat at Cravant was not 'a little local difficulty' and left Charles with a problem; his main army had been destroyed. In particular, the substantial casualties the Scots had suffered in the battle meant that Charles had to hire more of them if he could, since he and his advisors were fully aware of their quality. He had allowed the Earl of Buchan and later the Earl of Wigtown to return to Scotland to raise more Scottish troops. Archibald, Earl of Douglas decided to replace his son and heir the Earl of Wigtown as commander of this new force. Why would a man of just over 50 decide to risk himself in the hazards of war?

Douglas had always been keen to fight the English, although of late he had been involved in the diplomatic negotiations for the return of James I to Scotland. Once this had been agreed by the autumn of 1423, Douglas could look to other interests. He had been active in Scottish affairs for over a decade, particularly working to secure the position of the house of Douglas. He may have felt that the time had come when he could leave his son to maintain things in Scotland while he went to France to fight the English and see what honours and rewards he could extract from Charles VII. Given that Archibald Douglas, 4th Earl of that name, had always shown a very keen sense of his own worth and reputation, he may have been making a final effort to shake off his nickname, Tyneman or Loser. Charles's ambassadors agreed the levels of reward this new Scottish army under Douglas would receive for their service in France.

However, since Charles struggled to raise the money to pay the largely Castilian fleet which was to bring the Scots to France, Douglas and his men should have had some concerns about the actual rewards they might receive. Eventually the fleet brought Douglas and his men to La Rochelle by early April 1424. The delay in leaving Scotland caused by Charles's money problems came very near to causing another problem for Douglas and Charles. By the end of March 1424, James I was back in Scotland and had agreed a seven-year truce with the English. In the negotiations for this truce, the English had been determined to get James to commit to allowing no Scots to fight in France. In the end, they had to accept a vaguer promise that, while neither party would aid the enemies of the other, James couldn't speak for the Scots in France until they returned home.[155] This was agreed right at the end of March and Douglas and his men had been leaving for France throughout March, so it was probable that very few if any broke the truce, but it was a near thing.

Prior to the arrival of these reinforcements to the army of Scotland, Charles had been forced to a radical economic measure by his chronic lack of funds. In January 1424 he had disbanded all companies of men-at-arms except the Scots, Lombards and a few specified companies.[156] The exclusion of the Scots and the Lombards from this disbandment came about for two reasons. Firstly it no doubt reflected Charles's estimate of their effectiveness, and so their importance to any military plans he may have been developing. Secondly, if he disbanded these foreign forces it would take months rather than weeks to re-employ similar men, whereas the French forces could be recalled much more quickly.

Soon after the Scots arrived Charles summoned the Estates of Languedoc to provide funds to pay these and other troops. Meanwhile Charles rewarded Douglas with two titles. Firstly, Douglas was named 'Lieutenant General for waging war for the whole kingdom of France', a grandiose and unusual title that played on Douglas's self-love and appeared to give him equal status with the Earl of Buchan, who was Constable of France. Then Charles rewarded Douglas financially by making him Duke of Touraine. While this was a royal duchy, granting it to a foreigner upset a number of French nobles, who saw it as abusing the royal patrimony. Douglas visited his new duchy in the first week of May and the Council of Tours gave him a dutifully enthusiastic welcome.

However, in both June and July they sent deputations to Douglas to complain about the behaviour of his men and asking him to take them away from the city.[157] This evidence of bad behaviour by the Scottish troops may suggest that Charles was behind with their pay and that they were living off their commander's new duchy. In an attempt to increase support from the inhabitants of France south of the Loire, Charles also ordered Lafayette, the Master of the Crossbowmen and Admiral of France, to take 400 men and drive away all the companies or soldiers who were living off the people. Interestingly, and rather revealingly, any Scots and Lombards that Lafayette found were to be left alone. As will become apparent in the account of the Battle of Verneuil, these two 'nations' of soldiery were vital to any plans Charles had for defeating the English and he would not have wanted them antagonised into deserting his cause.

The other potentially significant actor in diplomatic affairs was Jean, Duke of Brittany. Aumale's success at La Brossonière and his subsequent sweep through Normandy, coupled with the arrival of Douglas and the Scottish reinforcements, seems to have overawed the vacillating Jean so that he started to negotiate a tripartite alliance between himself, Burgundy and Armagnac France which was agreed in the Treaty of Nantes in May 1424. While this was little more than a chivalric brotherhood in arms, news of it must have been very worrying to Bedford, because of the involvement of his brother-in-law Philip of Burgundy. In the end this treaty came to nothing because of the crushing English success at Verneuil. Meanwhile, Bedford held meetings of the council in Paris in May and June where plans were made for the further development of the English kingdom of France. Bedford would lead the conquest of Maine and Anjou to the south of the Duchy of Normandy proper. These two duchies had already been the scene of regular fighting, including the two major English defeats, Clarence's at Baugé and de la Pole's at La Brossonière. If the English gained control of these areas, Normandy would be much more secure. It would also open up a realistic possibility of crossing the Loire. However, Bedford also had to take some local action to consolidate the borders of Normandy. Lord Scales had to retake Gaillon, which had been lost in April to a surprise attack by the French. plans were also made for another attempt to take Mont St Michel, which had a symbolic value as an outpost of Armagnac France. It is possible that the dispatch of the

Earl of Suffolk to retake Ivry was a first step in this expansion into Anjou and Maine, but in fact it brought about the great confrontation which was to decide the fate of Henry's conquests in France.[158] The make-up of Suffolk's force of about 600 men shows how the English commanders always had to scratch around to raise forces for any offensive activity. His own retinue contained 69 men-at-arms and 204 archers, Salisbury sent 19 men-at-arms and 67 archers, the garrison of Cherbourg 15 men-at-arms and 45 archers, Evreux contributed 26 men-at-arms and 78 archers, and the Captain of Dreux seemed to be present in person with 17 men-at-arms and 54 archers.[159] The contribution from the last garrison in this list is a bit surprising, since Dreux was south of Ivry and might be thought of as at risk from the Armagnacs. But the way Suffolk gathered his little army together is a clear demonstration of the way the English commanders in France would build up 'scratch' field forces throughout this period as necessary. One of the major advantages of this practice was that the garrison troops were kept more battle experienced and their military quality did not lapse in the way that commonly happened with garrison troops. The other thing to note about this force is that it shows the 'classic' one to three ratio of men-at-arms to archers found only in the English armies of the period.

Suffolk quickly regained the town, but the castle held out for three weeks before coming to terms. He and the commander of the French garrison of Ivry castle made an agreement that the latter should surrender the castle on a specified day in August if he was not relieved. This chivalric device, known as the *journée*, was fairly common in the Hundred Years War.[160] The inability of Charles and his supporters to meet the terms of the *journée* has already been demonstrated with their failure before Cosne and Le Crotoy. So Suffolk had only to maintain a loose but effective blockade of Ivry while awaiting the Armagnac response, or lack of it if their previous behaviour was any guide. Even before he dispatched Suffolk to regain Ivry, Bedford would have known that Charles had been recruiting large forces in the preceding months, and that their most likely plan would be to sweep through Maine and Anjou into southern Normandy. Might this mean that on this occasion they would attend the *journée*? This possibility would have led Bedford to consider if they might be following a battle-seeking strategy in 1424. In fact it does seem that Charles had a well-developed campaign plan this time. He had brought together a large army made up of battle-winning components led by his most experienced, and in Aumale's case most successful, commanders. In addition there seem to have been a number of individuals and small groups in Normandy primed to rise up in revolt when Charles's army was successful in the battle, for which they were well prepared. This became apparent in the very immediate aftermath of the Battle of Verneuil when there were a number of small revolts in the Norman countryside stimulated by a false rumour of a French victory. Bedford and his advisors would have had a well-informed opinion of Aumale as a commander. They knew him to be a man who preferred a 'Fabian' strategy of avoiding battle from choice but who was also a skilled battlefield commander when the opportunity presented, itself, as his defeat of de la Pole had proved in the previous year. They may have taken Douglas less seriously because of his lack of military success. But that would not mean that they discounted him and the 'Army of Scotland'; he wanted to make a glorious reputation and the Scots were always formidable foes.

Charles's plans would become clear on 15 August 1424, the day of the *journée*, when the French must relieve the castle of Ivry by sunset or lose it.[161]

The armies

The army that Charles VII had built up painstakingly since late 1423 was as multinational as any he raised. It was not that he had found a new source of soldiers, just that this time he had put all the different contingents together in one army. He had had a similar multinational army at Cravant, but it had been smaller. Only part of the various national contingents available to him had been present on that occasion because of his financial problems. As has been mentioned above he seems to have been quite prepared for his commanders to risk all in battle. Why had such a usually cautious man decided to take this gamble? In large part because Charles knew that he had to use his army quickly, or lose it as a coherent force because he couldn't pay it. All the previous months' planning would come to nought if his commanders did not move quickly. The need to relieve Ivry by 15 August set the timetable.

The core of his army was the 'Army of Scotland' under the Earl of Douglas in his role as 'Lieutenant General for waging war for the whole kingdom of France'. He had his son-in-law, the Earl of Buchan, who was Constable of France, and his second son James with him. Out of these three men, Buchan was the most valuable because of his experience of the wars in France, although it seems that Douglas demanded the captaincy of the Scots because of his standing in Scotland. The 'Army of Scotland' itself consisted of between 6,000 and 6,500 men, most of whom were the new forces raised by Douglas and brought to France in 1424. These seem to have been about one third men-at-arms and two thirds archers since in April 1424 Hamon Raguier, Treasurer of Wars for Charles VII, recorded a payment that 'retained my said Lords Douglas and Buchan together with the number and charge of 2500 men at arms of the said country of Scotland'.[162]

The majority of the Scots recruited in the first half of the fifteenth century to fight in France seem to have come from the Western Lowlands, on the evidence of where their leaders held land.[163] Since Archibald Douglas, his son and son-in-law were the main leaders of the Scots in France in 1424, it is reasonable to assume that the majority of the men in the battle came from their estates, and those of their followers. However, these new men were probably largely inexperienced when compared with the Scots who had fought and died at Cravant. As we will see from the account of the battle, this may have had some effect on the outcome. Charles and his commanders clearly hoped that by putting such a large number of Scottish archers into the field they would be able to give the English a taste of their own medicine. This would have given the men-at-arms from the various nations making up the army the opportunity to win the battle, since they could reasonably expect to outnumber those in Bedford's army. It is possible that Douglas encouraged them in this since he was the one man present that we know had experience of fighting in a battle where both sides had substantial bodies of archers; the Battle of Shrewsbury. They had seen at the battles of Baugé and Cravant that the Scottish archers were good enough to delay assaults by men-at-arms, particularly in confined spaces such as assaults on bridges. What they hadn't noticed was that at Cravant the Scottish archers were not good enough to outshoot the English and Welsh archers.

The other key part of the French army of 1424 was the Lombard cavalry. These men had developed their skills and equipment in the well-financed world of Italian warfare where mercenaries were the dominant type of troops. The quality of their armour and their habit of armouring their horses has been noted above, and this led Charles and his advisors to feel that these heavy cavalrymen could also neutralise the English archers by being impervious to their arrows. They had proved their worth against the Burgundians at the Battle of La Buissière in the autumn of the previous year. In this battle they were no doubt used in the traditional way for heavy cavalry – a thunderous charge against the opposing armoured cavalry. But there had also been some Lombards at Cravant, where their behaviour was less creditable. They seem to have been fighting on foot in this battle, something that was outside their usual military experience. They fled when they saw that the English had stormed across the river and that the English archers were shooting into their flank. This act of self-preservation may have been normal practice in Italian warfare where the mercenaries were naturally concerned to limit casualties, but it didn't impress the observers and recorders of events at Cravant. It gave both French and Scottish chroniclers a scapegoat to explain the defeat, but it does not seem that the French and Scottish commanders read events at the battle the same way. The Battle of Verneuil proved that both views of the Lombards had validity. These men had another advantage besides their magnificent armour – the English had little experience of fighting them.

Their meeting at Cravant was atypical since the Lombards were not used in the classic way for heavy cavalry, to break the enemy's battle line by charging, but had been fighting on foot. If the actual events of the Battle of Verneuil are any guide, Charles and his advisors planned to use the Lombards in this traditional role to neutralise the English archers, in the same way that Aumale had used cavalry so effectively at La Brossonière. Charles had recruited about 2,000 Lombards under a well-established captain called Le Borgne Caqueran in the French records. Caqueran had first been in French service under Marshal Boucicaut in 1410. Since 1421 he and his men had been operating mainly in south-eastern France, away from the English. It was here in 1423 that they were responsible for the French victory over the Burgundians at La Bussière.[164] In 1424 he and his men are recorded passing through

Tours four days before the battle so they must have arrived just in time. The question is how many of these 2,000 men were in full armour. The number comes from records of the authorities at Tours and may be taken as a reasonable estimate of the total force.[165]

Did the Tours authorities see 2,000 Lombards in full armour or 2,000 Lombards in total? It is very unlikely that 2,000 fully armoured men, with their armoured horses, would be travelling without support. Indeed, it is quite likely that they wouldn't be riding their warhorses on this journey to the battle, and so would need servants to lead the horses they weren't riding. Finally, it is fair to assume that the authorities of Tours would record the total number of any company of soldiers travelling through their city since they were sensibly enough mistrustful of companies of soldiers after their experience with the Scots. Therefore it seems reasonable to suggest that Caqueran's force was about 2,000 men in total, or between 660 and 700 lances. However, the actual number of Italians who reached Verneuil in time for the fight may have been smaller since Basin says that there were 400 to 500 lances present.[166] Since it was normal practice for these Italian mercenaries to be organised in lances, Bedford's army would be facing up to 700 men equipped with excellent north Italian armour on armoured horses, supported by the same number of more lightly protected valets fighting on horseback, while the same number of pages kept out of the fighting if possible but may well have been expected to keep an eye on their masters to help them if necessary. The attack made by these men in the Battle of Verneuil was to be an unpleasant surprise for Bedford and his army.

The French forces in this army were probably a much more mixed bag than these two large foreign companies. The Count of Aumale was probably able to call together a fairly experienced body of troops since he had been fighting the English for at least six years now. He had about 1,700 with him on the banks of the Loire in June 1424.[167] These may have been something like a personal retinue or small army that formed the core of the forces he had led in previous years. In their ranks they may well have included a good number of displaced Normans who had been unwilling to accept Henry V as Duke of Normandy and who as a result, like Aumale himself, had a very personal interest in victory. Also, after his victory at La Brossonière in the previous autumn, his reputation would have been high so that experienced fighting men would be keen to fight under him.

It is likely that his men were the best French company at Verneuil. The other leading French commanders were the Count of Narbonne, the Count of Ventadour and the Duke of Alençon. Narbonne and Ventadour had previous experience fighting the English, indeed Ventadour had been captured at Cravant, and Alençon was a youth of about 15 whose father was a hero of Agincourt, dying there after reputedly killing the Duke of York. His enthusiasm for war exceeded his experience at this time, although he later became an important leader against the English.

The rest of the French troops were brought up from the regions of the Dauphine, the Auvergne and Limousin, a broad swathe of central and south-eastern France long loyal to Charles VII. It was also an area, with the possible exception of the western Limousin, that had had little contact with the English. However competent these men were, they were unlikely to have had much active military experience. The Count of Narbonne was leading a good-sized body of Spanish troops, probably mainly men-at-arms.[168] Many of these men probably had experience of war in France and some at least would have faced the English before. They were mercenaries who were effective fighting men but who had a reputation for living off the land.

The biggest problem for the French army was command. Aumale was in command but Douglas knew the value of his men and probably felt that his grandiose French title gave him equal standing. Then there were the other French nobles who felt that their advice should steer Aumale when it came to the fight. The other aspect of the command structure where there could be problems was basic communication: at least seven languages were spoken by the different contingents. These included langue d'oïl (the French spoken in the north and central parts), langue d'oc (southern French), Italian, Spanish, Scots English, Gaelic (still common in Galloway at this time) and Breton.[169] This would have caused little problem among the nobles and commanders of the various contingents. Probably as a consequence of the 'Auld Alliance' there seems to have been no problem between the Scots and the French commanders. The Italian leader Caqueran had served in France long enough to have sufficient understanding of French. The problems could arise among the junior captains and between the men themselves, as was shown at Cravant, particularly when the men were under the stress of battle and trying to communicate quickly.

A practical sign of these weaknesses in the command structure of the French army at Verneuil was that there is no evidence of the commanders having a council similar to Salisbury's at Auxerre before Cravant. Despite this, there is no evidence of the major commanders taking different tactical approaches in the forthcoming battle, although there was a major tactical contradiction in the plan as it unfolded. Even if they had wanted to hold a council of war, it would have been difficult because of the late arrival of Caqueran and his Lombards. He passed through Tours on 13 August, leaving him between three and four days to cover the 120 miles to Verneuil. Not impossible, but his men and their horses could not have been at their freshest for the battle!

When it came to the confrontation outside Verneuil on 17 August, Aumale headed an impressive army of between 14,000 and 16,000 men. The spirits of the whole army must have been lifted by the knowledge that they outnumbered their opponents, although they may not have realised that it was possibly by nearly two to one. The English army was more unified, although it was not made up of just one nation. The real unity of the English army centred on its commander, the Duke of Bedford, Regent of France. He was uncle to the infant Henry VI and brother to the renowned Henry V. In addition, he had successful military experience and had shown his qualities as a ruler and diplomat. He was fortunate in his subordinates. Thomas, Earl of Salisbury, his second-in-command, had proved that he was probably the best soldier in France at the time. Under them Bedford and Salisbury had a good number of experienced captains (see Appendix A) who could be relied upon to follow orders and use their experience and initiative when necessary. The English troops in the army at Verneuil came from three sources: the personal retinues of the main commanders, particularly Bedford and Salisbury; reinforcements sent over from England in 1424; and men drawn from the garrisons throughout Normandy. Although they were mainly employed through their captains and therefore had a unit loyalty to their fellows in the garrison, these garrison troops also had a loyalty to the Regent. He administered their pay and regulations in a way that made the whole English garrison in northern France effectively his own very large retinue.

About 3,400 newly mustered men arrived in Calais in April or May 1424 to reinforce the regent's efforts to expand the infant Henry VI's control in France.

By July Bedford was concerned by the desertions from these forces, which at that time were still rather underemployed. This is not to say that they were just sitting in tents or billets in and around Calais, since a good number of them had probably been brought south-east to join Bedford as he collected forces to meet the threat from Charles VII's army. It is likely that the majority were not doing much fighting, just marching, patrolling and preparing. Desertion was a problem that both armies faced. In the case of the English troops, where most of the men had volunteered, desertion does not seem to have been a sign of widespread unwillingness to be in the army. It seems that a number of men joined for primarily mercenary reasons and if underemployed, in activities where they were unlikely to find opportunities for gain, they were likely to look for better opportunities to profit.[170] While some of the deserters seem to have gone back to England with the wages they had received so far, others looked to make more profit by enlisting in other retinues based in Normandy. These might be those making up the English garrisons or the retinues of Norman landholders both Norman and English. Men who did this got paid a second time for being present at muster.[171] How experienced these reinforcements would be is unclear. Since they seemed to know a number of the common frauds, they may well have included quite a large number of men who had fought before and learnt bad habits, but there would have been a number of new men as well. English men had had more opportunity to gain military experience in the last ten years than the Scots, for example, so these new troops may not have been raw. Another reason why the men may well have had some experience was the simple fact that it takes years of practice to be able to use the war-bow. While as previously mentioned there were laws that required ordinary men to practise archery, it was the opportunity to profit in war from this practice that encouraged ordinary English and Welsh men to put the time in.

The Normandy garrisons provided about 2,000 men or about half their total strength according to Curry's calculations.[172] This shows more clearly than anything else the seriousness of the situation in the eyes of Bedford and his advisors. If this English army lost the battle, the Normandy garrisons would not have the strength to put up long, drawn-out resistance. It may also be a sign of Bedford's confidence that his men could beat any army Charles could put before them. This confidence was well founded, because of the English efforts to ensure that garrison troops maintained their military edge. The practice of regularly using detachments from garrisons in offensive operations has already been noted. But by April 1424, at the latest, the men administering the muster process to approve the pay of garrison troops were also testing that the archers were still effective war-bow archers by having them shoot at butts.[173]

The records of the administration of English-held France for 1423–24 are very patchy, so it is difficult to know how many men were in Bedford and Salisbury's personal retinues for the battle. Later in his Regency Bedford's retinue comprised 2 bannerets, 8 knights, 50 men-at-arms and 240 archers.[174] It is likely that the one he led at Verneuil was similar in size and make-up. Waurin describes it: '… his company … was large, fair and greatly to be feared, for they were all chosen men'.[175] No doubt, given his status and experience, the same could have been said of Salisbury's retinue. These men would have been the crack troops in the whole army, something that proved vitally important in the battle.

The English called upon their Norman subjects to contribute to the army that was gathering to defend Normandy. On 26 June a mandate was issued by the bailli of Rouen (no doubt at Bedford's behest) to muster troops at Vernon by 3 July to support Suffolk at Ivry. This required 'all those holding fiefs and arrière fiefs and others who have been wont to follow arms, should be ready, mounted and sufficiently armed …' This seems to be very much in the tradition of earlier French summons to arms with the emphasis on mounted men. Bedford issued a letter at Rouen on the same date, expanding on the mandate by specifically mentioning men-at-arms and archers.[176]

Whether this has any real significance is uncertain. It may just reflect the English military cast of mind or may be a deliberate emphasis for the information of tenants in Normandy, that what was required by this summons was different from what had been previously required. It also demonstrated that Bedford understood that there were a number of English and Welsh soldiers living in Normandy prepared to join the Norman landholders' retinues. Some of these might have been the recent deserters mentioned above but most would have been experienced men who had never returned home once their indenture was up, and who provided an important reserve for the English commanders to call upon in emergencies. No doubt Bedford was grateful for properly equipped troops of any kind from Normandy. Basin emphasises that there was a good turn out by the Norman landowners themselves, mentioning that 'the nobility of Normandy' were present at Verneuil.[177] The majority of these would have been men-at-arms, who were always needed to strengthen the battle line and take advantage of the disruption and damage caused by the archers. It is likely that this Norman contingent meant the English army was not made up to the standard of three archers to every man-at-arms that contemporary English administrative records suggest was the required make-up of companies and garrisons, but had a slightly higher proportion of men-at-arms.

Finally, L'Isle Adam, an experienced Burgundian commander, brought between 1,000 and 2,000 men to Rouen to join the force.[178] Bedford was reportedly pleased to receive this help, perhaps viewing it as payback for the substantial English help the Burgundians received at Cravant and Compiègne.

All in all, Bedford led over 10,000 men (maybe 11,000 if 2,000 Burgundians were present) to the *journée* at Ivry, although, as we shall see, he had fewer men at the Battle of Verneuil.

Manoeuvring before the battle

Aumale led the bulk of his army through Tours on about 6 August on his way north-east to the relief of Ivry. He had to cover about 125 miles in eight days to meet Bedford for the *journée* and satisfy the demands of chivalric code. This was an easy enough rate of march, which allowed for the scouts that Aumale would no doubt have sent ahead to be effective. This relatively gentle rate of march also gave the missing contingent, the Lombard cavalry, a chance to catch up. It is quite probable that Aumale didn't know just how far behind his main body these men were, since they passed through Tours a full week later. Bedford, meanwhile, had led his whole army, including his Burgundian allies under L'Isle Adam, to Ivry from Evreux by the evening of 14 August, so that they could take the field outside Ivry for the *journée* on 15 August. Once there he held a grand parade of the whole force. Bedford rode before his men splendidly clad in a blue velvet robe with a surcoat displaying a doubled cross; the white cross of France with the red cross of England superimposed. This was a clear statement that the men would understand. The surcoat with the doubled cross was an expression of the main point in the Treaty of Troyes, namely that Henry VI was heir to both thrones and that Bedford wore this as Regent. He also rode under the banner of St George, showing his well-known devotion to the saint, one shared with many of the soldiers in his army.[179] This parade was a great statement of purpose and unity for the English army.

In the morning of 15 August they took up their positions and awaited the arrival of the French. French scouts appeared at some point relatively early in the morning and inspected the English position. They realised that the English had taken advantage of arriving first before Ivry to take up an advantageous position that did not allow the French wide spaces to use their greater numbers or their supremacy in cavalry. They realised that it would not be to their advantage to fight before Ivry and their reports clearly impressed Aumale. But Aumale's reluctance to meet Bedford at the *journée* in front of Ivry may well have arisen not from timidity, but from calculation, because his army lacked one of its vital components – all or a large proportion of the Lombard cavalry. It has already been noted that a leading commander of Lombard cavalry in French service passed through Tours only four days before the Battle of Verneuil itself, so it would have been very difficult for him and his men to have reached the army approaching Ivry by 15 August in good fighting condition.

Because of this it is not unreasonable to suggest that Aumale, who had previously showed himself to be a very shrewd commander, decided to accept the smaller dishonour of not attending the *journée* under unfavourable circumstances, for the greater honour of winning a notable victory a few days later. Moreover, it is quite possible that Aumale was playing a much deeper strategic game, as will become clear below. This interpretation is supported in Jean de Waurin's account of the events, which is an important corroboration since Waurin, a Burgundian, was present in the English army and actually fought in the Battle of Verneuil. However, by not attending the *journée*, the French committed an offence against the code of chivalry. To modern people this code is one of the puzzles of medieval history. Knights and nobles, men trained for hand-to-hand combat from childhood in many cases, balanced their ferocious combat skills with a wide-reaching code of honour. In theory at least, women, children, the Church and its possessions and clergymen were to be protected from the grim reality of war. In addition, a knight's oath was expected to have real binding value. So in the case of the surrender of Ivry, some French nobles broke their words as knights by not attempting relief as agreed. Bedford, who genuinely seems to have put value on his word in all his dealings in France during his Regency, was angry and disappointed by this. But it seems strange to us that he should have expected the French to have obliged him by risking all in a battle on terms favourable to him just because they had sworn they would. In addition, on the English part at least, this was an age of professional armies made up of men most of whom were outside the chivalric classes and no doubt took a more pragmatic approach to war and the *journée* in particular. As has already been noted, this sort of agreement had become a convenient way for the commanders of both the besiegers and the garrison to agree an outcome without every siege having to be fought to a bloody conclusion. Maybe Bedford felt slighted; he would undoubtedly have felt frustrated that the campaign had not been resolved. At sunset on 15 August the castle of Ivry was handed over to the English. At this point, Bedford and his commanders may have felt that they had an advantage over Aumale and the Franco-Scottish army because they had achieved their immediate purpose, the recapture of Ivry, without any interference. But they also had reason to be worried because they seem to have been ignorant of the exact position of their enemy, whereas Aumale and his colleagues knew exactly where the English were.

While the English were keeping the *journée* to recover Ivry, the Franco-Scottish army seems to have been about 30 miles south-west of them approaching Verneuil. It is reasonable to assume that Aumale and his colleagues knew the lie of the land between the Loire and Maine better than most since they had campaigned over it for some years. Therefore, they may have decided to sacrifice Ivry, situated as it was in a more hilly landscape, to get round the English army and push northwards into Maine and Normandy. Doing this they would find themselves in more open, rolling countryside, suitable for the use of their 'surprise', the armoured Lombard cavalry. As a result, they found themselves at Verneuil, another small, fortified town in the hands of the English, on 15 August.

They gained the town not by violence but by a classic ruse. Heralds were sent to proclaim that the Franco-Scottish army had defeated the Regent outside Ivry, and to prove the claim that some 'English' prisoners were paraded outside the town walls. In fact these were members of the Scottish army daubed in blood and able to sound sufficiently English to fool the defenders of Verneuil into surrender. So by the end of 15 August another of the tit-for-tat exchanges of towns so typical of the wars in France at this time had happened. Aumale and colleagues had reason to feel particularly satisfied since they had outmanoeuvred Bedford, and were now on ground that favoured them, while they waited for the Lombards to catch up. They probably felt confident that Bedford had no choice but to confront them at Verneuil, on ground of their choosing. Otherwise they could drive northwards into Normandy and seriously threaten the survival of the English Duchy of Normandy.

12

The battle

The news of the fall of Verneuil to trickery increased the anger Bedford and the English felt towards the French over the events at Ivry. But at least they now knew exactly where the enemy was, and Bedford moved fast, but not recklessly. He sent the Earl of Suffolk with a small force to keep an eye on the Franco-Scottish army while he prepared to move the rest of his force to confront Aumale and Douglas at Verneuil. The army he led towards Verneuil on 16 August for this decisive meeting had been reduced from the numbers he had brought to Ivry. Firstly, he had had to leave men to garrison Ivry. Common sense suggests that the majority of these were likely to be the less fit and able men, perhaps those wounded in the siege of Ivry, so that his army was as unencumbered as possible for the forthcoming pursuit and battle. But the other two reductions of his army were much more worrying. Overnight, the news of the presence of this much bigger French army and its success at Verneuil seems to have worked on some of the Normans in the English army so that they deserted. Some simply quit, but others changed sides and joined Aumale outside Verneuil. One of these was Guillaume d'Estouteville, who took his whole retinue with him and fought in the battle against his erstwhile comrades.[180] This betrayal by men he had tried to treat fairly must have angered Bedford greatly, and worried him in that it showed how potentially frail the bonds of loyalty between the Norman knights and gentry and their English rulers could be. However, since the number of deserters was small, he must have been fairly confident that the vast majority of his Norman troops could be trusted, a faith that proved to be well founded in the battle.

More surprisingly, he dismissed L'Isle Adam and his Burgundians, sending them back to their siege at Nesle in Picardy, which they were undertaking at the Duke of Burgundy's behest. L'Isle Adam was one of the best Burgundian commanders and his men were likely to have been experienced troops, which is why this move has puzzled historians. It seems foolhardy of Bedford to send away at least 10 per cent of his strength when battle with a significantly superior force was likely. But Bedford was not a foolish man, so he must have had good reason. Burne's explanantion, that Bedford was so confident of victory that he dismissed these men, saying that he had no need of so large an army, seems unlikely to be the real reason.[181] Bedford knew from his brother Clarence's fate at Baugé that underestimating the French and Scots was a mistake. He was probably aware of how lucky (or favoured by God) Henry knew he had been to win at Agincourt. So why did he do it? The answer seems to have been lack of trust and politics. Three years earlier the English had arrested L'Isle Adam for conspiring with the French to betray Paris to the Armagnacs. He had not been cleared of these suspicions until November 1423. Whatever his virtues as a soldier, he had not had long to convince Bedford and the English of his good intentions towards their cause.

Moreover, the Duke of Burgundy was preparing for some negotiations with the French concerning the security of his interests in south central France while Bedford was marching to Ivry. Bedford's concerns over these negotiations proved well founded when Burgundy signed a treaty with Charles in the following month agreeing 'an abstinence of war' between them in the borders of the Duchy of Burgundy. Philip of Burgundy had already signed the Treaty of Nantes three months previously, which suggested that he was hedging his political bets. So Bedford was uncertain how much he could trust the Burgundians, and in a hard battle the last thing he needed was to have to watch his allies as well as the enemy. He may well have made the comment about not needing so large an army to deal with the Franco-Scottish army as a demonstration of confidence in his English and Norman troops and the importance of loyalty in an army. While he was not as charismatic as his brother Henry, Bedford was a popular leader who, as events would prove after the battle, tried to do right by his men, so remarks like these could have counted for something with them.

The English marched steadily towards Verneuil on 16 August, stopping at Damville, 12 miles from Verneuil, overnight. It is important to remember that very few if any of the fighting men would actually be marching on foot; archers were expected to have a horse so that they could more easily keep up with the men-at-arms. The relatively slow pace was set by the baggage train and common sense. While Bedford was determined to bring Aumale's army to battle he was not going to rush headlong towards them and be caught unprepared after a long day's march. No doubt he was scouting both his route ahead and the location of the enemy with care. The overnight stop also allowed the archers to cut a stake each from the surrounding woodland for their defence as Bedford had ordered. Waurin reports of the English at Damville that, 'they nearly all set in order their consciences that evening and in the morning, according to the custom of the English when they are awaiting the time for going into battle, for of their own nature they are very devout, especially before drinking'.[182] (This is one of a number of observations in medieval accounts about the English capacity for drinking.)

Preparations for the battle

The next day the English army marched on towards Verneuil, approaching through the forest of Piseux, about 3½ miles north-east of Verneuil. Somewhere about midday or early afternoon the English army came out of the forest into open ground that stretched about 2 miles to the walls of Verneuil. Aumale had clearly had his scouts out since his army was drawing up for battle across the road from Damville several hundred yards from the town walls. There could be no doubt that the French were going to fight. Waurin recorded his feelings on seeing the French army drawn up waiting for the English: '… the French arranged and set in order of battle, which was a very fair thing to see; for without a doubt I the author of this work had never seen a fairer company nor one where there were so many of the nobility as there were there, nor set in better order, nor showing a greater appearance of a desire to fight ...'[183] Clearly, the ranks of the French army looked splendid and somewhat daunting, standing barely a mile away, although they were not as well ordered as they appeared. The problem was the usual one with the French multinational armies of the time – the command structure. Jean d'Harcourt, Count of Aumale, was the designated commander, with Archibald Douglas, Duke of Touraine, and Guillaume, Count of Narbonne, as his senior colleagues.

The highly experienced leader of the Lombards, Caqueran, seems to have been content to be a loyal lieutenant and do as his commanders asked, but Douglas's son-in-law, the Earl of Buchan, was less content. There was some slight dispute among the Scottish nobles as to who was in overall command. Douglas won the arguments because of his age, experience, and noble status in both Scotland and France. He was also a problem as far as Aumale was concerned. As has been already mentioned, he had a high opinion of himself as a military man, despite his lack of military success. He had been shown great favour by Charles VII, who made him Duke of Touraine, and he commanded the largest single force in the French army at Verneuil. He felt that he was a most important figure and his opinions should carry great weight with his nominal commander, Aumale. Narbonne was no more or less of a problem for his commander than French noblemen usually were; he was likely to follow his version of any orders given. All this being said, the French army drew up in good order and waited to see what the English would do. But it was the next stage, the pre-battle diplomatic exchanges, where Douglas seemed to pre-empt Aumale.

There were the usual negotiations before the battle. These were not really a serious attempt to avoid fighting but a gesture to Christian values to show that the commanders of each side had tried to avoid the spilling of Christian blood. At Verneuil there was a particular edge to the negotiations, since, in modern parlance, Bedford and Douglas 'had history'. After Douglas had broken his parole and returned to Scotland, he resumed his post as Lord Warden of the Marches. In 1417 he and Albany decided to take advantage of Henry V's absence in France and attack Berwick-on-Tweed and Roxburgh Castle. Bedford led a powerful English army in response and Albany and Douglas hurriedly retired northwards, leaving the Scottish borders to be wasted by the English army.

This affair, very soon to become known as the Foul Raid, damaged Douglas's reputation, and lay behind the testy exchanges. Bedford invited Douglas to drink with him to which Douglas replied that he would be delighted to, since he had been unable to find Bedford in England so had had to come to France to meet him.[184] An interesting reversal of fact! Douglas also disparaged Bedford by referring to him as 'John with the leaded sword'. This was discourteous and cast doubt upon Bedford's standing as a soldier. In the sixteenth century, 'draw not a leaden sword from a painted scabbard' was a proverb meaning something like don't achieve bad results with fair words, or 'put your money where your mouth is'. Douglas was clearly suggesting that Bedford didn't know the military trade and was no danger to an experienced soldier like himself.

These exchanges would have been reported to the armies as far as practical before the onset. Even so, if this was regarded as pre-battle posturing and preening with the purpose of encouraging the Scottish soldiers to have less respect for the English commander, it was particularly arrogant coming from a man whose battle experience led to him being called Tyneman, or Loser, in his own lifetime. But Douglas may well have had a very serious purpose; to remind the Scots that this was not a man of Henry V's quality facing them, but only an English prince, and they had already killed one of those three years earlier. Other chivalric exchanges included a challenge from the Earl of Buchan, Douglas's second-in-command, to the Earl of Salisbury, to meet him in single combat. Bedford would not let Salisbury accept; such a chivalric gesture would achieve nothing before such a crucial battle.

The aftermath of these negotiations seem to have been declarations by both Douglas and Bedford that no quarter would be given between them. Why? On the English side two clear reasons can be found. Firstly, the instruction that no prisoners were to be taken until the battle was clearly won was normal practice in the ordinances of war issued by English commanders at this time. The purpose of this was to ensure that the English fighting men concentrated on the business of winning the battle rather than personal profit from taking ransom-worthy prisoners. It could have been a mere misunderstanding of emphasis by the chroniclers to turn such an order into a order of no quarter. But at Verneuil another matter came to the fore. It seems that Bedford viewed Douglas and the Scottish army as traitors to their king and Douglas personally as an oath breaker. The terms of the treaty by which James I was released to rule Scotland have been noted above, and while the Army of Scotland in France technically did not break them, the English did not see it that way. Douglas's oath to serve Henry V has also been noted, and Bedford felt quite rightly that Douglas was breaking this oath. Douglas is said to have '… had it proclaimed that there would be certain penalties if anyone took English men as prisoners and that they were to be killed indiscriminately without hope of ransom.'[185] While it is not certain that the soldiers on both sides knew of their opponents' orders in this regard, the author of the *Scotichronicon* wrote that the English *did* know of Douglas's order. These orders increased the ferocity of the forthcoming battle.

Contrasting deployments

At some time in the early afternoon Bedford drew up the English army in their usual formation, a solid line of dismounted men-at-arms in the centre several ranks deep, with the bulk of the archers making up two wings while the rest of them made a thin line in front of the men-at-arms. Since they were advancing out onto open ground without any hedges or woods to protect their flanks and rear, Bedford made specific arrangements to protect the army against encirclement. The baggage wagons, which were no doubt laagered, formed a sort of citadel well behind the army, with about 500 archers left as guards (this is Le Fevre's estimate). Men-at-arms were too valuable in the battle line to be put in this role. It is difficult to see how he could have spared more from the battle line since he only had around 8,500 men by this time after the various losses since the fall of Ivry. He ordered that the horses be tethered together to make a wall linking up to the baggage wagons. Since each one of his men would have had at least one horse, there would have been around 8,500 horses plus those that pulled the baggage wagons, which meant that this wall of horses would have been at least 2½ miles long.[186] This provided substantial protection against encirclement. Bedford *may* have thought of this baggage guard as a reserve, but this is far from certain since events were to prove that they were poorly led. Non-combatants like pages, servants and horse boys were also left with the horses and wagons for safety. His rank meant that Bedford would have commanded the right of the line and Salisbury the left.

The French army was drawn up in a more novel way. As a result of the disputes about precedence, Douglas and the Scots made up the right 'battle'. Since the Scots made up 'an army within an army', their archers almost certainly formed up around the Scottish men-at-arms probably on their right wing following the English practice. This meant that they faced the English and Welsh archers making up the left wing of the opposing army. But the only mention in any of the contemporary accounts of the battle of the Scottish archers does not say how they were deployed, just that they shot against the English archers. Since the Berry Herald's chronicle claims that Narbonne advanced and Douglas had to follow to try to maintain the line and his honour, it is probable that Narbonne and his largely Spanish troops made up the centre.[187] This would mean that Aumale led largely French troops forming the left battle facing the opposing commander, Bedford. These battles formed one solid line as Waurin reported: '… [the French army] put themselves in order for fighting without forming a vanguard or rearguard, but placed themselves together in one large body …'.[188] All of these men followed the English practice and fought on foot. The Berry Herald is the only contemporary to mention how the Lombard and French cavalry were positioned at the start of the battle, writing, 'the French had arranged two wings (*ailles*) of cavalry … the left wing led by Bourne Caqueran, Theode de Valpargue and Luquin Ris, Lombards, and the right wing Baron de Coulances, Poton de Sainterailles [sic] and other French knights …'.[189] These wings of cavalry seem to have had two roles in the French plan for the battle. Firstly, as accounts of the onset of the French army make clear, the heavily armoured Lombard horsemen were to move in front of the infantry ranks of the French army and smash into the English battle line. Secondly, the largely French cavalry on the right wing of the Franco-Scottish army were expected to swing wide and attack the English flank or rear. These men took up a position well out to the right because they needed to be beyond the large body of Scottish archers supporting Douglas and the Scottish men-at-arms. As a result they would have overlapped the English left wing, archers and all, and so must have felt confident of the success of their planned flanking attack. However, the reality of the battle proved to be very different.

Aumale and his colleagues would have planned the use of the Lombards carefully to achieve the greatest tactical benefit from them. The fully armoured men would have made up the front ranks, supported by their own more lightly armed valets. There were not enough of the heavily armoured men to attack the whole front of the English army, so while they might have faced more or less the whole line of men-at-arms, there would not have been enough of them to do more than menace part of the right wing of archers in the English army. This arrangement of the French battle line shows how Aumale and his colleagues had learnt from nearly ten years of fighting the English, particularly the events at Valmont in 1416 and La Brossonière in the previous year, where cavalry punched holes in the English battle line rather than just mounting flanking attacks.

The battle opened with the English army marching steadily towards the French until they were in bowshot, no more than 250yd. Then the archers set their stakes in the ground for defence and started to shoot. Waurin mentions an archery duel between the English and Scottish archers, saying, 'the archers of England and the Scots who were with the French began to shoot one against the other so murderously that it was horror to look upon them …'[190] The English archers may have been getting the better of this duel since it was the French army that advanced and the Scottish archers are not mentioned as having any particular effect in the later parts of the battle. However, there can be no doubt that the French plan for the battle relied on opening it with a thunderous cavalry charge. Firstly, the Lombard cavalry charged unscathed through the arrowstorm and smashed into the English line. Basin wrote, 'the Italian cavalry, who, perfectly protected both man and horse suffered nothing from the strikes of the arrows …'[191] They charged on a wide enough front to punch holes through the ranks of men-at-arms and disrupt the right wing of archers; the archers in front of the men-at-arms would have fallen back through them at the onset of the cavalry.

The archers' defensive stakes were either brushed aside by the armoured horses or the archers had been prevented from setting them securely by ground baked hard by the summer. Basin describes their effect on the English line graphically: 'the Italian cavalry charged the English infantry furiously creating fear in the ranks and seriously threatening them. Numbers of men-at-arms, struck by the shock [of the

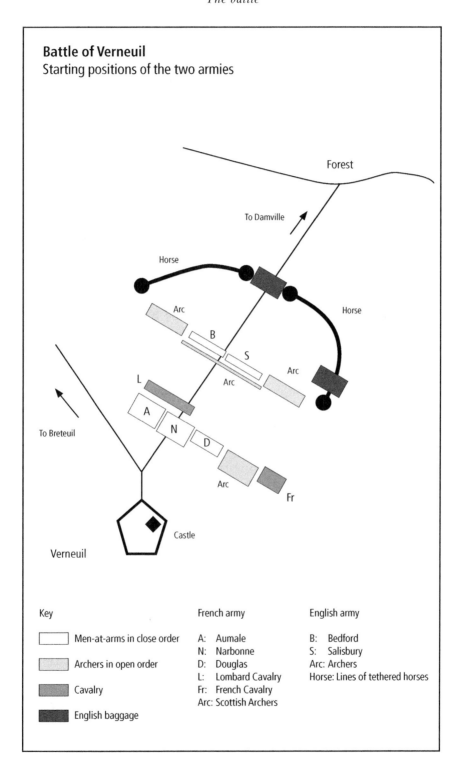

Battle of Verneuil
Starting positions of the two armies

Forest

To Damville

Horse

Arc

B

S

Arc

Arc

Horse

L

A

N

D

Arc

Fr

To Breteuil

Castle

Verneuil

Key

☐	Men-at-arms in close order
☐	Archers in open order
☐	Cavalry
☐	English baggage

French army

A: Aumale
N: Narbonne
D: Douglas
L: Lombard Cavalry
Fr: French Cavalry
Arc: Scottish Archers

English army

B: Bedford
S: Salisbury
Arc: Archers
Horse: Lines of tethered horses

attack], bit the dust (literally – *mordirent la poussière*) and the cavalry deeply penetrated the ranks of the English, army who opened their ranks to let the Italian cavalry pass through with the least damage possible.'[192] The Lombards, having broken through the English line, made no effort to reform and attack the English rear. They pressed on to attack the English baggage. But they had done their job well. They had broken the ranks of the English men-at-arms and disrupted one wing of archers. It was up to the French infantry to charge and finish the job.

But what of the French cavalry on the right wing of the French army? It is difficult to know how substantial a force they were, but later events make it clear that one wing of archers was relatively undisturbed by the cavalry attacks. Whether the English archers on the left wing had got their stakes more securely set or whether the French cavalry were less resolute in the face of an arrowstorm is not clear, but they acted as though their role in the battle plan was for them to swing wide round the archers to take the English in the rear, as Waurin suggests. Starting as they did from a position wide on the right of the French line, they swept very wide avoiding the archers and ended up on the wrong side of the English horse lines, which acted as a bulwark against them. Waurin describes this very clearly, writing that the French cavalry 'found there barriers and opposition, that is to say the wagons and the horses of their enemies coupled together by the halters and the tails and they also found two thousand stalwart archers'. This was the left wing of the English army who, once the enemy infantry advanced so that their archers had to stop shooting, had watched the French advance, wheeled round to face them, and using the horse lines as a barricade as had been planned, proceeded to shoot up the French cavalry who fled.[193] This was the body of archers that Burne called a reserve, following Waurin's misremembrance when he wrote that there was a baggage guard of that number. While Bedford did not have enough men to leave 2,000 archers as a reserve, that number would have been about right for one wing of archers. There are a number of other occasions where the English archers showed their professionalism and tactical awareness to adapt to the rapidly changing events in a battle.

To return to the French infantry, their role was to follow up the cavalry attack taking advantage of any disorder these caused. They would have seen the effect of the Lombards' attack on the English ranks, and no doubt Aumale, Narbonne and Douglas felt that the time for revenge on the English had come. It is clear from the contemporary accounts that the French onslaught was disordered by enthusiasm to attack and the tactical wisdom of spending as little time as possible under the English arrowstorm. One account claims that Douglas wanted to stand on the defensive, possibly to let his archers do their work, but that Narbonne advanced, leading Douglas to charge so as not to be outdone. Another states that Douglas and the Scots, confident in their superior numbers, 'rushed against their enemies neglecting the principles of sensible military practice'.[194] As the Scottish men-at-arms advanced, the Scottish archers, who before the archery duel had comprised nearly 60 per cent of the Scottish strength, probably fell in behind them to add weight to their charge and fight as light infantrymen. But would their slightly disjointed advance matter given the state of the English battle line after the Lombards' assault? The behaviour of the English and Norman men-at-arms at this point is one of the most remarkable episodes in the whole battle.

As the English line stood in some disorder after the Lombards' assault, Bedford showed his quality and exhorted the English and Normans 'not forto breke ner move theyr aray for wynnyng or kepyng wordly goodis, but only to wynne worship in the right of Englonde that day'.[195] While this may not be an exact report of Bedford's words, the point was that he was asking his men not to worry about their possessions in the baggage wagons that they could probably see being looted by the Lombards, nor to panic and flee as they had probably seen some men do already, but to reform and win fame and reputation. Such words would have been repeated by the captains to their men while Bedford and Salisbury would be making themselves and their standards very obvious as rallying points. But Bedford was also appealing to the well-known phenomenon in armies; the men fight as much for the good opinions of their comrades as for some nebulous idea of a national cause. Many of his men were professionals, the majority of whom were probably in companies that had fought together for a few years. Such men would steady themselves quickly knowing the difficult position they were in.

As a result, the English army received the disorderly charge of the French army in good order and settled down to the grim business of hand-to-hand fighting. If Narbonne did lead the attack as the Berry

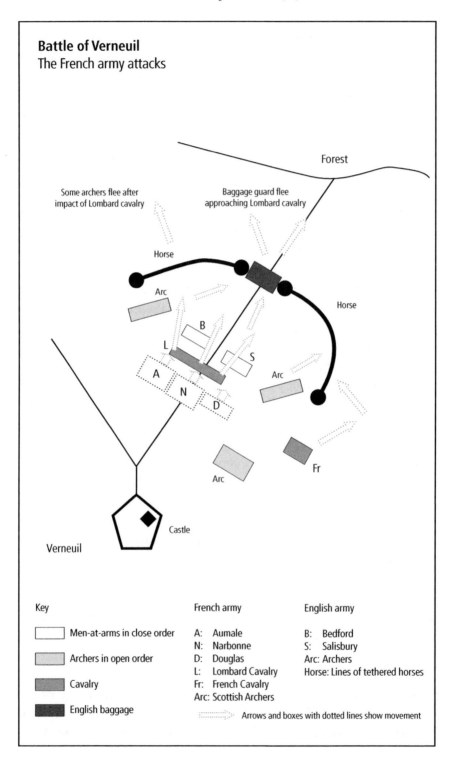

Battle of Verneuil
The French army attacks

Forest

Some archers flee after
impact of Lombard cavalry

Baggage guard flee
approaching Lombard cavalry

Horse

Arc

Horse

B

L

S

A

Arc

N

D

Arc

Fr

Arc

Castle

Verneuil

Key

☐	Men-at-arms in close order
☐	Archers in open order
☐	Cavalry
☐	English baggage

French army

A: Aumale
N: Narbonne
D: Douglas
L: Lombard Cavalry
Fr: French Cavalry
Arc: Scottish Archers

English army

B: Bedford
S: Salisbury
Arc: Archers
Horse: Lines of tethered horses

Arrows and boxes with dotted lines show movement

Herald records, then he may have hit the English line fairly centrally, while Aumale attacked Bedford, and Salisbury on the left received Douglas and the Scots. It was on the left that the situation for the English was particularly dire. Waurin wrote that, '… I the author know truly that that day the Earl of Salisbury sustained the greatest brunt, notwithstanding that he wavered greatly and had very much to do to maintain his position, and certainly if it had not been for the skill and great valour and conduct of his single person in the midst of the valiant men who fought under his banner after his example very vigorously, there is no doubt that the matter which was in great uncertainty would have gone very badly for the English …'[196] It seems that Salisbury was so hard pressed that he made a vow to go to Jerusalem on pilgrimage if he should be victorious.[197]

Waurin, writing in his old age of his experience of the hand-to-hand fighting at the Battle of Verneuil, says, 'I could not see or comprehend the whole since I was sufficiently occupied in defending myself.'[198] At the same time Bedford was also leading by example, with Waurin reporting other combatants accounts saying, '… the Duke of Bedford … did wonderful feats of arms and killed many a man, for with an axe which he held in his two hands he reached no one that he did not punish, since he was large in body and stout in limb, wise and brave in arms…'[199] Bedford showed how deadly the poleaxe could be in close-quarters fighting in the hands of a strong, skilled man.

The importance of commanders leading by example was immense in medieval battles as Henry V proved at Agincourt. Salisbury and Bedford, their standards high, supported and protected by their personal retinues, were the rocks on which the French and Scottish attacks foundered. They inspired their men to heroic deeds in the grim slogging match. The Norman men-at-arms in the English army also fought with great bravery, Jean de Saane being particularly prominent, recovering a banner from the French to provide a rallying point.[200] While men on both sides may have expected the Lombard cavalry to return to the battle and turn it Aumale and Douglas's way, it was actually the English archers who returned to the main battle. It is not clear whether these men were the archers of the right or the left wing of the English line. It is most likely that they were the men of the right wing who had pulled themselves together after the shock of the Lombards' charge.

The archers on the left wing had already been very busy, first fighting the Scottish archers and then repelling the French cavalry. The archers reorganised themselves and 'raising a wonderful shout' rejoined the main battle. Waurin's description of how they rejoined would have been impossible ('[they] put themselves in the front before the army'[201]) since the English and French armies were entangled in bloody fighting. So they must have wheeled round on to one flank of the battle. No doubt they first shot arrows into the enemy and then joined in hand-to-hand as they commonly did. Their intervention, showing great discipline and presence of mind, finally turned the battle in Bedford and Salisbury's favour. Their attack on the flank of the French infantry caused them to break, quickly followed by the largely Spanish infantry in the centre. As the English and Norman men-at-arms began to break up the French battle line, the French and Spanish troops started to flee towards the town of Verneuil. Aumale and other French leaders no doubt tried to rally their men and were killed in the rout. The Scots held their ground long enough to be surrounded and slaughtered. The garrison and citizens of Verneuil would not open the gates to let their fleeing comrades in for fear of the English getting in as well. Many of the fleeing men drowned in the ditches around the town or were slaughtered by the pursuing English and Norman troops.

But what of the Lombard cavalry who started the battle so well for the French? After they had broken through the English ranks they careered on to the laagered baggage train. Here they soon put the baggage guard, maybe 500 men, to flight, slaughtered the pages, servants and wagon men who had been left with the baggage for their own safety, and proceeded to thoroughly loot the baggage train. This may have just been the ill-discipline of cavalry fired up by a glorious charge losing sight of their tactical purpose. It may have been an example of mercenaries taking what gains they could, particularly since they may well have been owed pay given Charles's financial straits. Unknowingly they could have made a major contribution to the French strategy, since the fleeing baggage guard spread rumours of Bedford's defeat, which caused some small revolts in Normandy. But the French and Scottish infantry were unable to win the battle, so these revolts rapidly fizzled out. The cavalry reorganised themselves once they had gained all the booty they could and made a fairly orderly return to the battle; but they were too late! The French and Scottish forces had been destroyed and they were faced

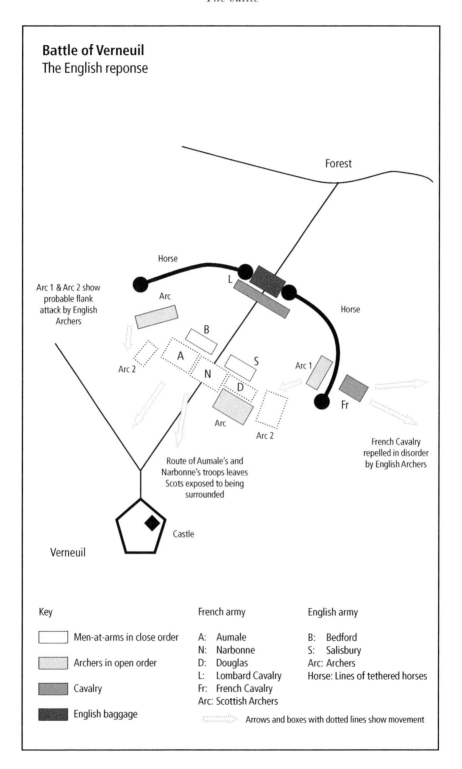

Battle of Verneuil
The English reponse

Forest

Horse

Arc 1 & Arc 2 show probable flank attack by English Archers

Arc

L

Horse

B

Arc 2

A

S

Arc 1

N

D

Fr

Arc

Arc 2

French Cavalry repelled in disorder by English Archers

Route of Aumale's and Narbonne's troops leaves Scots exposed to being surrounded

Castle

Verneuil

Key

	Men-at-arms in close order
	Archers in open order
	Cavalry
	English baggage

French army

A: Aumale
N: Narbonne
D: Douglas
L: Lombard Cavalry
Fr: French Cavalry
Arc: Scottish Archers

Arrows and boxes with dotted lines show movement

English army

B: Bedford
S: Salisbury
Arc: Archers
Horse: Lines of tethered horses

by a victorious enemy. The Lombards may have made an attempt at charging but it broke down, probably under flights of arrows, and they lost sixteen or twenty men while struggling across a small stream.[202] They decided that they could achieve nothing else and left the battlefield with their booty.

This was the end of the battle. Basin has left a graphic description of the field: 'There a horrible spectacle to see on the battlefield, the corpses in high, tightly packed heaps, especially where the Scots had fought. No prisoners were taken among them, and the heaps held the bodies of the dead English soldiers all mixed up with theirs.'[203] Waurin notes that Bedford called together his nobles and great captains to give thanks to God for the victory while the archers looted the dead as was their custom. Then they all camped around the town of Verneuil with a careful guard set.[204] The battle hadn't been a drawn-out affair; Waurin estimated it at about three quarters of an hour long. This may be rather short, since he was estimating without the help of any timepiece on a summer's day when the sun's movements were less marked. It perhaps reflects the length of the hand-to-hand fighting that he was involved in. But there seems no doubt that it was a relatively short, ferocious fight, which led to substantial casualties. Waurin writes that the French army lost more than 6,000 men, of which the majority were Scots, and the English army about 1,600, which he emphasises were both English and Norman. The French lost a minimum of about 40 per cent killed and the English 20 per cent. Bedford's letter to Sir Thomas Rempston written two days after the battle gives a very precise casualty figure for the French, 7,262 out of an army of 14,000, or about 52 per cent.[205] This casualty figure would have come from the heralds who had the grisly job of surveying the dead after a battle to identify casualties of note, and to asses the overall figure.

However, while Bedford may well be giving a much more accurate figure than Waurin's estimate, he also took a very positive view of the casualty ratio, since he wrote in the same letter that the English had only lost two gentlemen and very few archers. But the simple casualty numbers hide a very serious fact for Charles – he lost many experienced military leaders. The counts of Aumale, Ventadour and Narbonne were killed, along with another fifty-two French nobles and knights named by Waurin, who added, '… and many others whose names I know not'.[206]

Among the Scots the earls of Douglas and Buchan fell along with James, one of Douglas's sons. While few prisoners were taken – a reflection of the desperation of the fight – the young Duke of Alençon, his illegitimate half-brother, the bastard of Alençon, who died of wounds soon afterwards, and La Fayette, were the most significant. The casualty figures show two things very clearly: firstly it was a very bloody fight in which the English army had real difficulties; secondly the French army was effectively destroyed. The Battle of Verneuil has been called another Agincourt because it was a crushing victory won by an English army in a difficult situation. In particular Verneuil was an old-fashioned battle. There seems to have been no gunpowder artillery used in the battle, although Waurin mentions that the English had some small pieces in their baggage wagons. Charles and the French probably couldn't afford them. The English may just have been conservative in their military thinking, in that they knew gunpowder weapons were vital for sieges but thought that they were still too clumsy for field use. Despite events at Cravant showing that guns could be used in a battle, the English opinion may well have been correct in the 1420s, particularly since the war-bow still threatened all but the best armoured.

(Arguments concerning the interpretations of the accounts of the battle I have made, especially the conflicts between Waurin's account and the others, can be found in Appendix B. I have done this to try to avoid breaking up the flow of the narrative of the battle itself.)

How did the English win?

The French had a strategic plan which put the English at a disadvantage. They assembled what was a large army for the wars in France in the fifteenth century, made up of tested, good-quality troops. They refused to give battle until their whole army was assembled and they were able to lure the English army to ground which suited them. To do this they sacrificed Ivry, and some chivalric esteem, to gain the town of Verneuil and favourable ground for a battle. Tactically the French believed that they had the means to neutralise the English and Welsh archers. They would use exceptionally well-armoured cavalry and a large number of

Scottish archers. They also had a considerable advantage in numbers. The English, meanwhile, made the best of the open ground, using stakes and lines of tethered horses to make a defensive barrier to the rear with the laagered baggage wagons. But the ground still favoured the French. So, what went wrong?

Initially, nothing. The Italian heavy cavalry smashed through the English line, there was a vicious archery duel between some of the English archers and the Scottish archers, and the English baggage guard fled at the approach of the Italians. But there was a conflict of purpose within the French plan at this point. The infantry needed to follow up the Lombard charge quickly to take advantage of the disruption it caused, but, if the large number of Scottish archers were to inflict casualties on the English, they needed the infantry to hold back to give them clear shooting. It is probable that a rapid advance by the infantry was the best option, since the Lombards were so successful. Moreover, there is no evidence that the Scottish archers were good enough to win an archery duel with the English and Welsh archers, so it was important that the men-at-arms of the French army spent as little time as possible under English arrowshot. But instead things began to turn in favour of the English. Firstly, the English and Norman men-at-arms didn't panic after the cavalry attack but reformed and if anything advanced to receive the French infantry's attack, and secondly one of the archery wings of their army tracked the French cavalry who were trying to outflank the English army and shot them up at the horse lines. The French infantry attack was not a single uniform hammer blow, but a fragmented charge with each of the three major national groups – the French, the Spaniards and the Scots – seeming to compete to see who could come to grips first. This should not have mattered; numbers were still in their favour. But it did; the English line may have been forced back a little, but it did not break. The two English commanders, Bedford and Salisbury, seem to have set an heroic example. Then a large body of English archers returned to attack the flank of the Franco-Scottish army. The French army began to crumble, and bloody defeat was the outcome. If the Italian cavalry had reformed after breaking the English line, as the French tactical plan had probably required, the outcome would almost certainly have been different.

What made the difference between the two armies? The Anglo-Norman army was more unified, experienced and professional. The retinues and garrisons were used to fighting together and trusted each other. The men and their commanders were able to make their own decisions to react to the demands of the battle. Bedford and Salisbury were trusted by their men and they led by example, as was expected of medieval military leaders. Basically, the English and Norman soldiers didn't know when they were beaten, and so they won. They also had enough discipline not to get totally disordered in the pursuit of the defeated enemy, since they reformed to see off the belated return of the Lombard cavalry. The French army also contained many experienced professional fighting men but it was hampered by being multinational. While all the senior commanders seem to have shared a tactical plan for the battle, there is no evidence of any attempt to implement ordinances of war on the troops in the way that the English leaders did. Therefore nothing seems to have been done to improve trust between the different national contingents and reduce feelings of rivalry between them. The Scots, who probably thought of themselves as allies rather than mercenaries, seem to have stood and suffered heavy casualties. Given the number of French nobles killed, the French commanders, and no doubt their personal retinues, tried to hold things together as the line crumbled and paid the price. The Spaniards and Italians behaved as was expected of good mercenaries, fought well until the balance of the battle tilted against them and then they tried to save themselves. The Lombard cavalry failed to deliver the second part of their role, to reform and attack the English rear, but it was probably unrealistic to expect them to. Throughout medieval and modern military history, cavalry regularly found it difficult to reform and concentrate on their tactical objectives, as demonstrated by Prince Rupert and his Cavaliers, for example.

Ultimately, the English army won because overall it was made up of better soldiers, whether they are considered as individuals or as units.

13

The aftermath of the battle

The French garrison of Verneuil hurriedly negotiated their surrender the day after the battle and were allowed to march away. One grim piece of political display was the fate of the Count of Narbonne's corpse. After it was identified by the heralds, Bedford ordered it quartered and hung on a gibbet. Narbonne was close to Charles and his court and had been heavily involved in the assassination of Duke John of Burgundy in 1419. So Bedford gave him the fate of a traitor as an act of law enforcement and a gesture to his brother-in-law, Philip of Burgundy. Bedford restored the defences of Vernuil and established an Anglo-Norman garrison. Then he had the important task of spreading the good news of the victory as quickly as possible. On 19 August he wrote to Sir Thomas Rempston, outlining the victory, and no doubt he wrote to his wife Anne at Rouen. The news of the victory seems to have spread quickly, so he or others must have sent letters to the major towns and cities. It was important that it did because a number of small-scale, very localised revolts had broken out in Normandy.

While these had probably been planned as part of the French strategy, they were ignited by reports of defeat carried by the fleeing baggage guard. Inevitably these came to nothing. The completeness of their victory allowed the English administration to be magnanimous towards some of these rebels, issuing them with remissions of any penalty in 1424–25.[207] But the members of the baggage guard were less fortunate.

Some suffered the common fate of routed soldiers, being set upon and robbed by civilians who saw a chance to pay back some soldiers for the crimes of their fellows. One of them, a man named Yong, who may have been their captain, was taken later and hung, drawn and quartered as a traitor 'as he was well worthy'.[208]

Bedford sent parts of his army back to their garrisons while he returned to his capital of Rouen. Waurin describes how he was greeted by his wife and the citizenry of Rouen and how 'the streets were decorated with hangings and at all the crossways where he was to pass there were platforms erected where persons represented historical scenes; and there went to meet him the young people and children of the city in fair companies, showing a high degree of joy for his glorious and fair victory'.[209] At the gate of the town, Bedford showed proper humility and dismounted and walked to the church of Notre Dame to give thanks.

He went on to Paris to spread the message of the English success, arriving on 8 September. The author of *A Parisian Journal* recounts how the streets that he was to go through were cleaned and decorated. Parades of festively dressed citizens went out of the city to meet Bedford and escort him into the city, singing hymns and prayers. The children put on a mystery of the Old and New Testaments which seems to have gripped Bedford's attention before he went on to Notre Dame where he was greeted with religious singing and music and the cathedral bells were rung. The author of the *Journal* finished his account by writing, 'In short, more honour was never done at a Roman triumph than was done that day to him and his wife (she always accompanied him wherever he went).'[210]

The victory at Verneuil left the Duke of Bedford and the English in northern France confident that the Armagnacs were no longer any real threat. This gave them the liberty to concentrate on making the boundaries of Henry VI's French realm secure. The shock of the victory was such that a considerable number of Armagnac-held towns and fortresses despaired of support from Charles and surrendered or agreed dates to surrender to the English over the next six months. These included Nesle, La Ferté and various garrisons commanded by La Hire, who may have been at Verneuil. Aggressive as he was, even he recognised that he had to surrender a number of places that he used as bases to menace the marches of Normandy. Meanwhile, Bedford sent several of his captains from the Battle of Verneuil to consolidate the boundaries of the English kingdom of France. Salisbury and Suffolk went south and east from Verneuil, capturing Senonches, Nogent-le-Rotrou and other places broadly in the direction of Chartres and the Loire. Lord Scales, Sir John Fastolf and Sir John Montgomery headed into Maine and Anjou while Sir Nicholas Burdet went to revitalise the siege of Mont St Michel. In 1425, in another demonstration of Bedford's broad strategic vision, Sir Thomas Rempston took part in a joint operation with the Burgundian captain Jean de Luxembourg.

They eventually took Guise in Picardy after a five-month siege which showed that the English still had the skills they had developed under Henry V necessary to maintain a successful winter siege. This siege had been very much in Philip of Burgundy's interests since an Armagnac garrison at Guise could menace both his communications to Flanders and those to Paris. From Bedford's point of view this was a useful political success, since it helped relations with his brother-in-law. Salisbury took Rambouillet and then Le Mans without much trouble, consolidating the southern marches of Normandy. For the eighteen months after Verneuil, Mont St Michel was the only part of the fighting where the Armagnacs had any significant success. In 1424 the English captain of Avranches had unsuccessfully tried to bribe a member of the garrison, while in 1425, after Burdet had built a small siege castle at Ardevon overlooking the low, partially tidal flats before Mont St Michel, the French garrison broke the naval blockade and Burdet himself was captured. But the continued resistance of Mont St Michel was more a symbolic irritation to the English than a serious military problem.

These advances show how desperate Charles's position was now. While he was secure behind his moat, the River Loire, he could do nothing to protect his supporters north of it. As one modern historian put it, 'The knowledge that after Cravant and Verneuil he could not even hope for a speedy military victory, led him to adopt other means of survival.'[211] For the English the victory had benefits beyond Normandy. The destruction of Charles's main army, particularly the destruction of the Scots, left him unable to mount significant military activities for three or four years. The deaths of some of the most experienced French military men, such as Aumale and Narbonne, exacerbated this. But Charles still had some forces at his command. He also had two skilled commanders who survived the slaughter at Verneuil to remain active in these dark times for Charles and France. One was Étienne de Vignolles, better known as La Hire, an experienced commander who had first fought the English under Henry V in 1418 and, after fighting at Baugé, continued to be one of the most persistent opponents of the English until his death in 1443. He was still in the field in 1424 after Verneuil, but, as has already been noted, he did not have the resources to mount any real resistance to the English advances. The other, Jean Poton de Xaintrailles, survived the disaster at Verneuil and started to build his reputation as a skilled commander in the 1420s. He went on to be a major actor in the defeat of the English, dying in 1461 after their final expulsion from all of France but Calais. But, like La Hire, he could do very little to restrict English activity for some years. Charles's problems for much of the 1420s were lack of money, which of course meant lack of troops, and lack of morale. One consequence was that the 'Norman March' now moved south into Maine and Anjou. 'By deciding the fate of Normandy for a quarter of a century the battle of Verneuil marked a watershed. The victory gave Normandy, Paris and the surrounding areas something of the physical security from attack which they had previously lacked.'[212]

But it was not all bad for Charles. Yes, the defeat was a disaster for France, and the English gained some security for the southern borders of Normandy. Even the Duke of Burgundy settled into an appearance of loyal alliance with the English. But, since the army crushed at Verneuil had contained large numbers of mercenaries, particularly the Scots and Lombards, the French had an easy explanation for the disaster. It happened because of the failings of these foreigners, not those of their own soldiers. From a cynical, financial point of view, his debts to the mercenaries, particularly the Scots, died with them, and he was able to recover the Duchy of Touraine, which he had granted to Douglas. So in the short term his financial position improved. There seem to have been some efforts to vilify the reputation of the Scots under Douglas, so that their destruction was the end of another foreign threat to France. In other words, another achievement that went towards building Charles's reputation as 'Le Très Victorieux', a title applied to him immediately on his death if not in his lifetime.[213] Basin, who was a member of Charles VII's household later in his reign, reported some of this vilification in his history of Charles VII, writing that, 'they [the Scots] devised a plan whereby if they had beaten the English [in 1424] they would kill all that remained of the nobility in Anjou, Touraine and Berry and in neighbouring regions and seize their homes, their wives, their land and their valuable possessions'.[214] This seems ungrateful after the stalwart support the Scots gave Charles in the early 1420s, and inconsistent since he retained a guard of Scottish archers throughout his reign. But it reflects the pride and self-esteem that grew up in France because of their achievements in recovering their kingdom later in Charles's reign.

Another major problem for Charles VII was John, Duke of Bedford, the Regent of France himself. As the Battle of Verneuil proved, he was a brave, highly competent military leader in both a strategic sense and as a battle leader. But although this was very necessary in the circumstances found in France at the time, it was not a vital quality in a ruler, as the ultimate success of Charles VII proved. But this was only one side of Bedford's character. He was also a fair-minded, thoughtful administrator; even his enemies recognised this. Basin, who was informed by his personal experience as a cleric in Normandy under the English, wrote: 'France was governed with great energy and ability by the Duke of Bedford. Bedford was brave, humane and just: he loved many French seigneurs who gave loyalty to him and he gave them honours according to their merits.'[215] Charles had to be able to offer people something real and worthwhile if he was going to draw their support away from Bedford. In the end this problem was solved in 1435 when Bedford died.

But what of the consequences of the Battle of Verneuil for the third kingdom, Scotland? The destruction of the 'Army of Scotland' in the battle marked the end of significant Scottish involvement in the Hundred Years War. James I had agreed not to aid France as part of the treaty agreed at the time of his release. He stuck to this, and concentrated on establishing his royal power and trying to modernise the administration of his kingdom so that it more resembled what he had observed in his long detention in England. Meanwhile, in France, Sir John Stewart of Darnley became Constable of the Scots in France and led a relatively small force of Scots soldiers until 1429, when they were heavily defeated in the 'Battle of the Herrings'. After this, the king's guard of Scottish archers remained a symbol of the Auld Alliance, but one which had no military impact. But what would have happened in Scotland if the Franco-Scottish army had won at Verneuil?

Rewards for fighting in the battle

Bedford and Henry VI's administration in England recognised the importance of the victory at Verneuil and, just as Henry V did after his great victory at Agincourt, they made a serious effort to at least pay the men who had achieved the victory. A warrant issued in Henry VI's name in October 1424 ordered the collection of an aid by Humon de Belknap, Treasurer and Governor General of Finances in France and Normandy, to pay the arrears owed to the men who had taken part in various sieges that year and in the battles before Ivry and at Verneuil.[216] Bedford had already repaid the men who had lost money or goods when the Lombards plundered the baggage train out of his own resources. This was a gesture of gratitude for their steadiness in the battle and their willingness to sacrifice their possessions to ensure the order of their ranks. It was the sort of action that would be remembered by soldiers as showing that they could trust Bedford, so that they in turn would do their best for him.

Both Henry V and the Duke of Bedford as Regent of France granted lands to their soldiers. The most notable example of this was the land granted to each soldier present at Verneuil as reward for their significant service. This was a wider-reaching action than the common practice of granting lands to the captains and the men in particular retinues in the area where they were serving as garrisons. The recipients were vital to the consolidation of the English settlement in Normandy and the other conquered lands in northern France. By settling in France they introduced an English element into the towns and villages, which developed through marriage with local women. These men also provided a reserve that was a regular, convenient source of experienced soldiers who could be employed as necessary, given the tendency for the English administration to continue to issue relatively short-term indentures on financial grounds.[217] No doubt English administrators also hoped that by giving the soldiers a stake in France they would be less likely to maraud in times of unemployment. While these men could easily become targets for the French irregulars mentioned above in the discussion of brigandage, they might also be a source of local information about them.

The scale of the settlement after Verneuil was substantial. A document records the grant of lands to the English for 'their good deeds at the battle of Verneuil against the French'. These lands were specifically given to all the soldiers (of whatever rank) as inheritable grants in various sized parcels depending on their rank. The total amount of these grants was land worth 60,000 livre tournais or about 10,000 English marks.[218] The drawback for these Englishmen was that much of this land was in Maine, so if they were going to settle long-term they were going to be part of the effort by Bedford to establish a secure southern border to English-ruled France. But not all of these landholders settled in France. The problem of English absentee landholders increased in the state of relative peace that followed the victory at Verneuil. Some of these men would have held lands in France since the settlements Henry V made in the wake of his conquests of cities such as Caen and Rouen and the Duchy of Normandy in general, others would be more recently established settlers. While we might think, looking back over nearly 600 years, that the peace won at Verneuil would have brought opportunities for real prosperity for these men, they seem to have preferred the familiarity of living in England, while drawing some income from their French estates. This all meant that when Bedford issued a feudal summons to defend these lands, the forces he raised were significantly smaller than he expected because of these absentees. As a result he had to issue threats that he would recover the fiefs (in King Henry VI's name) for this failure of feudal duty, to get these absentees to at least provide an adequate substitute.[219] But it is also clear that a pool of English ex-soldiers developed in northern France who settled there, no doubt married and either worked landholdings or worked in small businesses. These men may have owned their land or businesses or rented them, but either way they became settled in France. In many cases, garrison service would have given them the opportunity to get to know the people and the place before they decided to become civilians. Many of these men were prepared to rejoin garrisons or field armies in times of need, as the crisis of 1429 proved.[220] They were the successful part of the English land settlement in that they fulfilled the military purpose behind it.

The war goes on

Fully aware of his military weakness, Charles continued the struggle through diplomacy. In October 1425 he agreed the Treaty of Saumur with Jean, Duke of Brittany, which made the duke firmly a member of his party. Jean was not a warlike man but one who preferred to consolidate his authority in his duchy and support the building of cathedrals. He is remembered in Breton history as Jean the Wise. This may explain his apparently vacillating behaviour; he wanted to avoid his strategically important duchy being drawn into the struggle between his two larger neighbours, England and France, something that had happened in the fourteenth century to the great detriment of the duchy.

His brother, Arthur de Richemont, was a very different character. He had fought with the French at Agincourt and been a long-standing supporter of the Armagnacs. By 1425 he was Constable of France and an important part of Charles's court. Arthur was forceful and no doubt influenced Jean's decision to openly ally with Charles (who in Armagnac eyes was his liege in any case) at this time when his fortunes seemed low. The gains for Charles were obvious. Having Brittany in his party opened another front for the English to watch. He had good lines of communication by both land and sea with Brittany, so he could easily send men (if he had any) to support any military activity there. In fact Charles gained new forces by the treaty, since Jean had built up a fairly professional army to maintain the peace in his duchy. Also the Breton sailors had a well-earned reputation as pirates preying on English and other shipping. If Charles could mobilise them he might be able to further distract the English.

Bedford's biggest problems after Verneuil did not come from the French loyal to Charles but from his relatives: his brother Humphrey, Duke of Gloucester and to a lesser degree his brother-in-law, Philip, Duke of Burgundy. Bedford must have found it difficult at times to understand his brother-in-law's approach to affairs in France, even with the help of his wife's advice and negotiations with Philip. Besides his political dealings with the Armagnac court, Philip's personal behaviour caused problems for the alliance. In October 1424 he attempted to seduce the Countess of Salisbury, the beautiful Alice Chaucer, at a ball.[221] Salisbury was personally angry; he felt that both his and his wife's honour had been besmirched, but more seriously it was another reason why Salisbury and other nobles felt that Burgundy was untrustworthy. This view was loudly espoused by Humphrey of Gloucester. Unlike Gloucester, Salisbury had the sense to realise that whatever he thought of the Duke of Burgundy personally, the English adventure in France could only succeed if the duke remained neutral at the very least. As a result, Salisbury remained in France and achieved much in Maine and Anjou, while Bedford was distracted by the consequences of Gloucester's activities in Flanders and England.

England in the 1420s

Henry V's will had broadly shared royal power between his brothers. However, it had also given the council of the great lords of the realm a powerful part to play as well. Bedford, the older surviving brother, was regent in France, and while he was pre-eminent in England when he was in England, he did not claim that he was regent there as well. Gloucester's power in England centred on his role as guardian of the infant King Henry VI, but he was unable to establish his claim that this guardianship extended to the realm. There were various reasons for this. Bedford was unprepared to compromise his status in England. Bishop Beaufort, uncle of Bedford and Gloucester, and the other lords of the council would not accept the idea of Gloucester having rule in England. So the lords of the council and Parliament declared that Gloucester was to be known as Protector and Defender of the king and the realm, while the council and Parliament held the king's power to govern.

Gloucester had some support among the members of the council, and soon cultivated the good opinions of the country at large, and London in particular, which he used to try to increase his power in the years immediately following Henry's death. Despite this support, he was largely unsuccessful in this quest for pre-eminence in England for four reasons: the terms of Henry V's will; Bedford's personal standing; the efforts of Beaufort, who had a good personal relationship with Bedford; and the determination of the other members of the council to keep the kingdom stable and prosperous. Parliament took advantage of the uncertainty of those holding royal power in Henry VI's minority that arose from these divisions to re-establish its tight control over taxation. It refused to grant direct taxation (such as tenths or fifteenths of property) between 1422 and 1427. This was in line with the English understanding of the Treaty of Troyes that the costs of the defence of Henry VI's kingdom of France should be borne by that kingdom. Also, possibly in reaction to Parliaments' generous grants to Henry V, the levels of customs duties and taxation on the wool trade were greatly reduced.

This tightfistedness by the English Parliament explains why Bedford and his lieutenants were unable to achieve large advances after the great victory at Verneuil. They simply couldn't afford to raise sufficient forces to engage in large-scale conquest. Many of the troops paid for by tax revenues raised in France were necessary as garrisons. The only way that funds could be found for the annual expeditions that enabled the expansionist campaigns between 1422 and 1427 was borrowing. Bishop Beaufort used his great wealth to help support the wars in France, which put Bedford in his debt literally and metaphorically, and gave the Bishop increasing control over the finances of England. Beaufort became chancellor in 1424, which, with his wealth and his influence in the council, made him the most powerful man in England, so long as Bedford remained in France. But Gloucester presented problems in two ways: firstly he was an enthusiastic political intriguer in England, trying to unpick this settlement. Secondly, in an attempt to win personal glory and wealth, he attacked the Duke of Burgundy's interests in Flanders. Besides his dissatisfaction with the terms of the Henrician settlement, Gloucester had a strong political rivalry and personal animosity for his uncle, Henry Beaufort, Bishop of Winchester.

Gloucester's military adventure in Flanders

Gloucester married Jacqueline, Countess of Hainault, in 1422, as a later chronicle put it 'either blynded with ambicion or dotyng for love'.[222] She had fled an unsatisfactory marriage to the Duke of Brabant and was soon enamoured with the handsome, cultured Gloucester. She seems to have been a feisty politician who made determined efforts to achieve her ends, and an English royal duke was just what she needed to further her claims in Flanders. The marriage gave Gloucester opportunities to fulfil his ambition to build a military reputation. He had no opinion of Philip of Burgundy and chose not to understand his importance to the prospects of English success in France. Instead, he looked back to the glory days of Edward III's reign when he believed (wrongly as it happens) that England succeeded without Continental support. Gloucester made sustained efforts to get funding for an expedition to Flanders to recover his wife's inheritance in 1423 and 1424. The council did what it could to stop him since the pro-Burgundian Beaufort made sure that it recognised that Humphrey's plans would antagonise Philip of Burgundy. Humphrey and Jacqueline finally invaded Hainault in October 1424. This was unbelievably crass timing, so soon after the victory at Verneuil which had given the English such an advantage. It demonstrates very clearly one of the reasons why the English attempts to hold the French Crown were doomed. English nobles (and many others) focused on short-term or personal interests rather than taking a wider, longer-term view of what could be achieved.

Initially, Humphrey and Jacqueline had some success in pressing her claim against her previous husband John, Duke of Brabant. Philip of Burgundy was very displeased by this, but, fortunately for English interests in France, Bedford was able to negotiate a peace agreement with Philip. This achievement shows Bedford's personal qualities and the value of his wife's good relations with her brother. Brabant accepted the terms of the agreement, Gloucester and Jacqueline did not. Philip of Burgundy was angered by this and prepared to support Brabant militarily. Bedford seems to have left Gloucester to take his chances against Philip and John of Brabant, since he concentrated on keeping on good terms with his brother-in-law. Waurin reports Bedford and Burgundy were, 'coming very often to see and visit one another very affectionately'.[223] Meanwhile on the ground, Gloucester and Jacqueline's army was moderately successful against the Burgundian-supported forces of the Count of St Pol over the winter and in early 1425. Frustrated by the lack of any solid progress in Flanders, Gloucester returned to England in April 1425 to raise reinforcements. He may also have tired of Jacqueline since he seems to have taken Eleanor Cobham, who was one of Jacqueline's ladies-in-waiting, as a mistress around this time. Jacqueline continued the struggle for her inheritance with some success. Humphrey sent some reinforcements from England under Lord Fitzwalter. But Jacqueline's efforts came to an end at the Battle of Brouwershaven in

January 1426, where the Burgundian knights destroyed her army despite the best efforts of the English troops who made up about a quarter of her forces. Gloucester's reputation in England was significantly diminished by this adventure, but he was still popular in London and with the merchants because of their distrust of Philip of Burgundy's ambitions in Flanders. Gloucester was the natural leader for these popular feelings and set himself determinedly against Beaufort, who was pro-Burgundian. The situation in England deteriorated to such an extent that in October 1425 armed supporters of Beaufort and Gloucester were facing each other in London. This was the point where Beaufort overreached himself because he was confident in his own power and didn't trust Gloucester's judgement. Gloucester declared his intention to ride to Eltham to see his nephew the king – a reasonable thing to do since he was officially the king's guardian. Beaufort was convinced that he meant to take the king under his control. As a result he had his armed retainers seize London Bridge and bar the duke's way. This was a serious mistake. Not only had he prevented Gloucester from undertaking a perfectly reasonable act as the king's guardian but he had done it in London where Gloucester had widespread support. Things had got to the point where a small incident would set off a fierce bout of civil strife in the capital, which might spread through the country. So Beaufort sent a desperate appeal to Bedford knowing that he was the only man with the status to curb Gloucester. He was also the only man that Beaufort would accept as arbitrator in this dispute because of his standing in the realm and his personal qualities.

Bedford knew he had no choice but to return to England to sort things out. He appointed the earls of Salisbury, Suffolk and Warwick as lieutenants in his absence, knowing that he could rely on them to look after English interests in France. But before he left France an attempt was made on his life, which showed the problems still faced by the English after the resounding victory at Verneuil. Sauvage de Frémainville, a brigand chief operating to the north of Paris, was the culprit. There is no evidence that de Frémainville was an Armagnac guerrilla; he was just a very successful bandit who showed that despite the sincere efforts of both the English and the Burgundians there were still men able to threaten the peace and security of the areas around Paris. He remained active until the end of 1427 when he was captured by the Burgundians and brought to Paris for execution.

Bedford landed in England on 20 December 1425, and he was not able to return to France until March 1427. In that time he struggled to find an arrangement which would bring peace to English politics so that he could return to what he regarded as his real task, gaining control of his nephew's French kingdom. He quickly recognised that Beaufort had overreached himself and had built up a position where he held too much power and influence. So Bedford forced him to resign as chancellor. Bedford then ensured that men of his party became chancellor and treasurer so that he could have some hope of funding for the French wars. Bedford eased Beaufort's pain by working for him to become a cardinal, something that Henry V had denied him. This still left the problem of his brother Gloucester.

While Gloucester had to accept Bedford's authority while he was in England, he made it clear that once Bedford went back to France he would not accept the authority of the council, declaring that he was answerable only to the king. This was unacceptable to the council who, quite possibly with Bedford's support, restated their powers and required both Bedford and Gloucester to accept them. But while Bedford had been able to bring some semblance of order to the government of England, he was much less successful in getting English money to pay for troops in France. While he extracted some from the clergy, Parliament refused any further direct taxation of the English people. So the new treasurer made his best efforts to get adequate funds from the customs dues the Crown could legitimately claim. This was the clearest demonstration of a significant downside to the victory and the relative security it brought to the English-dominated parts of France. The English Parliament, which had become increasingly reluctant to agree taxes on the English to pay for the wars in France in Henry V's reign, had become quite determined not to pay for these wars after his death. This great victory made it seem a sensible policy; there was no longer a need for large English field armies in France since the 'French Pretender' (as Henry VI's administration regarded Charles VII) had lost his army and some of his most experienced military leaders. The Normans, and the other French under English rule, could reasonably be expected to pay the costs of the English garrisons who protected them and maintained the peace. In general, as has already been noted, under Bedford's empathetic rule, the Estates of Normandy were quite prepared to pay for their own defence. But this was a very short-sighted approach by the English. Bedford, as Regent of France, and Salisbury, his most experienced and able colleague, knew that while they had preserved the English hold on France at Verneuil, sitting quietly in France was not an option. Some sort of agreement with Charles VII had to be achieved, and this would only happen if more military pressure was applied.

In March 1427, Bedford returned to France to continue his efforts to achieve great things with slight resources.

14

The tide of war begins to turn

The war 1426–28

While Bedford was in England trying to calm the tensions between the nobles, particularly his uncle and his brother, it was left to his lieutenants, the earls of Salisbury, Suffolk and Warwick, to prosecute the war. With Suffolk based at Avranches in support, Sir Thomas Rempston invaded Brittany with a small force of maybe 600 men. This seems to have been a small-scale chevauchée to show Duke Jean the folly of his alliance with Charles. Rempston got as far as Rennes, the capital of Brittany, before falling back to St James de Beuvron on the Normandy–Brittany border. Arthur de Richemont, Constable of France, raised a large army of French and Bretons to go to the assistance of his brother the duke. He besieged St James, battered breaches in the walls with his artillery and mounted prolonged assaults which Rempston and his much smaller force beat off.

However, the English knew that they couldn't hold out for long so they decided on an 'all or nothing' plan to try to defeat de Richemont. Probably near dusk, Rempston led part of his force out of St James and round behind the attacking army while the rest under Sir Nicholas Burdet held the battered defences. He then attacked the enemy rear with his men shouting 'Salisbury' and 'St George' while the defenders sallied out shouting 'Suffolk'. This caused panic; the French and Breton soldiers thought the feared Earl of Salisbury had come to St James' relief and fled back to their camp in disorder, suffering substantial casualties. That night, panic took hold of the troops and they fled the camp, abandoning their artillery.

Quite why de Richemont's army proved to be so fragile is unknown, but this remarkable English victory did his reputation no good at all and gave Duke Jean cause to reconsider his position. Two days later Suffolk brought up a relief force, which probably would have been too late but for the desperate daring of Rempston and his men. The combined force pushed into Brittany, taking Dol and approaching Rennes. Duke Jean asked for a short truce, which was granted. When this expired the Earl of Warwick mounted a siege of Pontorson, which was eventually successful. During this siege the French garrison of Mont St Michel proved their nuisance value by harassing Warwick's lines of communication. This led to another English success when a small force under Lord Scales defended a convoy so vigorously that it repulsed a much larger Franco-Breton attacking force. This fighting led the Duke of Brittany to change sides again, accepting that Henry VI was King of France and the rest of the terms of the Treaty of Troyes. All this had been achieved with little help from the Burgundians. Philip had drawn off his forces to deal with Jacqueline's attempts to regain her inheritance. The only Burgundian force active on behalf of Henry VI was that under John of Luxembourg, who was operating in the east of France.

Bedford returned to France with reinforcements in the spring of 1427. Many of these new men were sent under the command of the earls of Warwick and Suffolk, and Suffolk's brother Sir John de la Pole and Sir Henry Biset to attack Montargis. They began their siege in July and it dragged on through the summer for two months. Montargis was a difficult place to besiege because it was on the River Loing, which ran in more than one channel. Things were made more difficult because the inhabitants broke some of the dikes that helped to control the waters around the town. This led to the besiegers being based in three camps around the town, separated by water. They built at least one temporary pontoon bridge to help maintain contact with each other. Charles assembled a relief force under the Count of Dunois and La Hire, who were both competent commanders as subsequent events showed. They attacked the portion of the besiegers under de la Pole, who was caught by surprise; his men were scattered and he was captured.

Dunois went on to attack Biset's camp. Biset must have been more prepared, since, finding himself outnumbered, he attempted a fighting retreat towards Warwick's camp over one of the pontoon bridges. Unfortunately the bridge broke under the weight of men and a number were drowned. Warwick stood on the defensive ready to rebuff any French that attacked; Dunois and La Hire knew that there was no need to risk a fight since they had broken the siege and were able to enter Montargis. Warwick had lost maybe a third of his force, and so decided to withdraw. This meant that he abandoned his siege guns, making the French victory all the more emphatic. This was the second time that Sir John de la Pole had been responsible for a timely French victory that provided a morale boost out of all proportion to its military significance. The first was his defeat by Aumale in 1423 at La Brossonière. Just as on this previous occasion he was worsted by an able French commander who took advantage of his lack of preparation and watchfulness. While this defeat personally cost him another ransom payment, its cost to the English cause was much greater. His wasn't the only example of carelessness born of overconfidence, which may have been becoming a problem among the English soldiers. Another English force was ambushed and scattered at Ambrières in Maine at this time. The fallout of this defeat was that a number of fortifications in this disputed area fell to the French. The Earl of Salisbury was back in England at this time in 1427, but it is not clear exactly why. Hindsight suggests that it was to collect reinforcements, since he brought a comparatively large force to France in 1428. He may have been in dispute with Bedford over a lordship that he felt was his due. He may also have disagreed with the regent's strongly 'Burgundophile' policy in the light of the Duke of Burgundy's attempted seduction of his wife and military inactivity in support of English efforts. On a more personal level, he may have been sincerely considering honouring his oath to go on pilgrimage to the Holy Land that he had made in desperate circumstances in the Battle of Verneuil. He may have just been war-weary after years of sustained effort. Whatever the reason for his absence, he was missed.

Fortunately for the regent, he had brought another very able commander, John, Lord Talbot, with him when he returned to France. Talbot had a deal of military experience gained in tough, irregular fighting in Wales and Ireland, where he acquired a reputation for harshness. He proved to be a very energetic commander who, despite having a reputation for irascibility, was able to inspire his men to make great efforts against the French. He seems to have been a subordinate commander in the Earl of Warwick's forces initially, before becoming a more independent commander in 1428. He began the year with a raid into Maine that culminated in the rapid storming of Laval, which had never been in English hands before. Then he went eastwards towards Alençon, clearing out any Armagnac forces he found.

While at Alençon he heard that some inhabitants of Le Mans had betrayed the city to La Hire. The English garrison had escaped and were holding out in the castle. Talbot set out with about 300 men for a forced march of 32 miles, arriving at Le Mans in the early morning. The French, who were concentrating on the castle, were completely surprised when he stormed the city walls. The garrison sallied out on hearing Talbot's war cries and the French army fell apart with many captured. Talbot inflicted harsh summary justice on those who had let La Hire and his men into the city. His reputation was established among the English and the French of whichever party by this energetic campaign.

The turning point

Despite these successes, 1428 was the year when the tide of the war in France turned against the English. While this is a judgement with hindsight, since the English and Normans fought on for another twenty-five years, this was the year when the expansion of the English territories in France was stopped. The broad unity of purpose shown by the English up to this time broke down, leading to two major reverses. At the end of March 1428 the Earl of Salisbury, who was still in England, agreed an indenture to raise a little army of 600 men-at-arms and 1,800 archers. The terms of the indenture made it clear that this was an independent command; firstly because it gave Salisbury unusual independence from the authority of the regent, and secondly because it committed money specifically to cannons and the special equipment and skilled men necessary to serve them so that Salisbury had his own siege train.

It is likely that Gloucester was responsible for this independence from his brother's authority, encouraged by Salisbury's view that the time had come for a decisive stroke against Charles and the Armagnacs.

Their motives for this break in the unity of purpose previously shown in France differed. Salisbury may well have felt that it was time for a decisive blow against Charles while he was still reeling from Verneuil. He also had a well-founded confidence that he could take Orléans and so serve the greater strategic purpose of the English. Gloucester was politicking again. By ensuring Salisbury's independence from the Regent's authority, he was paying back Bedford for the way he contained Gloucester's bid for greater power in England. It was unfortunate because Bedford had agreed a different campaign agenda in the council in Paris, which had also provided adequate funding. In line with his steady expansionist policy, which met the needs of French and Norman subjects by aiming to establish secure borders for the English holdings, the council had agreed that he should take Angers, with the idea of securing Anjou and making the western Loire the boundary.

The two plans were equally valid, although Bedford's probably met the local needs better and built on Talbot's successes in Maine and Anjou. Salisbury's strike against Orléans raised three problems. One was that Philip of Burgundy could see it as an English attempt to restrict his influence, which would worry Bedford, but would probably be seen as a positive recommendation by Gloucester and Salisbury. The second problem was that it was an offence against the laws of chivalry, since the Duke of Orléans was an English prisoner. A prisoner's lands were meant to be left alone by his captors' forces since they were without their protector and were meant to be raising his ransom. The third was that it dissipated English efforts over a wide area rather than taking advantage of the momentum established in Maine and Anjou. But the real problem was that Salisbury did not seem to make his intentions known to Bedford until they became clear by his actions once he and his men had landed in France. They marched south towards the Loire, not south-west towards Anjou. Bedford was stunned and later remarked of this that Salisbury acted 'God knows by what advice'.[224]

The siege of Orléans

On his way south, Salisbury took Jenville in rather surprising circumstances. He had arrived at the town and surrounded it in preparation for an assault or siege. Salisbury had some unsatisfactory negotiations with the leaders of Jenville who refused to come to terms. In the aftermath of these, as the leaders on both sides considered the next step, the men of Salisbury's army saw the opportunity and stormed the town before the defenders could organise themselves. It was a brutal affair that left many of the population dead and the town destroyed. It emphasised Salisbury's reputation as a commander who achieved his aims and showed the quality of his army. The men and their captains understood the purpose of the campaign and were able to seize opportunities without direction from Salisbury. More importantly he took Jargeau, Meung and Beaugency, which gave him bridges over the Loire both east and west of Orléans. Salisbury rapidly established a vigorous siege of Orléans in the second week of October with the support of some 1,500 Burgundians, who made up about a third of his total strength. Their involvement shows that Philip was both covering his own interests in Orléans and supporting the aims of the Treaty of Troyes.

Salisbury still hadn't enough men (the curse of so many ambitious English operations after Henry V's death) to establish a complete blockade of Orléans, which was one of the largest cities in France and had old but very substantial walls. While these may not have been artillery-proof, the very size of the city and the fact that the Loire provided a substantial moat on the south side made it a difficult prospect for a siege. In addition, the city had a substantial garrison, including the city's militia led by the experienced and determined Raoul de Gaucourt, who hated the English after being imprisoned for nearly ten years for irritating Henry V by his heroic resistance while captain of Harfleur in 1415. At this stage of the siege, the besieging army may have exceeded the defenders – both soldiers and city militia – by maybe only 20 per cent.

In addition, the defenders had a good number of artillery pieces to make life difficult for the attackers. Salisbury established a loose siege by beginning the establishment of a ring of fortlets sited at key points around the city. His main endeavour was to attack La Tourelles, a substantial fort defending the southern end of the stone bridge over the Loire that led to the city. De Gaucourt had reinforced this with a substantial earthwork which restricted the damage Salisbury's artillery could do. The English assaulted the earthwork unsuccessfully after a bombardment. Two days later the French abandoned both the earthwork and the fort of La Tourelles. After the garrison had retired to the city the French broke two of the arches of the bridge to deny its use to the English. Salisbury repaired La Tourelles and its surrounding earthworks to use as a base from which to direct the siege. Then, on 27 October, two weeks after beginning the siege, the Earl of Salisbury was mortally wounded by a cannon shot when surveying the siege from a window in La Tourelles. Whether he habitually surveyed the city from this window, and the French gunners had carefully laid their guns, or whether it was a lucky chance, this single event helped change the course of the siege.

Bedford faced a difficult decision; should he continue a siege that was not part of his plans, or should he abandon it? He chose to send the Earl of Suffolk to continue the siege. Suffolk was both experienced and reasonably competent, but he had neither Salisbury's energy nor his vision, which doomed the siege. The English did little for two months, except consolidate their fortlets and sit out the winter in the neighbouring towns. While he may have been forced to this expedient by concern for the health of his troops, this was not a vigorous winter siege in the style of those Henry V led to success. As a result, de Gaucourt reinforced his defences as much as he could, enlarged and trained the militia and made what preparations as he might for a long siege. Early in December, three of the best Armagnac commanders – the Count of Dunois, known as the Bastard of Orléans, La Hire, and Poton de Xaintrailles – marched into the city with between 1,200 and 1,400 men to reinforce the garrison. Almost immediately after this Lord Scales and Lord Talbot arrived with about 2,500 men, possibly replacing those hired by Salisbury, whose indenture expired at this point and who no longer wished to remain in the besieging force.

With these reinforcements, the balance between attackers and defenders remained much as before. The difference was still one of morale; it is uncertain whether the average French fighting man really felt that his side could beat the English.

The English siege now regained some energy and direction, and work on the loose ring of fortlets (known as bastilles) and boulevards (earthworks sheltering one or more artillery piece to cover an avenue of approach to the city) was consolidated. It was now much more difficult for the defenders to get any significant supplies, despite persistent skirmishing. But the attackers were in a similar position; they depended on convoys to bring in supplies, which left them in difficulties if the Armagnacs could disrupt these convoys. In February 1429 they made a serious effort to destroy a large supply convoy of several hundred wagons that was on its way from Paris. A good number of men, led by Dunois, La Hire and Xaintrailles, managed to get out of Orléans to join up with another force under the Count of Clermont, which included the Scots who survived the defeats at Cravant and Verneuil. Sir John Fastolf and the Provost of Paris, who led the convoy and its substantial escort, got word of the approaching Armagnac army and circled the wagons to make a substantial temporary fort. When the Armagnacs saw this, despite the experience of most of their leaders, they fell to disputing how to attack the English.

Initially they seemed to have started well, using a number of small cannon to knock holes in the wagons and their cargo and inflict some casualties on the beleaguered English. But the commanders of the various contingents seemed to become impatient with this method of war and each contingent attacked as they saw fit. The Scots, under Sir John Stewart of Darnley, attacked on foot as they always did, while the Armagnacs attacked on horseback. The English and Parisian archers (many of the latter were probably crossbowmen) shot from the cover of the wagons and broke up the cavalry charges by shooting the horses and taking the force out of the Scottish attack. Then the English men-at-arms charged out of the wagons and destroyed the dogged Scots. The result was more than 400 dead among the attackers and many more taken prisoner. The blow to Armagnac morale both in Orléans and outside can be imagined. The battle, which has come to be known as the Battle of the Herrings because of the supplies being brought to the English outside Orléans, also showed the level of support Bedford's efforts had among the French, particularly in Paris and the north of the country.

At the end of February two things happened which showed the divided approach to the war at Charles VII's court. One party favoured continuing the diplomatic approaches to Philip of Burgundy knowing that if they could completely detach him from the English, then the English cause must fail. But there was another powerful party led by Yolande of Aragon, Charles VII's very able mother-in-law. She was against Charles coming to an agreement with Philip and continually pushed for determined military action. Both parties were engaged in efforts to save Orléans, although it was Yolande's party which had the greatest success.

Firstly, peace proposals were put forward to Philip of Burgundy by the leaders of the garrison and citizens of the city. The city would be given over to him and he would appoint governors if the siege was raised. The revenues of the city were to be divided between the prisoner Charles, Duke of Orléans and Henry VI. It is unlikely that this was their own decision alone; it was likely that it was part of a devious plan made with Charles VII's knowledge. There had been a long-standing concern in the Parlement of Poitiers that Orléans was vulnerable to just such a thrust by the English and these proposals would put its control beyond their reach. There is no reason to doubt that the English were aware of this French concern, and it may help to explain the Earl of Salisbury's ambitious assault; he felt that morale in the French camp at large was low and that this should be exploited.

But these peace proposals could begin to drive a wedge between Burgundy and England by exploiting the reservations some Burgundians had about the close relationship with the enemy of France. This was particularly pertinent since the Duke of Burgundy felt strongly that Orléans was important to his interests and, as a result, he felt his wishes with regard to these proposals should have great weight. If they were accepted, Orléans would survive relatively undamaged under mainly Burgundian control, although Henry VI's interests were also served, and Charles could carry on trying to excite tensions between the allies. If they were rejected then the time taken up in the negotiations would be useful to Charles to make more preparations to break the siege.

Whatever was behind these peace proposals, Philip of Burgundy, who like Charles preferred diplomacy and cunning plans to the hazards of war, responded favourably. Bedford and the royal council in France rejected the proposals because the Treaty of Troyes stated that all conquests became lands of the French Crown, meaning Henry VI by the terms of the treaty. Unsurprisingly, Philip was displeased by this decision and may even have taken this rejection as a sign that the English weren't really interested in power sharing with Burgundy.[225] By overriding the Duke of Burgundy's wishes, Bedford, acting as regent, behaved as the more powerful French kings did, putting their interests ahead of those of the great dukes of France. Philip of Burgundy wanted to continue to behave as the great dukes had done – for the last three decades at least – and pursue his ducal interest over those of the King of France. Certainly the rejection encouraged him in a diplomatic dance towards Charles, which was finally completed in 1435 with the Treaty of Arras. He immediately withdrew the Burgundian troops from the siege of Orléans, which left the English desperately short of men to continue it.

It is probable that Bedford's letters to the council in England urgently requesting the recruitment of 1,400 men arose in part from the need to reinforce the siege anyway, but also from the need to replace the Burgundian troops. He could not pull any more men out of the Normandy garrisons because all the underemployed men in the Normandy garrisons had been dispatched to the revitalised siege of Mont St Michel, funded by the Norman Estates General, who would not fund men for what they might regard as an adventure at Orléans anyway.

Secondly, Joan of Arc appeared at the French court. Her story and achievements are well known. What is less well known is the support amounting almost to sponsorship she received from Yolande of Aragon and her party. While Joan seems to have been genuine in her belief in the guidance her voices provided, and was one of a small number of female religious mystics guided by such voices, she was unique as far as I am aware because of her emphasis on a military solution to France's problems. This was exactly the approach favoured by Yolande.

Through a combination of her own inspirational sincerity and Yolande's discreet but powerful support, Joan gained access to Charles and tempted him with her mission of relieving Orléans and seeing him crowned in Reims. Charles raised a relieving force of maybe 4,000 men, which set out at the end of April under the command of the Duke of Alençon and morale-boosting leadership of Joan of Arc, who was splendidly clad in armour and under her banner showing Christ in judgement. Not only did she inspire the French soldiers to have real confidence in their cause but she also managed to get them to behave (to a large degree at least) as if they were on some sort of crusade. She insisted that whores and soldiers' lemans no longer followed the army and that the men forbore to swear, although the fiery La Hire for one found this latter requirement almost impossible to obey.

The army convoyed supplies to Orléans, which were successfully delivered before it returned to Blois, probably to bring a second convoy. Joan entered Orléans with the first convoy on 30 April. Three days later the relieving force also entered the city. The English seem to have made no effective efforts to hinder either of these reliefs, which may well reflect how stretched their forces were. The defenders of Orléans now outnumbered the besiegers. The garrison of Orléans attacked the fortified church at St Loup, one of the English fortlets isolated to the east of the city, probably as a diversion, while the relieving force entered the city with the second convoy. Once Joan realised that this attack was underway, she galloped out of the city and inspired the French soldiers to take St Loup. Talbot was coming to its relief, skirmishing with the French on the way when he realised that he was too late and the fortlet had fallen. This small success added to the effect Joan had on the French, but it is far from clear that the English paid her any great heed at this time.

The French commanders decided that the next step was for them to regain control of the bridge over the Loire. On 6 May they began this with an attack on another fortified church, Augustins, which acted as an outwork for the boulevard in front of La Tourelles. It was an epic two-day fight notable for two things. One was the way that Joan exposed herself to risk to inspire the French soldiers in their assaults. Despite her armour she was wounded at one point but recovered sufficiently to return to plant her banner on the edge of the ditch and so urged the men on to one final effort. The other was the way that the heavily outnumbered English under William Glasdale fought for two days. In the end they couldn't hold the positions and attempted a fighting retreat. This was only partially successful, as a damaged bridge collapsed under the weight of the men casting Glasdale, among others, into the river.

Suffolk, Talbot and Scales knew that the loss of St Loup and La Tourelles, along with the loss of the bridge across the Loire, meant that they could no longer maintain anything resembling a siege. So they drew up their forces in good order and marched away to their secure bases along the Loire. The failure in front of Orléans damaged the reputation of the English, not least because they had had to abandon their heaviest artillery. But the real significance was the way that morale among the French rose, in large part attributable to Joan of Arc. Her contribution was not over.

She urged Charles to take advantage of the English discomfiture and go to Reims to be crowned. He did not have her sense of divine mission, so he took the more sensible course of action and raised an army to retake those cities on the Loire still held by the English. A powerful army several thousand strong led by the Duke of Alençon and Joan began a siege at Jargeau, commanded by the Earl of Suffolk. Joan was the most important figure in this army because the superstitious Alençon would do her bidding with little question. Suffolk attempted to negotiate terms but Alençon refused. He made a second attempt as a major assault began, which was also ignored by Alençon. When the town was taken, the French killed the majority of the prisoners.

These three affronts to the common rules of war and chivalry were probably Joan's doing, since she had the zeal of a religious warrior, not a professional fighting man. After this success the army marched west past Orléans, largely ignored Meung as too powerful to assault and went on to prepare a siege on Beaugency, commanded by Matthew Gough. The large Armagnac army was reinforced by the unexpected arrival of Arthur de Richemont with about 1,200 Breton troops. Soon afterwards La Hire's scouts discovered a large English force near Meung, but the Armagnacs managed to keep this news from the garrison of Beaugency. As a result, Gough made terms to surrender Beaugency in two days time.

No sooner had Gough led his men out of the town than the Armagnacs heard that Talbot had pulled his men out of Meung as well and was retreating north. This struck Richemont, La Hire and Xaintrailles as too good an opportunity to miss, so, with Joan's encouragement, they set out in pursuit. The English force of 3,000 men that was meant to be relieving the towns was led by Sir John Fastolf, and the question that comes to mind is why did he do nothing offensive? Fastolf was not one of England's great fighting commanders, despite his success in the Battle of the Herrings; he was a cautious man who may not have been confident in the steadiness of his men. Talbot, commander of the garrison at Meung, could not have been more different. But Fastolf had been put in overall command by Bedford, so he and Talbot wrangled over what to do.

This confusion soon came to a head, with Talbot declaring he would set out to relieve Beaugency with those men who would follow him, just as news that it had surrendered came to Meung. So he reluctantly agreed with Fastolf that they should retreat towards Paris. However, there can be no doubt that the English command was fractured, and that Fastolf and Talbot would imitate French commanders in earlier battles and not fight a concerted battle. The Armagnacs caught up with the English at Patay, so Fastolf and Talbot recognised that they would have to fight. Fastolf drew his men up on a rise while Talbot tried to draw up his archers in advance and possibly to one side of Fastolf's front. The French heavily armoured cavalry arrived before the English had finished their preparations. They rode down the archers and broke through Fastolf's line. Fastolf and maybe half of his men fled, doing his reputation serious harm. Lords Talbot and Scales and a number of lesser commanders were captured, and most importantly the aura of invincibility the English had held since Verneuil was shattered.

While Joan was able to lead Charles to Reims for his coronation, she achieved little else militarily. Bedford managed to stabilise the situation using men drawn for the garrisons because he could rely on the passive support of the population in the English-ruled parts of France, who did not suddenly rise in support of Charles. But Joan did not need to do anything else; her greatest achievement was to get the French commanders and fighting men to believe in themselves and to get Charles to believe he could win. While it was almost certainly inevitable that the French would eventually contain the English for a number of reasons, it didn't have to happen in 1428–29. The English could have continued their advance for a number of years if they had remained united in purpose, and if the Earl of Salisbury hadn't looked out of a window. It took Charles another twenty-three years to drive the English out.

15

Verneuil: The forgotten battle of the Hundred Years War

The four great land battles in the Hundred Years War are Crécy in 1346, Poitiers in 1356, Agincourt in 1415 and Verneuil in 1424.[226] In terms of popular knowledge of what are thought of as key events in English history, they probably fall into the following order: Agincourt, Crécy, Poitiers and Verneuil. In fact, in terms of popular knowledge it's doubtful that Verneuil should even be on the list. Why is this? Agincourt was seen as a great victory at the time, a reputation it has never really lost. It was not only Henry V who saw the apparently miraculous victory of a smaller, less splendid, tired and desperate English army over the military nobility of France as a sign of God's favour – a number of contemporary chroniclers did the same. The shock of it affected the French for years. It was an important battle in medieval terms because a reigning king led one army against the royal army of another. For this reason alone the outcome was bound to have real consequences for the kingdoms involved. Victory made Henry's reputation in Europe as a warrior king without equal; a reputation he was able to use to achieve his ends, on paper at least, with the Treaty of Troyes five years later. No other English king came so close to holding both the English and French thrones.

Soon after it happened, the battle was being celebrated in popular songs, one of which, the Agincourt Carol, survives. But it was two later writers who fixed its fame in the popular history of England – William Shakespeare and Michael Drayton. Shakespeare's *Henry V* was first performed in around 1599. It told a rousing tale of how England beat its enemies in Continental Europe in the past and was written to inspire the people to resist the external threats that faced late Tudor England. With this play Shakespeare ensured that Agincourt stayed in the popular mind, and his play was used to boost civilian morale in later difficult times, such as when Laurence Olivier made a film of it in 1944. Kenneth Branagh's 1989 film brought the mud and blood of Agincourt to the fore, but this did nothing to reduce either the battle's or Henry's mythic reputation.

Michael Drayton is less well known now, although in his own lifetime he built up enough of a reputation to be buried in Poets' Corner in Westminster Abbey. He wrote a number of historical poems which brought him some fame under Elizabeth I, but the court of her successor James I was much less appreciative of his talents. In 1605 he published *Poems Lyric and Pastoral*, a collection of his shorter works, which included the first publication of his 'Ballad of Agincourt'. Drayton retained his reputation among his fellow poets and playwrights and may have known Shakespeare. The ballad was an influence on the growth of the legend of Agincourt, particularly in the nineteenth century.

Crécy was one of a small number of battles in the first half of the fourteenth century where fighting men drawn from the non-noble population, including ordinary peasants, were a significant factor in the defeat of an army largely made up of armoured knights and men-at-arms. Since two ruling kings faced each other at the head of large armies it was bound to be an important battle. This importance was increased because Edward had been trying to provoke Philip of France to face him in battle for some time, so the outcome was going to be decisive. Victory established Edward III and the English as one of the major military forces in Europe after about a century and a half of insignificance. It also established a fairly widespread point of view among the populace of fourteenth- and fifteenth-century England that war could be a very profitable activity.

Both contemporary chroniclers and historians since then have viewed the battle as marking the arrival of the English longbowman as a battle winner in military practice. Crécy was the biggest of these four battles in terms of numbers of men engaged. In popular history for the last 200 years Crécy was the first major victory for the English longbowman, a sort of prototype John Bull character with all sorts of plain, homely virtues. No contemporary songs survive and Crécy appears very little in English literature.

Poitiers is a battle that some historians have argued neither side really wanted to happen. Edward of Woodstock, later called the Black Prince, seems to have engaged with the efforts of Cardinal Talleyrand to find some way of avoiding battle, as did Jean II of France. Edward may have felt that the French army was too big to fight and was looking for a way out; he may have just been spinning things out to gain time to avoid a fight or, if he had to fight, to find the best ground for it.

Jean II was not a king who sought war, although his personal efforts in the battle showed him to be a brave and skilful fighter, so negotiation may have seemed the best course to him.[227] In reality it is probable that neither side could afford a truce because of the cost in money, land and reputation. Like Crécy, the status of the leaders of both armies meant that the battle was significant. The English commander Edward was heir to the renowned Edward III of England, while the French army was led by the king, Jean II, who was accompanied by the Dauphin Charles and two more of his sons.

As was true to a varying degree with all four battles, the French outnumbered the English. It was a battle where both sides showed some tactical acuity, although the French made the fundamental mistake of fighting on ground that suited the English way of war and allowing them time to prepare their position, which they put to good use. The French recognised the danger the English archers posed to their horses and so chose to advance on foot for the main part. They also attempted to sweep the archers away with flanking cavalry charges. The experience of the English archers suggests that the horses of these mounted men may have worn some reinforced protection in addition to the thick cloth trappers bearing heraldic symbols.

Once the battle started, the French showed no ability to adapt their tactics in an attempt to overcome the English resistance. This was also true at Crécy and Agincourt. The English had reinforced their position by digging small pits to trip man and horse. Once the battle started, one wing of the experienced English archers realised their arrows were having no effect on the charging cavalry so moved out to the flank and were able to break up the charge by shooting the horses where they were less protected. After a slogging match in the centre of the battle where Edwards's army managed to beat off the French attacks, he sent the Captal (an ancient Gascon feudal title meaning 'chief') de Buch out to make a flank attack, which broke the morale of the French force. This flexibility of approach won the battle for Edward. Despite Edward's presence and the capture of the French king, Poitiers seems to have had little or no presence in medieval song, possibly because it happened in appallingly difficult times, just six years after the Black Death and five before the Children's Plague.

If you have read this far you will be aware of the significance of the Battle of Verneuil. While it is the only one of the four battles without a reigning king on the field, a king's direct representative, John, Duke of Bedford, regent in France, was present. Like Crécy, both sides had sought battle, so when it came the battle would be bound to have significant consequences for them both. It is probable that it was the second biggest of the four battles in terms of numbers of men involved. The English victory broke the morale of the Armagnacs, leaving them in the sort of paralysis that affected the French after Agincourt whenever Henry V was campaigning. If the English had lost, it is difficult to know how much of northern France they would have been able to hang on to.

It is also likely that the Duke of Burgundy would have reconsidered his position very quickly. The writer of the *Parisian Chronicle*, who was a supporter of the English and Burgundians, as were many citizens of Paris, makes clear the sense of impending disaster that they felt if the Armagnacs won at Verneuil, 'for it was said that they had boasted that if they had beaten our people they would have spared neither women nor children, heralds nor musicians; all would have been put to the sword'.[228]

Like the small-scale uprisings in Normandy after the false reports of an English defeat at Verneuil, these blood-curdling statements may have been part of a deliberate attempt by the Armagnacs to destabilise Paris as part of the strategic objectives of the battle-seeking campaign which culminated at Verneuil. If the Armagnacs had won at Verneuil, it is quite likely that the small uprisings in Normandy would have increased in scale and scope, if only because Bedford had had to draw so many men from the Normandy garrisons to make up his army for Verneuil. If these men had not returned because of a defeat, the English garrisons would have been too thinly spread to restore civil order, and resist the resurgent Armagnacs. So one of the reasons that the Battle of Verneuil is largely forgotten is that the English victory achieved a negative result! Because the English won, disaster *did not* befall the English-ruled lands in northern France, and so the event that prevented disaster was soon forgotten. There is plenty of evidence that men recognised the battle as important at the time but it soon fell out of memory. Why? One reason has already been noted – victory meant that things continued to go well for the English in France. Maintaining the status quo in France, the state of steady English progress towards the young Henry VI being king of both countries, was not something that fired up the imaginations of the mass of the English people in the way that the rich booty Edward III brought back from France did in the fourteenth century. While Bedford made sure that his nephew's subjects in France were aware of their deliverance from the Armagnac peril, he doesn't seem to have broadcast it widely in England. He probably left it to the council to do so, and they had more parochial matters on their minds, as has been noted above.

Unlike the aftermath of Agincourt or Edward III's victories, it is uncertain how many soldiers went back to England at the end of their indentures with tales of glorious deeds told around the fireside to excite their friends. Many of these men seem to have stayed in France awaiting the next military employment opportunity. These two reasons may go far to explain why the battle seems not to have attracted literary renown. Early histories like *The Brut* (the part mentioning the French wars of the fifteenth century was probably written in the 1460s) and Edward Hall's *Chronicle* (first published in 1542) mention it very favourably. But it was overshadowed to some extent by great historical figures – Henry V, particularly as portrayed by Shakespeare, and Joan of Arc, literally a sainted figure.

The victory ensured that the war in France went on, which pleased the military classes in England. These included men from all social and economic groups because of the importance of archers for the English military effort. But these military men seem to have been becoming detached from English society at large for two reasons. Firstly, the English forces fighting in France were becoming increasingly professional, with men serving for years through a sequence of contracts. This probably led to them having relatively little contact with English civilians to tell their stories. Also, many of them settled in France, either on land grants received as rewards for service or as veterans/settlers who just remained in the area they had served in because that was where they knew people.

Secondly, unlike the French wars under Edward III in the 1340s and 1350s, the wars between 1418 and 1430 did not bring great wealth into England from the ransoms and the spoils of war. In fact they cost money. Even before the death of Henry V, who had achieved so much to boost English self-esteem, the English were becoming very reluctant to keep on paying for the wars. After his death it was a continual problem for Bedford and subsequent English commanders in France to find enough money to pay for anything like enough troops to keep the French at bay. All this meant that the events of the wars in France after Verneuil were probably not that well known in England and there was no reason for them to be widely popular. So, the victory at Verneuil appears to have had less importance than the other great battles because the people of England were not greatly concerned about the wars in France, so long as they didn't have to pay taxes to support them. But, if the battle had been lost, with the result that the English holdings in France were under serious threat, it is probable that there would have been some sort of popular outcry about it. There certainly was in the early 1450s when the French regained all of their country except Calais.

How was the importance of the Battle of Verneuil seen at the time? In November 1433 the records of Parliament include the following after a long encomium on the Duke of Bedford:

> and in especial ye Batayle of Vernule, ye which was ye grettest dede doon by English men in our days save the Bataille of Agyncourte, in the which Bataille of Vernule was slayne and taken ye flour of knyghthede, as well of ye Kyngs partie adverse of ye same cuntre, as of Scotland and of oyer strange nations yat were yere in assistance and help of ye kings partie adverse.[229]

Jean de Waurin, who fought at Agincourt, Cravant and Verneuil, wrote: 'I saw the assembly at Azincourt (sic), where there were many more princes and troops, and also that at Cravant, which was a very fine affair, but certainly that at Verneuil was of all the most formidable and the best fought.'[230]

The celebrations of the victory at Rouen and Paris have already been noted. Even allowing for an element of sycophancy by the citizens, there is good evidence of the popularity of the Duke and Duchess of Bedford and that the celebrations of the victory arose from genuine feelings.

Allmand, a modern historian, as quoted earlier thought that 'by deciding the fate of Normandy for a quarter of a century the battle of Verneuil marked a watershed …' A French academic, writing slightly earlier, reflected the same judgement writing that, 'certain [French] historians have judged that if the fortunes of war had been different, Normandy would have been liberated 25 years earlier'.[231] Allmand went on to be dismissive of Verneuil, writing, 'Verneuil was no Agincourt yet its effects were greater.'[232] Perhaps he meant that the Battle of Verneuil itself was not such a near-miraculous victory as Agincourt can appear. I feel that this judgement belittles Verneuil.

Verneuil showed the qualities of the English and Welsh soldiers, their personal skill, their discipline and loyalty to one another and their leaders, and their raw courage in just the same way that Agincourt did. Verneuil was an actively sought battle whereas Agincourt was one where the English army was caught by a superior force. It is notable that Henry V never took such a risk again as the march from Harfleur to Calais which led to Agincourt. He knew that he could not rely on God's favour and the courage of his men to such a degree for a second time. Henry was a great military commander because he learnt from his actions. Bedford had the strategic vision to know that he had to fight a great battle in 1424; it was up to Charles and his commanders if they wanted to see their plans through to the hazards of battle. His tactics in the battle itself were conservative, relying on the skills of his men. He was proved right in this, but with hindsight it was a risk, as the events of the battle demonstrated. So the question is, why did the Armagnacs lose? Their plan was a good one; they had an army which had the elements to beat the English. They had more men. They fought on a field which favoured them more than the English. The answer lies in the make-up of the Armagnac army itself. Aumale, who was a good, experienced commander, seems to have been unable to take firm command of his army. Having to command Douglas and Narbonne was an unenviable task because Aumale did not have the rank or status to dominate them. Moreover, Charles had complicated Aumale's situation by giving Douglas great favour and a grandiose title. Narbonne was not incompetent, just impetuous. But despite this, these men agreed and broadly implemented a plan for the battle.

The contradiction in the plan for the battle, the need for the infantry to follow up the charge of the heavy cavalry to take advantage of any disruption it caused, as against the need for the Scottish archers to have time to damage the English troops, may have led to the slightly disordered advance of the infantry. But the real problem in the army of Charles VII at Verneuil was that no one seems to have made anything like the efforts Salisbury did in his preparations for the relief of Cravant to establish ordinances to bring the disparate elements of the army together.

In fact, with the late arrival of some at least of the Lombards, the army had had very little time to come together and build any sort of trust between the various national groups making it up. This was the classic problem for an army made up of mercenary companies. While they may have been good soldiers in the main, as was the case with Charles's army at Verneuil, the different companies often knew each other more by prejudiced reputation than any real experience of their respective qualities. The events of the battle showed that this was a vital difference between the two armies. The English and Welsh soldiers knew and trusted each other and their commanders.

Despite the eve of battle desertions, Bedford seems to have trusted the Norman men-at-arms in his army, a trust which their behaviour in the battle proved to be well placed. The various national units in the Armagnac army may have trusted their own commanders, but they certainly didn't trust each other. In the follow up to the successful charge by the Lombards, the French and Scottish infantry seemed to be competing with each other to reach the English line first rather than co-operating to hit the line together. Then, with the Scots being the honourable exception, when the English started to put pressure on the men-at-arms of the French army, the different national groups seem to have looked to try to save themselves rather than work together to save the battle.

Nothing in this account of the Battle of Verneuil shows a good reason why it is forgotten. In fact it shows all the reasons why the battle should be remembered as one of the great victories of the English soldier. It also shows that it had as great a political and historical consequence as any of the other three battles.

English captains at the battles of Cravant and Verneuil[233]

This appendix provides a small insight into why the English armies were so successful in France in the fifteenth century – experienced captains who were used to serving together and individuals with substantial experience. Those in italics definitely fought in both battles, and those underlined probably did, allowing for the well-known flexibility in spelling of personal names at the time and later.

Cravant – 31 July 1423

Earl of Salisbury

Lords *Willoughby, Poynings* and Mollyns

Sirs John Arthur, *Henry Biset*, Thomas Bourgh, John Crafford, Thomas Flemmyng, *John Gray, Ranald Gray, Gilbert Halsall*, Edmond Heren, *Lancelot Lisle, William Oldhall, John Pasheley*, William Peito, Richard le Wike

Untitled: *Rhys ap Madoc*, Digon ap Marc, Jenkin Banester, *William Glasdale, Matthew Gough*

Verneuil – 17 August 1424

Duke of Bedford

Earl of Salisbury

Lords *Willoughby, Poynings* and Scales

Sirs *Henry Bissett*, Thomas Blount, Raynould Boutieller, Philip Branche, Aleyn Bukessall, Nicholas Burdet, Thomas a Burgh, William Crafford, John Fastolfe, Thomas Gargrave, *William Glasdale, John Gray, Ranald*

Gray, Raynald Gray, John Grey de North, *Gilbert Halsall*, Robert Harling, John Harpelles, John Harthur, John Kyrkeley, *Lancelot Lisle*, Richard Merbury, John Montgomery, *William Oldhall, John Pasheley*, John Robessard, John Salvern, Raynold Staundeche, William Tarbroke
Untitled: *Rhys ap Madoc*, John Bannester, John Burgh, Thomas Everyngham, Richard Gethyn, *Matthew Gough*, William Kirkby, Thomas Lounde, William Minore, William Rygmaden, Richard Waller.

William Glasdale was an example of a professional soldier in France at this time.[234] A man of this name first appeared in 1417 as an archer in the Earl of Salisbury's company, which was part of the Duke of Gloucester's expedition to France. In 1420 he was 'maitre d'hotel' for Salisbury in Normandy. This household service shows that he was a trusted servant and possibly companion of Salisbury in France. It also shows how men could hold both military and household roles in the professional armies of this time.

By 1423 he was fighting as a man-at-arms and captain in Salisbury's service at Cravant, and did the same at Verneuil in the following year. (The scribe responsible for the list of commanders at Verneuil causes confusion when he calls Glasdale 'Sir William'. William Glasdale was probably plain William at this time.) Salisbury awarded heraldic arms to men who loyally and bravely fought with him, and Glasdale seems to have been one who earned this advancement.[235] By 1426 he is recorded as William Glasdale esquire in the garrison Fresnay, and by this time he might be called Sir William as a sign of respect rather than a formal title.[236] By 1428 he was sufficiently well established in France to be in receipt of protections from legal action while on military service issued on the orders of the Duke of Bedford as Regent. These continued until his death in May 1429 at Orléans, where he served with some distinction. At the time of his death, Glasdale was bailli of Alençon (a bailli was a royal administrator of an area; Glasdale with his military experience would have been an ideal man to hold a 'marcher' city like Alençon).

One sign of how much these captains were a community is found in the records of the Clerks of Chancery of proceedings of 1433. William Glasdale's widow, who was bringing matters before the court, had remarried to Glasdale's comrade in arms Sir Thomas Blount.

Other captains who had long military careers are Lord Poynings and Thomas Burgh (some records have him as Thomas a Burgh). Lord Poynings is first recorded in 1404 when he served at sea. Later he was involved in the relief of Harfleur in 1416 and the blockade of Le Crotoy in 1423. He also fought in land campaigns, culminating in the Battle of Verneuil when he was 41 years old. Thomas Burgh is recorded as a man-at-arms and captain between 1418 and 1433.[237]

APPENDIX B:

Reconstructing events at the Battle of Verneuil

This appendix contains various points of argument and interpretation showing how and why I decided on some of the features of my reconstruction of the battle. The reason for putting these in a separate appendix rather than including them in the main account is simply that, necessary as these arguments and interpretations are, they would disrupt the story of the battle if they were embedded in it.

Reconstructing a battle as complicated as the Battle of Verneuil requires a considerable amount of deduction and interpretation to produce a coherent and convincing account. But that does not mean that this or any other reconstruction of the battle is just guesswork. We are fortunate that there are a number of contemporary or near contemporary accounts of the battle written by members of the main three nations involved. The best three of these are: Waurin's, since it was written by a man who took part in the battle; the Berry Herald's, written by someone who had considerable contact with heralds and other men who were present at the battle; and Thomas Basin's, written by someone who had access to much local information from both sides since he was born in Normandy, he went to Paris University in the year of the battle and was later a canon at Rouen. In addition, there are two well-thought-through modern reconstructions of the battle, those by Burne and Jones. All these have contributed towards my account.

Col. A.H. Burne published two books in the 1950s, *The Crécy War* and *The Agincourt War*, which have been very influential on the accounts of the battles of the Hundred Years War written by subsequent writers. There has been much debate about the principle of 'Inherent Military Probability' which he used in his reconstructions of events. However, in general he used his sources fairly. M.K. Jones writing almost half a century later produced a more detailed account of the battle than Burne, largely because he had access to a wider selection of sources. He raises a number of significant questions about Burne's reconstruction and offers a new reconstruction that is both more detailed and more convincing.

1. The numbers involved

By the fifteenth century it is no longer necessary to rely on chroniclers' estimates of the numbers of men involved in a battle, because there are often administrative records which enable much more accurate estimates to be made. In general, the estimates of the numbers of combatants on each side at Verneuil are much less exaggerated than is the case for many other battles in medieval Europe. Waurin does not provide actual numbers, but makes a clear statement of relative sizes of the armies, writing that 'the French … had more men by one half than the English'.[238] Basin overestimates the numbers in the English army, but makes the same point, that the French '… had a good advantage …' in numbers.[239] The Duke of Bedford estimated that the French army was about 14,000 men strong in his letter to Sir Thomas Rempston, written two days after the battle.[240] This is an estimate that deserves to be valued, since Bedford had plenty of opportunity to view the enemy forces and had no interest in seriously underestimating their numbers. Bedford also wrote that 7,262 of these were left dead on the battlefield – an appalling toll.

Modern historians have been hampered by the very patchy survival of records for 1424. Newhall calculated that Charles had at least 8,000 French and Spanish troops and 6,500 Scots in June, and eventually about 3,000 Lombards in addition. But this is a figure for his total forces in that month, not the force that went to Ivry and Verneuil in mid-August. The numbers of French and Spanish troops in particular would have been reduced by desertion and the demands of garrison duty. Of the English forces that Bedford was able to lead to meet the French threat, Newhall writes that '… all things considered, 10,000 men does not seem an overestimate'.[241] This figure included Lord Scales' men besieging Ivry and the Norman retinues. It seems not to include the Burgundians, who of course were not present at the battle in any case. He may well have overestimated the contribution made by the reinforcements sent from England, whom we know caused Bedford concerns about the number of desertions from them. So it is likely that both of Newhall's figures are a little high. Burne, followed by Jones, reduced the English force to c.8,000 and increased the size of the French army from Bedford's estimate to between 14,000 and 16,000. These are reasonable figures, although I think it is likely that the English army was slightly larger, somewhere between 8,000 and 9,000. The important thing about these modern estimates is that they fit well with Waurin's remark about the relative sizes of the two armies.

2. Who faced whom?

It is clear from the accounts that both the French and the English formed up in good order, but it seems that neither side formed a conventional medieval battle line made up of three distinct 'battles' with discernible spaces between them. The English army seems to have formed up in two 'battles', with Bedford and Salisbury commanding approximately one half of the English line each. This demonstrates the importance of personal leadership in medieval battles. Bedford and Salisbury, with their retinues of selected highly skilled men (Waurin's description of Bedford's retinue has been noted above) gathered around them under their standards, were the leaders and rallying points for the English 'battles'. From accounts of the battle it is clear that both men led by example in the actual fighting. The archers took their now traditional positions on the flanks of the line of men-at-arms and as a screen in front of them. The organisation of the Franco-Scottish line was more complex because there were more men of high standing in their army. Douglas commanded the Scots. Aumale and Narbonne seem to have been the main commanders of the rest, leaving aside the Lombard cavalry for the moment. Conventionally the right was the place of honour, and it seems that Bedford led the English right. But who faced him? Waurin is not clear. He seems to use the term French to mean the French army in general, rather than just the French fighting men. He mentions the Scots only twice once the battle has started, once to describe the archery duel between the English and Scottish archers and once to report that Bedford 'was very greatly harassed by the Scots'.[242] This second mention does not say explicitly that Bedford faced Douglas and the Scots, just that they were a great aggravation to him, which is an accurate estimation of their effect on the English cause. Both Monstrelet and *The Book of Pluscarden* have the Scots facing Salisbury. This has the attraction of allowing Douglas and the 'Army of Scotland' the place of honour on the right of the battle line.

Taken together, the contemporary accounts make it clear that the Armagnac battle line was a solid line made up of three blocks under (from the left) Aumale, Narbonne and Douglas. I have followed these two contemporary sources over Waurin's vaguer remark, as did both Burne and Jones.

3. Where were the French and Lombard cavalry at the start of the battle?

Gilles le Bouvier, the Berry Herald, is clear about this, writing, 'the French had arranged two wings (*ailes*) of cavalry … the left wing led by Bourne Caqueran, Theode de Valpargue and Luquin Ris, Lombards, and the right wing Baron de Coulances, Poton de Sainterailles [sic] and other French knights …'.[243] Waurin appears to have the cavalry, both French and Lombard, in one block under the leadership of 'Le Bourn Quaqeran, Theaulde de Valpergue … La Hire, Pothon [sic] and others' which was 'for the purpose of dashing into their enemies in the rear, either right through them or otherwise, so as to their greatest advantage they might be able to do them damage'.[244] [*Note flexible spellings of personal names.*]

He later makes clear mention of the French cavalry coming to grief against the horse lines under heavy arrowshot. He seems to have remembered the attack of the French cavalry, probably because it was on the side of the battle he was part of, but completely misses the charge of the Lombards. But in his confusion over the deployment and activities of the cavalry of the Armagnac army, he has his baggage guard of archers repel both cavalry 'whose chief was Le Borgne Kaquetan a Lombard knight [sic]'[245] and the French cavalry mentioned above.

This latter event may be a garbled memory of the repelling of the belated return of the Lombards to the battle after the rest of the Armagnac army had been defeated. Basin's account is clearer, emphasising the position of the Lombards when the French army began to advance on the English, '(with) the Italian cavalry in the lead, the battalions of infantry and the body of Scots began to advance on the English …'[246] Basin's account complements that of le Bouvier.

4. The attacks made by the French and Lombard cavalry

What did these two wings of cavalry achieve?

Basin gives a graphic account of the impact of the Lombards on the English and makes it clear that they advanced ahead of the French infantry, and broke through the battle line, before going on to pillage the baggage. *The Book of Pluscarden* gives a similar account of their success. The *Book*'s account is slightly confused by having the Lombards and others looting the baggage before stating how they got to it. But then it records that 'in fact at the first onset they charged the English archers and broke their ranks; and, on others coming up, they made a gap through them and passed on to the booty …'[247]

These two accounts each give a very important statement of the position and role of the Lombard cavalry, and make it equally clear that they fulfilled their role. There is no mention of significant French cavalry being part of this charge. This is no surprise, since the superior quality of the Italians' armour was the key to their tactical purpose in this battle. Although the account of the battle given in *The Book of Pluscarden* and Basin's *History* share a number of features, it is difficult to see how Basin, whose account is the later, could have seen the *Book*. *The Book of Pluscarden* was compiled at Pluscarden Priory around 1461, while Basin wrote his great history of Charles VII in exile from France in 1471–73.

The Berry Herald is less clear about how the Lombards got to the baggage, but is clear that they lost order in their rush to this booty. Waurin doesn't mention the Lombards in the battle after his very first mention of them as being in one block with the French horse. All this suggests that while the Lombards may have started the battle on the left wing, they made their attack fairly directly at the English men-at-arms as Basin makes clear. Both *The Book of Pluscarden* and Basin have the English ranks opening to let the Lombards through in an effort to minimise the damaging impact, and then reforming afterwards.

The right wing consisting of French cavalry were less successful. When Waurin mentions the activities of the cavalry in the battle it is as French cavalry, following their purpose of attacking 'the English in the rear or in the flank' who found 'barriers and opposition' made up of the horse lines and the baggage. 'They also found there two thousand stalwart archers' who drove them off. This suggests that at least some of the French cavalry went wide enough round the English army to end up on the outside of the horse lines that protected the English flank and rear. The archers who drove them off Waurin described as, 'appointed to guard the baggage … in order that their army might not be attacked in the rear or thrown into any confusion'.[248]

The Berry Herald has them making an attack after the English have started to win the infantry fight but retreating after one of their leaders was killed. Basin and *The Book of Pluscarden* make no mention of a body of specifically French cavalry in their accounts of the battle. I think that it is likely that the right wing of French cavalry started the battle overlapping the English line because it was to the right of the Scots. There was a large number of Scottish archers present – Waurin mentions the duel between them and the English archers at the start of the battle – and they probably flanked their men-at-arms in imitation of the English tactical practice. Their presence would have pushed the French cavalry wide. Since there is no hint that the French cavalry attacked early like the Lombards, they would have to swing wide to attack the English because of the need to avoid the Scots and try to attack the English from behind, as was the French battle plan. This led to them getting caught up on the bulwark formed by the English horse lines.

For some reason Waurin doesn't make any unambiguous mention of the activities of the Lombards in the battle. Maybe he overlooked them because they added nothing in his view to his chivalric account of the deeds of arms of the Duke of Bedford and Earl of Salisbury. However, he does record the French cavalry attack noted above, which got caught up in the English horse lines. There are two possible interpretations of what he was recording here. The simplest was that the body of French cavalry on the right wing of the Franco-Scottish army made a circuitous flank attack, which came to grief as described.

Waurin didn't mention the Lombards breaking through the English line because he personally was far enough left not to experience the consequences and he was soon distracted by the hand-to-hand fighting, 'for I could not see or comprehend the whole since I was sufficiently occupied in defending myself …'[249] The other possibility is that Waurin was giving a *very* garbled account of what the Lombards actually did. I have already noted that he tends to use 'French' to mean any of the troops in the multinational French army. An example of the confusion that this can cause is found at this point in his account, where he records that the French cavalry driven off by this baggage guard of archers were led by 'Le Borgne Kaqueran, a Lombard knight'! He notes that, 'according to what I can understand, and I have also since heard many of this opinion about it', before writing that the archers in his baggage guard rejoined the main battle making a decisive attack on the flank of the Franco-Scottish army. This suggests that his memory of some of the details of the battle was vague and he was trying to construct his account in discussion with others. He links two events involving the Lombards: their attack on the baggage and their being driven off by archers in the final part of the battle. But he completely misses out the Lombards' most dramatic achievement, breaking through the English battle line.[250]

Waurin's account shows the problem facing Bedford, Salisbury and the other English leaders at Verneuil. While they were prepared for cavalry making encircling attacks, as the wall of horses shows, they were probably not prepared for a frontal assault by cavalry. So the tactical plans of the French only became apparent with hindsight after the battle. Waurin's account suggests that he and his correspondents either never understood the detail of the French plans or had forgotten them by the time he was writing. So he made his account from his experience and missed the key fact that the whole French plan hinged on starting the battle with cavalry attacks. But the major problem with accepting Waurin's account of the battle in its entirety is that to do so it requires that all comments made by other contemporary historians and chroniclers that contradict Waurin's account should be ignored. This cannot be done since although Waurin has left us a valuable account that includes much personal experience, his account is vague and lacking in details at many points. Therefore, I came to the reconstruction of the activities of the cavalry in the French army given in the chapter above, rather than attempting to make sense of Waurin's account of the activities of the cavalry.

5. The English baggage guard

Waurin alone of the major accounts records the appointment by Bedford of 2,000 archers to guard the baggage and the horse lines. The problem with this has already been noted; Bedford could ill afford to put about 25 per cent of his strength in reserve, since he was outnumbered at least 3:2 if not 2:1. Jean Le Fevre, another herald, also left an account of this period. In general it is much less valuable than any of the other accounts because Le Fevre's account of the Battle of Verneuil and the 1420s as a whole was copied extensively from Waurin and Monstrelet. However, he does provide one significant detail. He gives a much more credible figure of '500 archers lightly armed' for the number ordered to guard the baggage and horses.[251] There seems to be no doubt that the group deployed as a baggage guard fled, and the *Brut*'s comments about the fate of one of them is noted above. Waurin was clear, he was not thinking of a reserve but a baggage guard.

Mention is made in section 2 above of the lack of clarity in Waurin's account of the activities of the cavalry in the battle. *The Book of Pluscarden* mentions a rearguard, noting that, '(the Lombards) began to fall on the baggage behind the rearguard'.[252] However, it makes this comment before explaining that the Lombards had broken through the battle line as noted above. It also makes no mention of this rearguard turning the battle for the English in the way that Waurin's 2,000 archers do. Both Waurin and Basin have the cavalry that get behind the English battle line looting the baggage and killing the servants and pages sheltering there. As has been mentioned, Waurin has his reserve drive off the cavalry whereas Basin makes no mention of an heroic baggage guard driving off the cavalry. In fact he, like the author of *The Book of Pluscarden*, suggests that the Lombards were able to loot the baggage train almost at their leisure. In truth, as has been noted above, the actual baggage guard seems to have been anything but heroic, fleeing at the sight of the oncoming Lombards, leaving the pages and horse boys to their fate. There is no doubt that some men fled the battle because of the legal records of the English administration of Normandy and the comments in the English *Brut* noted above.

So who were Waurin's archers who 'gave a great shout' and turned the battle? There are two possibilities, which are not mutually exclusive, since it is possible that archers from both wings of the English army contributed to the collapse of the Franco–Scottish infantry. The first, and most likely, is that they were the reformed right wing of archers. Some of these may have fled like the baggage guard but there is no reason to believe that this wing suffered heavily from the Lombards. The reason for this assertion is that the Lombards did not attack on an especially wide front because, as has been noted above, only one third of them were heavily armoured. The number of heavily armoured men set the width of the front of the Lombard attack so that they shielded their lighter armoured colleagues. Since there is a clear statement that they hit the men-at-arms, they could not have seriously damaged the right wing of archers as well. So it's reasonable to suggest that the majority of the right wing pulled themselves together after the disruption caused by the charge of the Lombards. If these were the archers who gave Waurin's 'great shout' as they attacked it would explain the sudden and disastrous collapse of the French and Spanish troops making up the left and centre of the French army, which led to the Scots being surrounded and slaughtered.

The second possibility is that they were the archers on the English left wing. These men were involved in an archery duel with the Scottish archers, which was foreshortened by the rapid advance of the French and Scottish infantry. Then they were able to watch the French cavalry ride wide round the English flank and charge into the horse lines where they got stuck. Before the cavalry could force their way through the horse lines, the archers shot at them with enough vigour that the French cavalry withdrew and took no further part in the battle. These men, whose fighting spirits would have been very high after their successes, could then have reorganised themselves and, as the archers had done at Agincourt, attacked the enemy in the flank. However, this could well be expecting too much of the archers on the English left. Therefore I think it is likely that the archers who helped to turn the battle were those who had made up the English right wing, since they had had less to do up to that point.

APPENDIX C:

The most important contemporary sources[253]

Jean de Waurin

Waurin was probably born in 1394, the illegitimate son of the Seneschal of Flanders, who was closely connected to the dukes of Burgundy. He was a constant member of the Burgundian party throughout his life. It was this loyalty to the dukes of Burgundy that led him to fight in English armies in the 1420s, despite his father and half-brother being killed at Agincourt fighting for the French. He took part in the battles of Cravant, Verneuil and Patay. He remained loyal to the Duke of Burgundy and so later fought against the English when the duke had made his peace with Charles VII of France. Waurin retired from military activity somewhere in the early to mid-1440s, but remained an active servant of the Duke of Burgundy.

He probably wrote the parts of his chronicle that covered Henry V's conquests and the events of the 1420s in his old age, at some time in the 1460s. Much of his chronicle before the fifteenth century is taken directly from other chroniclers, but when he comes to write of his own times he is much more useful. Even for the fifteenth century he used other written accounts of the times, particularly Monstrelet's. However, he may also have used information from other veterans of the wars and certainly drew on his extensive personal experience. His account is always limited by one factor – he was writing a chivalric history. The deeds of men of title, knights and esquires figure larger than those of the mass of the fighting men. This is frustrating but unsurprising.

Despite his use of this lens in his writing, his account of the Battle of Verneuil is important because he was actually there fighting in the thick of things, probably under Salisbury's banner. His account of the actual battle is far from clear at times, but then he was an active participant in the battle, not a spectator. Also, his memory of certain features of the battle may have faded with time or been coloured by later experience and reading. Despite this, his account remains that rare thing in medieval history, a detailed account of a battle by someone who took part in it.

Thomas Basin

Basin was born in Normandy in 1412, and his family must have taken the oath of loyalty to Henry V since Thomas held benefices in English-held Normandy after studying at Paris University. He rose to be a teacher at the English-established university at Caen. He obtained a bishopric and was a significant figure in the English administration in Normandy. When Charles VII conquered the duchy, Basin changed sides and soon became a royal councillor. He fell out with Charles's successor and became an exile. He took both the classical Roman historians and the developing contemporary early Renaissance style of historiography as his models when he wrote most of his history of Charles VI in 1471–73.[254] He probably used some of his contemporaries' accounts as sources, but was able to add a great deal from personal experience and enquiry.

His modern editor, Samaran, emphasises the clarity and seeming truthfulness of his account of the battle because of his opportunities to hear the stories of some of those involved.[255] His history had the purpose of exposing what he saw as increasing royal tyranny that began as Charles recovered the kingdom of France and became more extreme especially under his son Louis XI. Despite this, he is fair about the English administration in Normandy, particularly in its golden days in the 1420s. He had a bias towards Norman affairs, as his richly coloured account of the English efforts against the brigands shows, and this is something that becomes more marked in his account of Charles's recovery of the duchy in the 1440s. While he is in no sense neutral, his history is not unlike some of the great histories of the eighteenth and nineteenth century with magisterial judgements garnishing his account.

Gilles le Bouvier, the Berry Herald

Gilles le Bouvier was born in 1386. By 1416 he was in the household of the then Dauphin, Jean, and on his death in 1417 he moved into the household of the new Dauphin, Charles. When Charles fled Paris in 1418, Gilles went with him and he served Charles as a herald and envoy for the rest of his life. Gilles, like other heralds, wrote a chronicle of Charles VII's reign, as well as an Armorial of France as his role required. Heralds were able to write valuable chronicles since they were in key positions in royal courts that gave them knowledge of political and military discussions and activities, and were often present at major battles. Anne Curry has observed that 'the whole of his chronicle is useful for its military detail' so his account of the actions of the French and Lombard cavalry at Verneuil is significant.

Bibliography

48th Annual Report of the Deputy Keeper of Public Records (London, 1887).

Actes de la Chancellerie d'Henri VI, edited by P. le Cacheux (Paris, 1901).

AHRC-funded 'The Soldier in Later Medieval England Online Database', www.medievalsoldier.org.

Allmand, C.T., *Lancastrian Normandy 1415–1450* (Oxford, 1983).

Allmand, C.T. (editor), *Society at War* (Woodbridge, 1988).

Askew, G.N., Formenti, F. and Minetti, A.E., 'Limitations imposed by wearing armour on Medieval soldiers' locomotor performance', Proceedings of the Royal Society B., published online, 20 July 2011.

Ayton, A. and Preston, P., *The Battle of Crécy 1346* (Woodbridge, 2005).

Barker, J., *Conquest* (London, 2009).

Barker, J., *England Arise* (London, 2014)

Basin, T., *Histoire de Charles VII*, edited & translated by C. Samaran (Paris, 1933).

Bell, A.R., Curry, A., King, A. and Simpkin, D., *The Soldier in Later Medieval England* (Oxford, 2013).

Blair, C., *European Armour c. 1066–c. 1700* (London, 1958 (1972)).

Bongrain, Gilles, 'La Bataille de Verneuil, le 17 aout' *1424, Histoire Medieval* no. 29, May 2002.

Brie, F.W.D. (editor), *The Brut or the Chronicles of England* (London, 1908).

Burne, Col A.H., *The Agincourt War* (Ware, 1999).

Calendar of Close Rolls 1363 & 1368 (Nendeln, Lichtenstein, reproduced 1972).

Calendar of Close Rolls 1413–19 (London, 1929–32).

Campbell, J., 'England Scotland and the Hundred Years War in the 14th Century' in Hale, J. et al (editors), *Europe in the Late Middle Ages* (London, 1965).

Cannan, F., *Scottish Arms and Armour* (Oxford, 2009).

Capwell, T., *Masterpieces of European Arms and Armour* (London, 2011).

Chroniques de Normendie, edited by A. Hellot (1881).

Les Chroniques du roi Charles VII par Gilles le Bouvier dit le herault Berry, edited by H. Courteault and L. Celier (Paris, 1979).

Clements, J., 'Wielding the Weapons of War: Arms, Armour and Training Manuals During the Late Middle Ages' in Villalon, L.J.A., and Kagay, D.J. (editors), *The Hundred Years War: A Wider Focus* (Leiden, 2005).

Cohn, N., *The Pursuit of the Millennium* (London, 2004).

Contamine, P., *Guerre, Etat et Société à la fin du Moyen Age* (Paris, 1972).

Curry, A., 'The First English Standing Army', p. 195 in Ross, C. (editor), *Patronage, Pedigree and Power* (Gloucester, 1979).

Curry, A., 'English Armies in the Fifteenth Century' in Curry, A. and Hughes, M. (editors), *Arms, Armies and Fortifications in the Hundred Years War* (Woodbridge, 1994).

Curry, A., *Battle of Agincourt: Sources and Interpretations* (Woodbridge, 2000).

Curry, A., *The Hundred Years War* (Basingstoke, 2003).

Curry, A., *Agincourt: A New History* (Stroud, 2005).

Ditcham, B.G.H., 'The Employment of Foreign Mercenary Troops in the French Royal Armies 1415–1470', Phd dissertation Edinburgh University, http://deremilitari.org/articles/.

Ditcham, B.G.H., 'Mutton Guzzlers and Wine Bags: Foreign Soldiers and Native Reactions' in *Power, Culture and Religion in France c.1350–1550*, edited by Allmand, C. (Woodbridge, 1989).

Dockray, K. *Henry V* (Stroud, 2004).

Duffus Hardy, Sir T., 'Syllabus of the documents relating to England and other kingdoms …' in *Rymer's Foedera* (London, 1873).

Gesta Henrici Quinti, translated by Taylor, F. and Roskill, J.S. (Oxford, 1975).

Goodman, A. *The Wars of the Roses: The Soldiers Experience* (Stroud, 2005).

Grant, A., *Independence and Nationhood: Scotland 1306–1469* (Edinburgh, 1984).

Hall, E., *Chronicle* (London, 1809).

Harriss, G., *Shaping the Nation: England 1360–1461* (Oxford, 2005).

Hildred, A. (editor), *Weapons of Warre* (Portsmouth, 2011).

Jones, D., 'Arrows against linen and leather armour', *Journal of the Society of Archer Antiquaries*, vol. 55 (2012).

Jones, M.K., 'The Battle of Verneuil (17th August 1424): Towards a history of courage', *War in History*, vol. 9, part 4 (2002).

Jones, R., *The Knight: The Warrior and the World of Chivalry* (Oxford, 2011).

Keen, M. in Archer, R.E. and Walter, S. (editors), *Rulers and Ruled in Late Medieval England* (London, 1995).

Le Fevre, J. *Chronique*, edited by Morand, F. (Paris, 1876–81).

Liber Pluscardiensis, edited and translated by Skene, F.J.H. (Edinburgh, 1877–80).

Little, R.G., *The Parlement of Poitiers* (London, 1984).

'Le Livre des Trahisons de France' in Lettenhove, Baron Kervyn de (ed.), *Chroniques relatives à l'histoire de la Belgique sous la domination des ducs de Bourgogne* (Brussels, 1870–76).

McCulloch, A., *Galloway: A Land Apart* (Edinburgh, 2000).

Maxwell, S.H. *A History of the House of Douglas* (London, 1902).

Newhall, R.A., *The English Conquest of Normandy* (New Haven, 1924).

Newhall, R.A., *Muster and Review* (Cambridge, Mass., 1940).

Nicholson, R., *Scotland: The Later Middle Ages* (Edinburgh, 1974).

Oakeshott, R.E., *The Sword in the Age of Chivalry* (London, 1964).

A Parisian Journal, translated by Shirley, J. (Oxford, 1968).

Plaisse, A., 'La Bataille de Verneuil', in the *Bulletin Municiple de Verneuil sur Avre*, no. 4 (June 1968).

Register of the Freemen of the City of York, vol. 1 at www.British-history.ac.uk.

Reid, P., *By Fire and Sword* (London, 2007).

Rotuli Parliamentorum, vol. iv (London).

Rowe, B.J.H., 'John Duke of Bedford and the Norman "Brigands"', *English Historical Review*, vol. 47 (1932).

Small, G., *Late Medieval France* (London, 2009).

Smith, R.D. and DeVries, K., *The Artillery of the Dukes of Burgundy* (Woodbridge, 2005).

Spencer, M., *Thomas Basin: The History of Charles VII and Louis XI* (Nieuwkoop, 1997).

Statutes of the Realm, vol. 1 (London, 1735).

Stevenson, J., *Letters and papers illustrative of the wars of the English in France during the reign of Henry VI* (London, 1861–64).

Sumption, J., *Trial by Fire: The Hundred Years War, Volume 2* (London, 1999).

Sumption, J., *Divided Houses: The Hundred Years War, Volume 3* (London, 2009).

Usk, A., *The Chronicle of Adam Usk 1377–1421*, edited and translated by Given-Wilson, C. (Oxford, 1997).

Vale, M.G.A., *English Gascony 1399–1453* (Oxford, 1970).

Vale, M., *War and Chivalry* (London, 1981).

Vale, M.G.A., *Charles VII* (London, 1974).

Vaughan, R., *Philip the Good* (Woodbridge, 2002).

Wadge, R., 'Agincourt: Where were the archers stationed in the battle line?' in Bickerstaffe, P., *Medieval War Bows: A Bowyers Thoughts* (Kegworth, 2006).

Wadge, R., *Arrowstorm: The World of the Archer in the Hundred Years War* (Stroud, 2009).

Wadge R., *Archery in Medieval England* (Stroud, 2012).

Waldman, J., *Hafted Weapons in Medieval and Renaissance Europe* (Boston, 2005).

Warner, M., 'Chivalry in Action: Thomas Montague and the War in France 1417–28', *Nottingham Medieval Studies*, vol. xlii (1998).

Watt, D.E.R. (editor), *Scotichronicon* by Walter Bower, vol. 8 (Aberdeen, 1987).

Waurin, J. de, *A collection of the chronicles and ancient histories of Great Britain now called England*, translated by Hardy, E.L.C.P. (London, 1891).

Williams, A., 'The Metallurgy of Medieval Arms and Armour' in Nicolle, D. (editor), *A Companion to Medieval Arms and Armour* (Woodbridge, 2002).

Wylie, J.H. and Waugh, W.T., *The Reign of King Henry V* (Cambridge, 1914–29).

Notes and references

Chapter 1. The Hundred Years War

1 This term is used for convenience to describe the longbow used by the English and Welsh archers in particular in this period. Also I will on occasion use the term 'English archers' for the sake of brevity. In no way should this be taken as a denial of the contribution that the Welsh archers made both to the development of heavy bow military archery and to the success of the archers in English armies in these wars. For a detailed discussion of the development of English and Welsh archery leading up to the Hundred Years War please see Wadge R., *Archery in Medieval England* (Stroud, 2012).

2 For more information about this see Curry, A., 'The First English Standing Army', in Ross, C. (editor), *Patronage, Pedigree and Power in Later Medieval England* (Stroud, Gloucester, 1979) p. 195.

3 Hall, E., *Hall's Chronicle* (London, 1809), p. 122.

4 McCulloch, A., *Galloway: A Land Apart* (Edinburgh, 2000), p. 206.

Chapter 2. England and France at the beginning of the fifteenth century

5 Quoted in Sumption, J., *Divided Houses* (London, 2009), p. 864.

6 Nicholson, R. *Scotland: The Later Middle Ages* (Edinburgh, 1974), p. 220.

7 Recent historians have cast doubt on whether this battle happened at all because of the weakness of the original historical sources that mentioned it. There is also dispute over whether it happened in 1403 or 1405.

8 More details of the politics of the time can be found in Harriss, G., *Shaping the Nation: England 1360–1461* (Oxford, 2005), pp. 498–505.

9 Small, G., *Late Medieval France* (London, 2009), p. 134.

10 Small, G. (2009), p. 135.

11 *A Parisian Journal*, translated by Shirley, J. (Oxford, 1968), p. 114.

12 Small, G. (2009), p. 142.

13 See Little, R.G., *The Parlement of Poitiers* (London, 1984), for more details of this administration.

14 *A Parisian Journal* (Oxford, 1968), p. 137.

15 Curry, A., *The Hundred Years War* (Basingstoke, 2003), p. 112.

Chapter 3. Scotland and the Auld Alliance

16 Quoted in Grant, A., *Independence and Nationhood: Scotland 1306–1469* (Edinburgh, 1984), p. 178.

17 Nicholson, R. (1974), p. 211.

18 Nicholson, R. (1974), p. 228.

19 His picturesque nickname first appears in Walter Bower's *Scotichronicon* written in the 1440s.

20 See Grant, A. (1984), pp. 208–9 for more on Alexander Stewart's career.

21 Grant, A. (1984), p. 213.

22 This description comes from the account of the affair written by Wyntoun in his 'Orygynale Chronykil of Scotland' probably written before 1425.

23 Caterans: this term was derived from the Gaelic for a lightly armed fighting man, and was used by the 'Lowland' Scots as a pejorative term meaning bandit or raider in the late fourteenth century. In 1384 a Council General decreed that all caterans should be arrested and killed on sight. Grant, A. (1984), p. 205.

24 Nicholson, R. (1974), p. 208.

25 Gallowglasses were basically heavy infantry, who in the fifteenth and sixteenth centuries often fought as mercenaries in Ireland. Whereas the caterans wore no armour and would have only a shield for protection at best, the gallowglasses wore mail shirts, sometimes about knee-length, and helmets. Offensive weapons included swords, both one- and two-handed; axes, one type of which resembled the English bill; and daggers.

26 Nicholson, R. (1974), p. 208.

27 This account is based on that in Nicholson, R. (1974), pp. 235–6.

28 Grant, A. (1984), pp. 171–4.

29 See Campbell, J., 'England, Scotland and the Hundred Years War in the 14th Century' in Hale, J. et al (editors), *Europe in the Late Middle Ages* (London, 1965) for more on Scotland's part in the first half of the Hundred Years War.

30 See Grant, A. (1984) for a lively account of this complicated period.

31 Grant, A. (1984), p. 42.

32 Campbell, J. (1965), p. 209.

33 Goodman, A., *The Wars of the Roses: The Soldiers Experience* (Stroud, 2005), p. 128.

34 Grant, A. (1984), p. 45.

35 Ditcham, B.G.H., 'The Employment of Foreign Mercenary Troops in the French Royal Armies 1415–1470', Phd dissertation (Edinburgh, 1979), http://deremilitari.org/articles/, p. 176.

Chapter 4. Tactics and strategy in the Hundred Years War

36 I will use the term war-bow and occasionally English war-bow for convenience and brevity to describe the bow used by English and Welsh archers at this time. Archers from other European nations probably used very similar bows in imitation. The term longbow, which can be traced back to the fifteenth century, is a much more general term just describing a man-length bow regardless of its power.

37 For Agincourt see Wadge, R., 'Agincourt: Where were the archers stationed in the battle line?' in Bickerstaffe, P., *Medieval War Bows: A Bowyer's Thoughts* (Kegworth, 2006). For Verneuil, see below.

38 Askew, G.N., Formenti, F. and Minetti, A.E. (2011). 'Limitations imposed by wearing armour on medieval soldiers' locomotor performance.' *Proceedings of the Royal Society*, published online 20 July 2011.

39 See Ayton, A. and Preston, Sir Philip, *The Battle of Crécy 1346* (Woodbridge, 2005), for the clearest discussion of the lie of the land at Crécy and the way it affected the onset of the French.

40 Curry, A., *Agincourt: A New History* (Stroud, 2005), pp. 140–2.

Chapter 5. Recruiting armies in England, Scotland and France in the Middle Ages

41 For a fuller discussion of this see Wadge, R., *Archery in Medieval England* (Stroud, 2012), pp. 24–8.

42 Statutes of the Realm, vol. 1 (London, 1735), pp. 97–8.

43 Calendar of Close Rolls 1363 (reproduced 1972), pp. 534–5.

44 Wadge, R., *Arrowstorm: The World of the Archer in the Hundred Years War* (Stroud, 2009), pp. 37–9.

45 Curry, A., 'English Armies in the Fifteenth Century' in Curry, A. and Hughes, M. (editors), *Arms, Armies and Fortifications in the Hundred Years War* (Woodbridge, 1994), p. 43.

46 Curry, A. (1979), p. 195.

47 Bell, A.R., Curry, A., King, A. and Simpkin, D., *The Soldier in Later Medieval England* (Oxford, 2013), p. 116.

48 For figures demonstrating this trend see Appendix 2 in Wadge, R., *Arrowstorm: The World of the Archer in the Hundred Years War* (History Press, 2009).

49 Allmand, C. (editor), *Society at War* (Woodbridge, Suffolk, 1988), p. 48.

50 Philippe de Mézières quoted in Allmand, C. (editor) (1988), p. 50.

51 Curry, A., 'English Armies in the Fifteenth Century' in *Arms, Armies and Fortifications in the Hundred Years War*, edited by Curry, A. and Hughes, M. (Woodbridge, 1994), p. 64.

52 Allmand, C. (editor) (1988), p. 47.

53 Curry, A., *Agincourt: A New History* (Stroud, 2005), pp. 99 and 184–5.

54 Contamine, P., *Guerre, Etat et Société à la fin du Moyen Age* (Paris, 1972), pp. 235–71 in passing.

55 See Wadge, R. (2009), pp. 216–35 and Appendix 4 for more information about this trade.

56 Ditcham, B.G.H., 'The Employment of Foreign Mercenary Troops in the French Royal Armies 1415–1470', Phd dissertation (Edinburgh, 1979), p. 168.

57 Ditcham, B.G.H., 'The Employment of Foreign Mercenary Troops in the French Royal Armies 1415–1470', Phd dissertation (Edinburgh, 1979), p. 170.

58 Ditcham, B.G.H., 'The Employment of Foreign Mercenary Troops in the French Royal Armies 1415–1470', Phd dissertation (Edinburgh, 1979), p. 172.

59 Grant, A. (1984), p. 34.
60 Nicholson, R. (1978), pp. 212–13.
61 Nicholson, R. (1978), p. 207.
62 Keen, M. in Archer, R.E. and Walter, S. (editors), *Rules and Ruled in Late Medieval England* (London, 1995).

Chapter 6. Arms and armour at the time of the Battle of Verneuil

63 Williams, A., 'The Metallurgy of Medieval Arms and Armour' in Nicolle, D. (editor), *A Companion to Medieval Arms and Armour* (Woodbridge, 2002), p. 51.
64 Vale, M., *War and Chivalry* (London, 1981), pp. 105–6.
65 Askew, G.N., Formenti, F. and Minetti, A.E., 'Limitations imposed by wearing armour on Medieval soldiers' locomotor performance'. *Proceedings of the Royal Society*, published online 20 July 2011.
66 Blair, C., *European Armour c.1066–c.1700* (London, 1958 (1972)), p. 80.
67 Calendar of Close Rolls 1368 (reproduced 1972), p. 414.
68 Jones, D., 'Arrows against linen and leather armour'. *Journal of the Society of Archer Antiquaries*, vol. 55, pp. 74–81.
69 Hildred, A. (editor), *Weapons of Warre* (Portsmouth, 2011), pp. 774–91.
70 Jones, R., *The Knight: The Warrior and the World of Chivalry* (Oxford, 2011), p. 45.
71 Oakeshott, R.E., *The Sword in the Age of Chivalry* (London, 1964).
72 Capwell, T., *Masterpieces of European Arms and Armour in the Wallace Collection* (London, 2011), p. 26.
73 Clements, J., 'Wielding the Weapons of War: Arms, armour and training manuals during the Late Middle Ages' in Villalon, L.J.A. and Kagay, D.J. (editors), *The Hundred Years War: A Wider Focus* (Leiden, 2005), pp. 464–5.
74 Register of the Freemen of the City of York, vol. 1 at www.British-history. ac.uk.
75 This discussion of fighting manuals owes much to Clements, J. (2005).
76 Quoted in Clements, J. (2005), p. 455.
77 Hildred, A. (editor), *Weapons of Warre* (Portsmouth, 2011), pp. 676–8.
78 This data comes from the English War-bow Society, *www.theenglishwar-bowsociety.com*.
79 48th Annual Report of the Deputy Keeper of Public Records (London, 1887), p. 241.
80 See Wadge. R. (2009), pp. 155–93 for more details of this.
81 Waldman, J., *Hafted Weapons in Medieval and Renaissance Europe* (2005), p. 156.
82 Jones, R. (2011), p. 47.
83 Wadge, R. (2009), p. 44–5.
84 Cannan, F., *Scottish Arms and Armour* (Oxford, 2009) is an invaluable summary of the development arms and armour in Scotland.
85 Maxwell, S.H., *A History of the House of Douglas* (London, 1902), p. 137.
86 Quoted in Sumption, J., *Divided Houses* (London, 2009), pp. 556–7.

87 Ditcham, B.G.H., 'The Employment of Foreign Mercenary Troops in the French Royal Armies 1415–1470', Phd dissertation (Edinburgh, 1979), http://deremilitari.org/articles/, chapter 2, p. 7.

Chapter 7. Henry V and the conquest of Normandy

88 Allmand, C.T., *Lancastrian Normandy 1415–50* (Oxford, 1983), p. 6.

89 Ditcham, B.G.H., 'The Employment of Foreign Mercenary Troops in the French Royal Armies 1415–1470', Phd dissertation (Edinburgh, 1979), http://deremilitari.org/articles/, chapter 1, p. 2.

90 Casualty figure Wylie, J.H. and Waugh W.T., *The Reign of King Henry V* (Cambridge, 1914–29), vol. II, p. 331.

91 Newhall, R.A., *The English Conquest of Normandy* (New Haven, 1924), p. 20.

92 Calendar of Close Rolls 1413–1419 (1929–32), p. 364.

93 Reid, P., *By Fire and Sword* (London, 2007), p. 283.

94 Newhall, R.A. (1924), p. 55.

95 *Gesta Henrici Quinti*, translated by Taylor, F. and Roskill, J.S. (Oxford, 1975), p. 175.

96 Harriss, G. (2005), pp. 545–6.

97 Allmand, C.T. (1983), p. 14.

98 Newhall, R.A. (1924), p. 68.

99 When his great grandfather Edward III undertook a similar exercise in his sustained siege of Calais, his men were less keen since there are forceful dispatches from the king complaining about desertion from his army (see Rymer, T. *Foedera* quoted in Wadge, R. *Arrowstorm* (2009), p. 105). Although to be fair, the siege of Calais was a more drawn-out affair.

100 Newhall, R.A. (1924), p. 97.

101 Allmand, C.T. (1983).

102 Harriss, G. (2005), p. 546.

103 Burne, Col A.H., *The Agincourt War* (Ware, Herts., reproduced 1999), p. 128.

104 *A Parisian Journal* (1968), pp. 139–40.

105 Newhall, R.A. (1924), p. 136.

106 Harriss, G. (2005), pp. 548–9.

107 Wylie, J.H. and Waugh, W.T. (1914–29), vol. III, p. 197.

108 Burne, A.H. (reproduced 1999), p. 145.

109 Wylie, J.H. and Waugh, W.T. (1914–29), vol. III, p. 216.

Chapter 8. Henry V as Regent of France

110 Summary from Allmand, C.T. (1983), pp. 19–20.

111 Harriss, G. (2005), p. 550.

112 Wylie, J.H. and Waugh, W.T. (1914–29), vol. III, p. 266.

113 Barker, J., *Conquest* (London, 2009), p. 33.

114 The accounts of the Battle of Baugé give few precise dates, so while Clarence was definitely at Beaufort for two days, he may have been there for slightly longer.

115 *A Parisian Journal* (1968), p. 159.

116 *Scotichronicon* by Bower, W., edited by Watt, D.E.R., vol. 8 (Aberdeen, 1987), p. 121.

117 Wylie, J.H. and Waugh, W.T. (1914–29), vol. III, p. 310.

118 Wylie, J.H. and Waugh, W.T. (1914–29), vol. III, p. 311.

119 Newhall, R.A. (1924), p. 280.

120 Newhall, R.A. (1924), p. 276.

121 Grant, A. (1984), p. 47.

122 Grant, A. (1984), p. 47.

123 Ditcham, B.G.H., 'The Employment of Foreign Mercenary Troops in the French Royal Armies 1415–1470', Phd dissertation (Edinburgh, 1979), http://deremilitari.org/articles/, chapter 2, p. 6.

124 Quoted in Dockray, K., *Henry V* (Stroud, 2004), p. 199.

125 Quoted in Newhall, R.A. (1924), p. 276n.

126 Usk, Adam, *The Chronicle of Adam Usk 1377–1421*, edited and translated by Given Wilson, C. (Oxford, 1997), p. 271.

127 Figures for the strength of both Clarence's army at Baugé and Henry's army from Harriss, G. (2005), p. 550.

128 Duffus Hardy, Sir T., 'Syllabus of the documents relating to England and other kingdoms … Rymer's Foedera' (London, 1873), vol. 2.

Chapter 9. The legacy of Henry V

129 Usk, Adam (1997), p. 259.

130 Usk, Adam (1997), p. 271.

131 Curry, A. (1979).

132 Curry, A. (1994), p. 41.

133 Vaughan, R., *Philip the Good* (reproduced by Woodbridge, 2002), p. 6.

134 Curry, A. (1979), p. 197.

135 Ditcham, B.G.H., 'Mutton Guzzlers and Wine Bags: Foreign Soldiers and Native Reactions' in *Power, Culture and Religion in France c.1350–1550*, edited by Allmand, C. (Woodbridge, 1989), p. 3.

136 Vale, M.G.A., *Charles VII* (London, 1974), p. 17.

137 Quoted in Rowe, B.J.H., 'John Duke of Bedford and the Norman "Brigands"', *English Historical Review* (1932), vol. 47, p. 585.

138 *A Parisian Journal* (1968), p. 161.

Chapter 10. 1423: The Regent of France versus the King of France

139 'Jean de Waurin (1864–91)'. In *A Collection of the Chronicles and Ancient Histories of Great Britain Now Called England* edited by Hardy, Sir W. and Hardy, E.L.C.P. (London), vol. 1422–31, pp. 6–7.

140 Ditcham, B.G.H. (1989), p. 205.

141 'Jean de Waurin (1864–91)', vol. 1422–31. For more on the medieval ordinances of war issued by the English kings and commanders, see Wadge, R. (2009), pp. 80–2.

142 Smith, R.D. and DeVries, K., *The Artillery of the Dukes of Burgundy* (Woodbridge: Boydell Press, 2005), p. 92.

143 Smith, R.D. and DeVries, K. (2005), p. 29.

144 'Jean de Waurin (1864–91)', vol. 1422–31, p. 45.

145 'Le Livre des Trahisons de France (1870–76)', p. 170 in *Chroniques relatives à l'histoire de la Belgique sous la domination des ducs de Bourgogne*, edited by Baron Kervyn de Lettenhove, (Brussels).

146 This account of the Battle of Cravant owes much to the account in 'Le Livre des Trahisons de France', pp. 168–71.

147 *A Parisian Journal* (1968), p. 189.

148 Quoted by Ditcham, B.G.H. (1989), p. 1.

149 Ditcham, B.G.H. (1989), p. 220. Money equivalent derived from information in Sumption, J. (2009), p. 876.

150 'Jean de Waurin (1864–91)', vol. 1422–31, pp. 15–16.

151 Stevenson, J., *Letters and papers illustrative of the wars of the English in France during the reign of Henry VI* (London, 1861–64), vol. 2, p. 11.

152 *A Parisian Journal* (1968), p. 191.

153 Newhall, R.A., *The English Conquest of Normandy* (New Haven, 1924), p. 307.

154 *Les Chroniques du roi Charles VII par Gilles le Bouvier dit le herault Berry*, edited by Courteault, H. and Celier, L. (Paris, 1979), p. 114.

Chapter 11. The road to Verneuil

155 Duffus Hardy, Sir T., 'Syllabus of the documents relating to England and other kingdoms ... Rymer's Foedera' (London, 1873), vol. 2, p. 641.

156 Ditcham, B.G.H., 'The Employment of Foreign Mercenary Troops in the French Royal Armies 1415–1470, Phd dissertation (Edinburgh, 1979), http://deremilitari.org/articles/, chapter 2, p. 12.

157 Ditcham, B.G.H., 'The Employment of Foreign Mercenary Troops in the French Royal Armies 1415–1470, Phd dissertation (Edinburgh, 1979), http://deremilitari.org/articles/, chapter 2, p. 13.

158 This is R.A. Newhall's estimation of the significance of the Battle of Verneuil, which I wholeheartedly agree with. See Newhall, R.A. (1924), p. 315.

159 Newhall, R.A. (1924), p. 314n.

160 The account of the events immediately before the battle and some aspects of the battle itself in this chapter owes much to Jones, M.K., 'The Battle of Verneuil (17 August 1424): Towards a History of Courage', *War in History*, vol. 9, part 4, pp. 375–411. Although he disagrees with it substantially, he builds his account on that found in Burne, A. (reproduced in 1999), pp. 196–215. In common with both these other authors, I rely on the contemporary accounts. My views on a number of aspects of the actual fighting and the context of the battle differ significantly from both Burne's and Jones' accounts because of my reading of those contemporary accounts.

161 See Jones, M.K. (2002), pp. 384–86 for the argument for dating the *journée* to 15 August, and therefore for the timescale of the pre-battle manoeuvring.

162 Stevenson, J. (1861–64), vol. 2, pp. 15–16.

163 Ditcham, B.G.H., 'The Employment of Foreign Mercenary Troops in the

French Royal Armies 1415–1470', Phd dissertation (Edinburgh, 1979), http://deremilitari.org/articles/, p. 182.

164 *Les Chroniques du roi Charles VII par Gilles le Bouvier dit le herault Berry* (1979), p. 114.

165 Jones, M.K. (2002), p. 391n.

166 Basin, T., *Histoire de Charles VII*, edited and translated by Samaran, C. (Paris, 1933), p. 93.

167 Newhall, R.A. (1924), p. 312n.

168 Ditcham, B.G.H., 'The Employment of Foreign Mercenary Troops in the French Royal Armies 1415–1470'. Phd dissertation (Edinburgh, 1979), http://deremilitari.org/articles/, chapter 2, p. 13.

169 Bongrain, Gilles, 'La Bataille de Verneuil, le 17 aout 1424', *Histoire Medieval*, no. 29 (May 2002), p. 27.

170 See Wadge, R. (2009), pp. 102–36 for more on the rewards of military service at the time and for desertion, pp. 56–9 in particular and the other references as well.

171 Newhall, R.A. (1924), p. 315.

172 Curry, A. (1994), p. 51.

173 Newhall, R.A. (1940), *Muster and Review*, Cambridge, Mass., p. 33.

174 Stevenson, J. (1861–64), vol. 2, p. 560.

175 'Jean de Waurin (1864–91)', vol. 1422–31, p. 72.

176 Stevenson, J. (1861–64), vol. 2, pp. 24–7.

177 Basin, T. (1933), p. 93.

178 Numbers from Jones, M.K. (2002), p. 402.

179 See Jones, M.K. (2002), pp. 400–3 for a fuller discussion of the symbolism around this parade.

Chapter 12. The battle

180 Jones, M.K. (2002), p. 381.

181 Burne, A. (reproduced 1999), pp. 200–1.

182 'Jean de Waurin (1864–91)', vol. 1422–31, p. 73.

183 'Jean de Waurin (1864–91)', vol. 1422–31, p. 73.

184 *Les Chroniques du roi Charles VII par Gilles le Bouvier dit le herault Berry* (1979), p. 116.

185 *Scotichronicon* by Bower, W. (1987), vol. 8, p. 127.

186 A horse can be estimated at about 8ft long by about 18in wide. If the horses were tethered nose to tail in three ranks the wall would be about 4¼ miles long, if tethered side by side it would be about 2½ miles long. Waurin suggests that they were arranged nose to tail, 'coupled together by the halters and the tails', 'Jean de Waurin (1864–91)', vol. 1422–31, p. 76.

187 *Les Chroniques du roi Charles VII par Gilles le Bouvier dit le herault Berry* (1979), p. 117.

188 'Jean de Waurin (1864–91)', vol. 1422–31, p. 74.

189 *Les Chroniques du roi Charles VII par Gilles le Bouvier dit le herault Berry* (1979), p. 117.

190 'Jean de Waurin (1864–91)', vol. 1422–31, p. 75.

191 Basin, T. (1933), p. 93.

192 Basin, T. (1933), p. 95.

193 'Jean de Waurin (1864–91)', vol. 1422–31, p. 76.

194 For Narbonne's advance see *Les Chroniques du roi Charles VII par Gilles le Bouvier dit le herault Berry* (1979), p. 117: for the Scots charge see *Scotichronicon* by Bower, W. (1987), vol. 8, p. 127.

195 Boke of Noblesse quoted in Jones, M.K. (2002), p. 409. This was written in 1475 to encourage Edward IV in his plans to renew the wars in France.

196 'Jean de Waurin (1864–91)', vol. 1422–31, p. 76.

197 Jones, M.K. (2002), p. 398.

198 'Jean de Waurin (1864–91)', vol. 1422–31, p. 76.

199 'Jean de Waurin (1864–91)', vol. 1422–31, pp. 76–7.

200 *Chroniques de Normendie*, edited by Hellot, A., p. 76, quoted in Jones, M.K. (2002), p. 398.

201 'Jean de Waurin (1864–91)', vol. 1422–31, p. 77.

202 *Les Chroniques du roi Charles VII par Gilles le Bouvier dit le herault Berry* (1979), p. 119.

203 Basin, T. (1933), p. 95.

204 'Jean de Waurin (1864–91)', vol. 1422–31, pp. 79–80.

205 'Jean de Waurin (1864–91)', vol. 1422–31, p. 78 and Newhall, R.A. (1924), pp. 319–20.

206 'Jean de Waurin (1864–91)', vol. 1422–31, p. 79.

Chapter 13. The aftermath of the battle

207 *Actes de la Chancellerie d'Henri VI*, edited by Cacheux, P. le (Paris, 1901), pp. 104–5.

208 *The Brut or The Chronicles of England*, edited by Brie, F.W.D. (London, 1908), vol. 2, p. 565.

209 'Jean de Waurin (1864–91)', vol. 1422–31, p. 81.

210 *A Parisian Journal*, translated Shirley, J. (1968), p. 200–1.

211 Vale, M.G.A. (1974), p. 35.

212 Allmand, C.T. (1983), p. 29.

213 Vale, M.G.A. (1974), p. 4.

214 Basin, T. (1933), p. 101.

215 Basin, T. (1933), p. 101.

216 Stevenson, J. (1861–64), vol. 2, pp. 32–3.

217 Curry, A. (1979).

218 Stevenson, J. (1861–64), vol. 3, pp. 550–1.

219 Curry, A., 'English Armies in the Fifteenth Century' in Curry, A. and Hughes, M. (editors), *Arms, Armies and Fortifications in the Hundred Years War* (Woodbridge, 1994), p. 65.

220 Curry, A. (1994), p. 48.

221 Warner, M. (1998), *Chivalry in Action: Thomas Montague and the War in France 1417–28 Nottingham Medieval Studies* (1998), vol. xlii, p. 168.

222 Hall, E., *Chronicle* (1809), p. 116.
223 'Jean de Waurin (1864–91)' vol. 1422–31, p. 87.

Chapter 14. The tide of war begins to turn
224 Quoted in Barker, J., *Conquest* (London, 2009), p. 96.
225 This argument is put forward in Little, R.G. (1984), p. 93.

Chapter 15. Verneuil: The forgotten battle of the Hundred Years War
226 The Battle of Cravant is not included because it is the smallest in terms of numbers engaged and there was no reigning king or regent actively involved. Also, whoever won it wasn't going to have major effects on the war in France. However, it is a very interesting battle for the military historian because of the quality of Salisbury's leadership and the performance of the various elements of his army.
227 See Sumption, J., *Trial by Fire* (London, 1999), pp. 231–7 for the detail of these negotiations and their significance.
228 *A Parisian Journal* (1968), p. 200.
229 *Rotuli Parliamentorum*, vol. IV (London), p. 423.
230 'Jean de Waurin (1864–91)', vol. 1422–31, p. 73.
231 Plaisse, A., 'La Bataille de Verneuil', in *The Bulletin Municiple de Verneuil sur Avre*, no. 4 (June 1968), p. 4.
232 Allmand, C.T. (1983), p. 29.

Appendix A
233 Stevenson, J. (1861–64), vol. 2, p. 385 for Cravant, vol. 2, p. 394 for Verneuil.
234 AHRC-funded 'The Soldier in Later Medieval England Online Database', www.medievalsoldier.org, 22 May 2013.
235 Warner, M., *Chivalry in Action: Thomas Montagu and the War in France 1417–28* (Nottingham Medieval Studies, 1998), vol. xlii, p. 153.
236 Bell, A.R., Curry, A., King, A. and Simpkin, D. (2013), *The Soldier in Later Medieval England* (Oxford, 2013), p. 164.
237 Bell, A.R., Curry, A., King, A. and Simpkin, D. (2013), pp. 30 and 69.

Appendix B
238 'Jean de Waurin (1864–91)', vol. 1422–31, p. 77.
239 Basin, T. (1933), p. 95.
240 Newhall, R.A. (1924), p. 319.
241 Newhall, R.A. (1924), p. 312 for the French army and p. 316 for the English.
242 'Jean de Waurin (1864–91)', vol. 1422–31, p. 77.
243 *Les Chroniques du roi Charles VII par Gilles le Bouvier dit le herault Berry* (1979), p. 117.
244 'Jean de Waurin (1864–91)', vol. 1422–31, p. 74.
245 'Jean de Waurin (1864–91)', vol. 1422–31, p. 77.
246 Basin, T. (1933), p. 95.

247 *Liber Pluscardiensis*, edited and translated by Skene, F.J.H. (Edinburgh, 1877–80), vol. 2, p. 272.
248 'Jean de Waurin (1864–91)', vol. 1422–31, pp. 74–6.
249 'Jean de Waurin (1864–91)', vol. 1422–31, p. 76.
250 'Jean de Waurin (1864–91)', vol. 1422–31, p. 77.
251 Le Fevre, J., *Chronique*, edited by Morand, F. (Paris, 1876–81), p. 85.
252 *Liber Pluscardiensis* (1877–80), vol. 2, p. 272.

Appendix C

253 These notes owe much to Curry, A., *Battle of Agincourt: Sources and Interpretations* (Woodbridge, 2000), pp. 136–9, 178–9 and 187.
254 Spencer, M., *Thomas Basin: The History of Charles VII and Louis XI* (Nieuwkoop, 1997), p. 10.
255 Basin, T. (1933), p. 99 n3.

Index